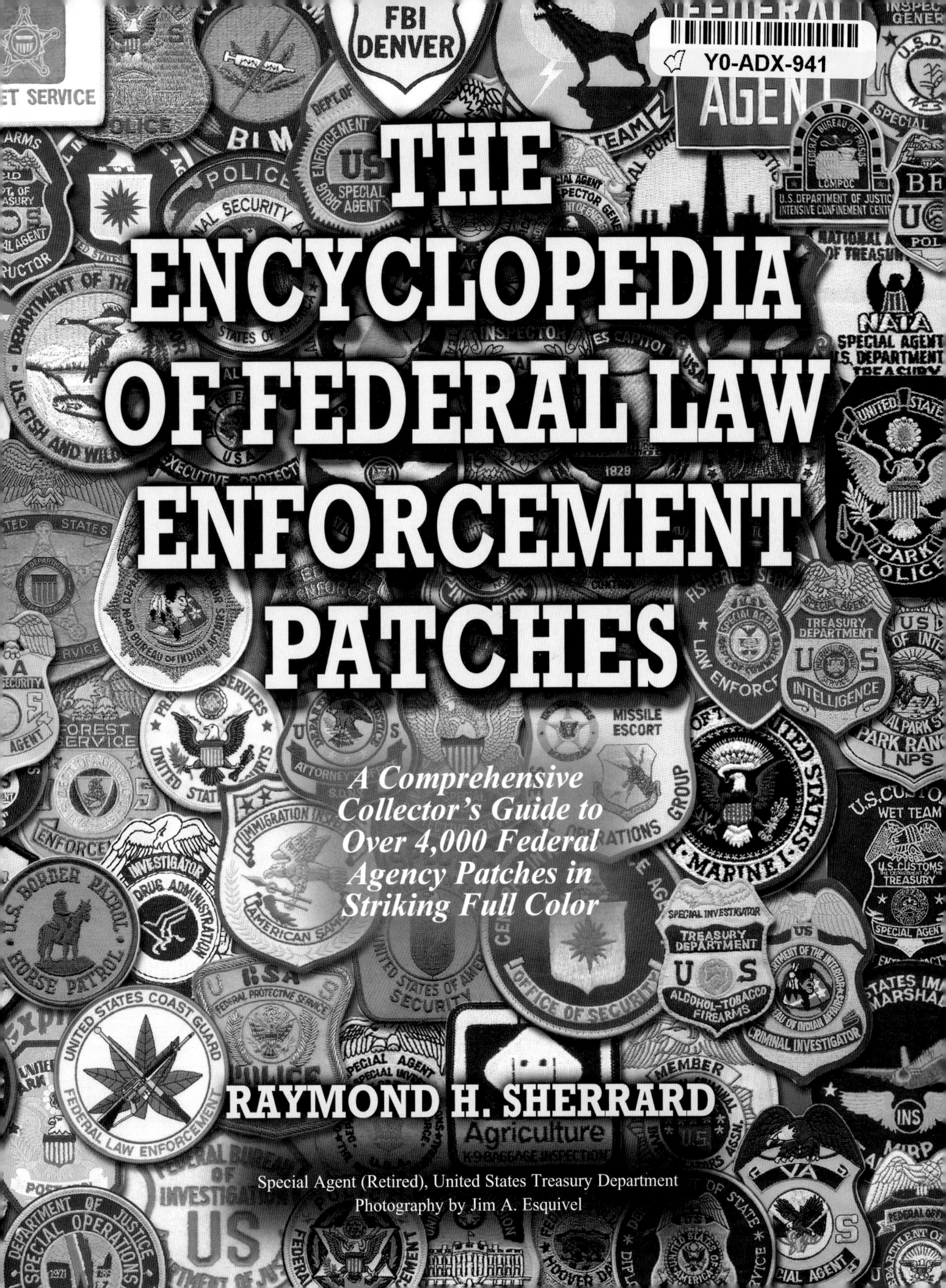

THE ENCYCLOPEDIA OF FEDERAL LAW ENFORCEMENT PATCHES

A Comprehensive Collector's Guide to Over 4,000 Federal Agency Patches in Striking Full Color

RAYMOND H. SHERRARD

Special Agent (Retired), United States Treasury Department
Photography by Jim A. Esquivel

Publishers Cataloguing In Publication Data
(Provided by Quality Books, Inc.)

Sherrard, Raymond
  The Encyclopedia of Federal Law Enforcement Patches: an
Illustrated Reference Manual / by Raymond Sherrard. — 1st ed.
  p. cm.
  Includes bibliographical references and index.

  LCCN 99-70173
  ISBN 0-914503-07-3

  1. Police—United States—Uniforms—Encyclopedias.
  2. Insignia—United States—Encyclopedias.   I. Title

HV8143.S44 1999   363.2'3'027
              QBI99-900116

First Printing February, 2000
Manufactured in Korea

Copyright © 1999 by Raymond H. Sherrard

Copyright acknowledgment: Every reasonable effort to trace the owners
of copyrighted materials has been made, but in some instances it has
proven impossible. The author and publisher will welcome information
leading to more complete acknowledgments in subsequent printings of
this book, and in the meantime, extend apologies for any omissions.

All rights reserved. This book may not be reproduced in whole or in part
by any means, electronic or mechanical, without the written permission of
the copyright holder.

Additional copies may be obtained from the publisher:

RHS ENTERPRISES
Post Office Box 5779
Garden Grove, California 92846-0779 USA
Telephone/Fax 714-892-9012

Contents

Dedication iv
Preface v
Special Thanks vi
Acknowledgments vii
Introduction 1
    Why This Book? 1
    Emblem Manufacturing 1
    How to Collect 4
    Legal Aspects of Collecting 4
    Reproduction Insignia 5
    Types of Collectors 5
    "Issue" Patches 6
    Patch Prices 6
    Abbreviations 7
    Seal Heraldry 7
    How Many Federal Patches are There? 8
    Future Editions 8
    Future Titles 8
Organization and Numbering of Patch Exhibits 8
Task Force Patches 8
Exhibits 9
    Executive Departments
        Department of Agriculture 9
        Department of Commerce 14
        Central Intelligence Agency / National Security
        Agency 16
        Department of Defense 18
        Department of Education 42
        Department of Energy 42
        Environmental Protection Agency 49
        Federal Law Enforcement Associations 50
        FDA / HHS / SSA / HUD / OPM 51
        Department of the Interior 54

        Department of Justice 69
            Drug Enforcement Administration 77
            Federal Bureau of Investigation 93
            United States Border Patrol 120
            Immigration and Naturalization Service 123
            United States Marshal Service 130
        Department of Labor 142
        United States Postal Service 143
        Department of State 149
        Interpol / United Nations / USIA 153
        Department of Transportation 154
            Amtrak 156
            United States Coast Guard 157
            Federal Aviation Administration 160
        Department of the Treasury 163
            Bureau of Alcohol, Tobacco and Firearms . . .166
            United States Customs Service 171
            Internal Revenue Service 185
            United States Secret Service 188
    Judicial Branch / Federal Courts 201
    Veterans Administration /
    Department of Veterans Affairs 202
    Legislative Branch / United States Congress 204
    Independent and Quasi-Federal Agencies 208
    National Aeronautics and Space Administration 218
    National Science Foundation 220
    Tennessee Valley Authority .220
    U.S. Trusts, Territories, and Possessions 221
Insignia Suppliers 227
Related Reading 229
Appendix: Laws Relating to Federal Insignia 231
About the Author . . . . .Inside Back Cover

Dedication

I dedicate this book to all of the hosts of the various local, regional, and national police insignia swap meets. These fellow collectors are the first to arrive and the last to leave each meet, where they spend so much time attending to the problems and concerns of other collectors that they neglect their own collecting. They try to please everyone, and rarely receive much in the way of thanks. Putting on a meet, particularly a national meet, may take a year's work, or more, but without that work this hobby would be moribund. Thanks to you all. Please keep up the good work.

Secondly, Mike Bondarenko and the staff at *PCNews* are the glue that holds this hobby together. They provide a venue for collectors to share their knowledge, to buy and sell and trade for additions to their collections, to learn where swap meets are being held, and (very importantly) to "vent" their feelings about the hobby and the personalities in it. *PCNews* has been called "the Bible of police insignia collecting" by the Los Angeles *Times*, and rightfully so. Thanks Mike, Paula, and Donna.

Finally, a special note of thanks must go to Lt. Nick DeMarco of the Department of Defense Police. Nick wrote the "Fed Scene" column about federal patches for many years, and was responsible for many new federal collectors entering the hobby. We all owe Nick a debt of gratitude for his many years of unpaid service to the hobby. Thanks again, Nick.

Preface

While federal badges have been a part of American law enforcement since at least the Civil War era, federal cloth insignia are a much more recent invention. Noted police historian George Virgines, in his book entitled *Police Relics*, states that American law enforcement agencies did not begin the use of cloth insignia until the 1930s. Customs did not issue a standarized shoulder patch until 1959.

Of course, military units have always used cloth and metal insignia to instill a sense of organizational pride and identity in their members, and uniformed federal police officers and guards have made shoulder emblems and armbands a part of their equipment for several decades.

The rise of multi-agency task forces and coordinated raids, where agents of many different jurisdictions come together for selected enforcement activities, has shown the need of a highly visible means of identity for officers who generally work in plainclothes. Large cloth badges are filling that need, enabling friend and foe alike to take immediate note of the wearer's identity and authority. Many federal agencies now issue, or allow their agents to use, raid jackets and/or baseball-type caps bearing some sort of agency identification.

The use of these cloth badges, etc., has caught the attention of the many thousands of police officers and others who collect patches, adding yet another category of cloth collectibles. The attractiveness of federal patches is enhanced by the fact that they are generally harder to come by than most local and county insignia.

Special Thanks

A great number of collectors gave unselfishly of their time and expertise in the compilation of this volume, most of whom I have tried to list on the Acknowledgments page. In addition, the individuals named below also helped in the editing and proofreading of the chapters dealing with their agencies, and corrected many (but I bet not all) of my errors. Some of them copied their entire patch collections, made laser copies of patches I needed, or actually loaned me some of the rarest federal patches around, in order to make this book more complete.

Needless to say, I owe them a great deal for their unpaid help, and all readers of this volume will benefit from their input.

In some instances, even collaborators from the same agency disagreed over some patches; *i.e.*, which is the original, what is a "novelty" patch versus an issue patch, etc., and I have attempted to resolve such disputes to the best of my ability. In the process I'm sure some errors on my part crept in. For that I apologize in advance, and welcome input from readers to correct such mistakes in future editions.

While I have tried to recall and list the names of all who helped, this book is the culmination of a twelve-year project and inevitably I omitted some people. For this I also apologize in advance, and can only hope that you will take some satisfaction in the fact that this book is much better for your contribution.

Rudy Basurto	Darrell Klasey	Rich Pontes
Kevin Corr	David Kolberson	Mark Preuss
Luke Flannery	Steve LaBier	Bill Simmonds
Gary Grant	Ryder Lusk	Gary Teragawa
Frank Gulich	Wes Maroney	Al Tukey
Darrell Haynes	Robert Matia	Steve & Vicki White
Thom Houk	George Mitchell	Fred Winker
Kent Jeffries	Tom Owens	Bryce Workman
Doug Jones	Steve Petro	

In addition, the folks named below were essential to putting all the exhibits and actual book together, and I thank them all:

Anna Bae
Joann Bae
Rose Bae
Jim A. Esquivel
Shelley Ginsburg
Chris Lloyd
Jeff Millet
Kristin Popovich
Terri Speakman

Acknowledgments

The author is by no means an expert on law enforcement patches, and without a great deal of help from the following individuals and organizations this book could never have been completed.

Abramson, Larry
Ackiss, F.
Adler, Sandy
Aery, Peter
Ainsworth, Phillip
Alexander, Wayne
Allen, Steve
Anderson, Jack
Anderson, William A.
Argonish, Bob
Armstrong, Jim
Arnold, Dave
Asher, Mike
Assad, Mike
Austin, Jim
Banco, Joseph
Bankus, Bryan
Baron, Scott
Barosko, Tom
Barrera, Rudolph S.
Bartlett, Jay
Bassett, Thomas W.
Basurto, Rudy
Benedict, Floyd M.
Benjamin, Stan
Benton, Ed
Berry, Will
Bitzer, John
Blackburn, Larry
Boeckmann, Tom
Bondarenko, Mike
Bonner, Mark H.
Book 'Em Insignia
Borton, Lee
Boster, Mark
Boushh, J.C.
Boyden, Nolan
Bramscher, Robert
Brandt, Jim
Brockman, Donald E.
Broncato, Joseph "Bronc"
Broshous, Charlie
Brown, Lesley
Broyles, Rob
Buchanan, Sean
Burnett, Bob
Burnette, Jeff
Burton, Jim
Bushey, Alyssa Mary
Bushey, Keith
Bushey, Jake
Bushery, Tom
Campisi, Charles V.
Canaris, Mike
Canfield, John
Carlton, Bob
Carlton, Kenneth
Carlton, Robert
Carter, Carolyn
Carter, Stan
Casalese, Paul
Casas, Rich
Casey, Rick
Cassidy, Marty
Castro, Andy
Cates, Ken
Catterall, Logan
Cereno, David
Chang, Myron
Charles, Joseph
Chumley, Tom
Cicala, Bob
Clark, Vincent
Coajou, Pat
Collins, Dan
Commercial Emblem Supply
Conley, Lawrence
Corr, Kevin
Crawford, Fred
Cresthohl, Michael
Cron, Bernard
Crow, Brian
Crumpacker, Jim
Cumings, Scott
Currie, George
Cutrone, Lou
Daddio, William
Dale, David
Davis, Bob
David, Gerard Jr.
Davis, Russ
Davis, Stephanie
Delgado, William J.
Demarco, Betty
Demarco, Nick
Dempsey, Bill
Dever, Bill
Diaz, Vinnie
Dietterick, Stephen
Di Rubba, Joe
Doser, Virginia
Dowling, Jerry L.
Drewitt, Bruce
Driver, Grant
Dugan, Frank
Edwards, Dan
Elmendorf, Frank
Enochs, Jack
Epps, Sterling
Erickson, Peter
Fagel, Mike
Fahy, Jim
Falcone, Anthony
Fallon, Denny
Falzone, Dominick
Federal Criminal Investigators Association
Federal Law Enforcement Officers Association
Fellmann, John
Few, Edward
Fire Magazine
Fitz-Patrick, Dennis
Flannery, Luke
Flynn, Pete
Foley, Bob
Foley, "Doc"
Foster, David
Fujimoto, Alan
Galloway, David
Garrett, Bill
Garrison, Michelle
Gaschke, David
Ghio, Fred
Gianuzzi, Gene
Gibb, Charlie
Giblin, Charlie
Gidley, Karen
Gieseke, Gary
Giles, Don
Ginsburg, Al
Ginsburg, David and Dena
Ginsburg, Rochelle
Gist, Doug
Gist, Walt
Goldmark, Josh
Gonzales, Adam
Gonzales, Ambrosio "Gonzo"
Grago, Randy
Grant, Gary
Grasska, Denis
Griffin, Henry
Gripon, Peter
Grodin, Jay
Gulich, Frank
Gustafson, Bob
Gustafson, Robert
Haig, Joe
Hall, Dave
Hall, Rick
Halpern, Natalie
Hamilton, Rick
Hamm, Chuck
Hansen, Rod
Harris, Dan
Hart, James
Hathaway, Marty
Haynes, Darrell
Hearn, Thomas G.
Hedges, Bill
Heffler, Joe
Heiser, Gioia
Henry, Darryl
Herron, Joe
Hester, Laurel
Hollywood, Tom
Hoos, John
Horne, Tony
Houk, Thom
Hurry, Gerald
Hutcheson, Kevin
In-Gear Promotions, Inc.
Ingleby, Kenneth
International Police Association
Irish, John
Irwin, Robert M. II
J&G Enterprises
Jacobson, Dorothy
Jackson, James
Jackson, Rob
Jaffe, Joel
James, Gary
Janzen, Linda
Jared, Lou
Jeffries, Kent

Johnson, Kelly
Jorgenson, Jim "J.J."
Kalicki, Tony
Karas, Jim
Karotseris, Charlie
Keim, Don
Kelly, Joe
Kelly, Norma
Kelly, Owen J.
Kelly, Pam
Kessler, Ed
Kimball, Mike
Klasey, Darrell
Knight, Bruce
Kolberson, Dave
Kozol, Phil
Krohn, David L.
Kruger, Frank
La Bier, Steve
La Jeunesse, Roger
Latham, Frank
Lauro, Gene
Leaf, Rick
Lee, Bill
Leffler, Eric
Leibowitz, Irwin
Leno, Jay
Levine, Ron
Lindsay, Andy
Lion Brothers Co., Inc.
Loar, Dave
Long, Sean
Lowery, Randy
Lusk, Ryder
Ly, Mau
Lynch, Carol
Lynch, Mike
Lynch, Pat
Lyon, Charles
Mac Martin, Steve
Machinski, Mike
Mack, Scott
Magill, Robert
Magyar, Richard
Marcello, John
Mahony, Michael
Margulies, Paul
Markardt, Steve
Maroney, Wes
Martin, Phil
Martin, Steve
Matens, Bill
Matia, Bob
Matzke, Gene
Mc Carthy, Pat
Mc Cormick, Bill
Mc Ewan, Wayne
McLellan, Dennis
Meany, Dan
Mendoza, Alex
Menzies, Dave
Messer, Doug

Middleton, Samuel L.
Miles, Ed
Miller, Douglas
Miller, Edward
Miller, Richard
Millet, Jeffrey R.
Mitchell, George A.
Mixon, Brian
Money, Larry
Morales, Manny
Morris, J.D.
Mullins, John
Mullins, Leslie
Mulvihill, Jim
Mumma, Danny
Murphy, Anthony
Murphy, Richard
Murray, Robyn Stewart
Nadel, Seth
National Association of
   Federal Investigators
Nemec, Brian
Nevins, Victor
Neyens, Duane
Nordeen, Al and Debbie
Norton, Marcy
Novak, Ben
Nunes, Ken
Nunez, Clint
Nurse, Douglas
O'Callaghan, John V.
Oda, Pat
Ohlfs, Jeff
Oliver, Robert
Olvey, Pat
O'Meara, Ed
Otto, Rob
Owens, Tom
Pace, William
Pappin, Craig
Parker, Michael
Patchula, Count
Pate, David
Patterson, Chuck
Peel, Michael
Perry, Richard
Peters, David
Peterson, Jim
Petro, Steve
Pfeifle, Greg
Philpott, Marty
Piwowarczyk, Ron
Police Insignia Collectors
   Association
Pontes, Richard
Post, Dave
Post, Mike
Poulsen, Soeren
Preuss, Mark
Price, Bill (deceased)
Reff, Sam
Reifke, Art

Reimer, John
Rembisz, Frank
Rice, Jerry
Richards, Ron
Riehn, Delbert
Richard, Lew
Richardson, Dave
Richardson, Donald
Ritchie, Lee
Rivers, Steve
Roberts, Glen
Robertson, LeRoy
Robertson, Steve
Robins, Tad
Robinson, John
Rodriguez, Ed
Rodriguez, Jesse
Roek, Paul
Rogers, Leo D.
Ruiz, George C.
Runyon, Doug
Russell, Ed
Russell, Jeffrey
Russell, Paul
Russo, Lisa
Rutt, Robert
Sachs, Ed
Saitta, Joe V.
Salchunas, Richard
Salen, J. Richard
Sally's Cop Shop
Saunders, Tim
Schreiber, Al
Schulberg, Dave
Schwartz, Ned
Searle, Frank
Serrano, Angelo
Shattuck, Jim
Shaw, Jim
Shell, Dennis
Shepherd, Mike
Shiohama, Mike
Sigona, Robert
Simon, P.
Sitek, Jerry
Skaggs, J.R.
Smeets, Rene
Smith, "Hoss"
Smith, Marvin
Solomon, Isaac
Solter, Erik
Sorenson, Norm
Spohn, Shawn
Springer, Ed
Sprinkle, Dave
Squadron Flight Shop
Stahl, John William
Stanley, Richard
Star Emblems
Starkman, Robert
Stechmann, Chris
Steiner, Bill

Stielow, Curtis
Stumpf, George
Sullivan, J.J.
Sviland, Marty
Swyter, Wendy and Steve
Tagni, Peter
Taylor, Howard
Taylor, Ken
Taylor, Terry
Terjesen, Robert
Teragawa, Gary
Thompson, John H.
Thread Letter Embr. Co.
Trevis, Mike
Trivilino, Mark
Truxal, Dan
Truxal, Dave
Tukey, Al
Uland, Rick
Underwood, Dave
United Insignia
U.S. Attorney's Office
Van Horn, Dwight
Van Schuyver, Larry
Veich, Mickey
Venables, George
Venables, Mary
Vicki White Enterprises
Vida, Herb
Virgines, George
Vitaletti, James
Von Dust Bunny, Baron
Walden, Mike
Wambaugh, Joe
Ward, Mort
Waterman, Warren
Watts, Frank
Watts, Gary
Wayne, Dennis
Weinstock, George
Wellesley, Brian T.
Wessling, Wes
Wheeler, George
White, Jim
White, Steve
Whitfield, Tim
Widup, Kim
Wilhelm, Frank
Wilhite, Art
Wills, John
Winget, Richard
Winker, Fred
Winker, Tom
Workman, Bryce
Worldwide Insignia
Yarton, Chuck
Yee, George
Zaback, Jerry
Zagami, James

Introduction

Why This Book?

Volume One of this series, *Federal Law Enforcement Patches*, grew out of the author's frustration at being unable to find reference works of any kind that dealt with federal cloth insignia. As a collector, I needed one, and I felt other collectors probably did, too.

Necessity really is the Mother of Invention, so I published my first book, which featured around 300 color photos of federal patches, in 1983. Four years later, with both my own collection and the hobby itself having grown exponentially, it clearly was time for a supplementary work. Volume Two debuted in 1987, containing about 500 new exhibits.

By 1998, my own collection of federals had grown to over five thousand patches, and more kept coming out every month. I knew it was time for a new edition of the book, and started pestering many of the major federal insignia collectors to let me borrow some of their items and began scanning them into digital color images, then to be transferred onto CDs as the nucleus of a new "encyclopedia" of federal patches.

Since I was sold out of Volume One, and nearly out of Volume Two, I decided to partially incorporate those volumes into the new one (with some omissions, as explained below), and to correct errors and color reproduction problems.

I originally had planned and budgeted for about 2800 to 3000 images, but soon found that I had about 6000 to choose from. I ended up with over 4000, but had to omit some very colorful and collectible Coast Guard, Military, and Tribal patches. Other collectors already have published books on these categories, and I urge readers to buy them (see the Related Reading section in the back of this book).

Emblem Manufacturing

Like the Village People, federal patches come in many colors, shapes, and sizes. In prior editions of this book the then-current manufacturing processes were described. Since 1987, the year that Volume Two was published, computerized patch design and manufacturing have come of age. The updated material below is excerpted from the sales brochure entitled *Law Enforcement Insignia Design and Manufacture*, used with the permission of Star Emblems. I urge all collectors to order and maintain a copy as useful reference material. Write to Star Emblems at 31518 Anacapa Drive, Malibu, California 90265. Telephone (310) 457-5023, fax (310) 457-3622, E-mail Bconnect@aol.com.

The Star Emblems brochure is twelve pages long, and contains nearly 200 photos of federal, state, and local law enforcement patches separated by type. It is a bargain at just $2.00!

Law Enforcement Insignia Design and Manufacture
During the 12th century the use of pictures and emblems on shields and coats of arms was introduced into England from western Europe. This was the origin of the heraldic system. Early uses were on the battlefield as a means of identification for otherwise unrecognizable armor-clad knights. The knight's name and a bold emblem were embroidered on his surcoat, the garment worn over his armor, which became known as the "coat of arms." At the time many people were unable to read or write, so seals were used to authenticate official documents. The messengers of royal or noble households—heralds—had the duty to identify knights. Thus heralds became interested in colorful means of identification, and heraldry as it is known today began.

Law enforcement agencies have adopted insignia in the same way as the Knights of the Round Table, for the purpose of identification. In particular, embroidered insignia have been used for identification on jackets, shirts, and caps. Most commonly, cloth insignia is applied to the shoulder sleeves and metal badges are worn on the front of shirts and jackets. Special applications can be used, such as cloth badges on jackets or shirts, and large patches for the backs of jumpsuits, jackets, or raid gear. In every instance the insignia is designed for identification. There are over 12,000 law enforcement agencies and departments in the United States, and in each department there are a variety of different groups who all require specialized identification.

The ultimate decision for the type and design of the insignia may rest with the chief, sheriff, or leading official of the department. The quality and uniqueness of the design is limnited only by the imagination and creativity of the artist. Knowledge of the design and manufacture of insignia is a key element in assisting the artist in the creation of both a visually apppealing and a functional design.

FABRIC AND THREAD: The majority of insignia are manufactured using a cotton twill material as a base, with cotton or polycotton thread embroidered onto the base fabric. Most thread is designated as colorfast, meaning that it can be laundered and exposed to heat and ultra-violet (sunlight) without fading or discoloring. Also used is metallic thread, which is thicker than the 30mm size thread used on most multi-head machines. Metallic thread adds a rich brilliance to the design, and may be best suited for commemorative or award patches. While metallic thread is very durable, it can be difficult to embroider because it frequently breaks during the embroidery process. As metallic thread has a high degree of reflectivity it may not be suitable for tactical purposes. A recent innovation is the use of reflective material as a base for embroidery, which has become popular for use in traffic situations such as bike and motor details. Reflectivity is rated in candlepower, with visibility of the material from a distance of 3,000 feet. Reflective material is 300 times brighter than white fabric.

BACKING: After the insignia is embroidered there are several options in finishing the back of the patch. It can have no backing, meaning that the cotton twill and thread are exposed on the back. A thin layer of plastic can be applied to the back of the patch, designated as plastic backing. Plastic backing keeps the patch from shrinking when laundered, and extends the life of the patch. Another type of backing is heat seal applied, which allows the patch to be ironed or heat-applied onto a garment or cap. It is best suited to caps, and not advised for application to shirts or jackets which are laundered more frequently. Sewing on the emblem is the best application for shirts and jackets. Other backings available are velcro material, or felt backing for display patches. In general, most law enforcement patches have the plastic backing applied. It is universal, and gives the patch a longer life than the garment it is attached to.

THREAD COLORS: There is a wide range of color choice in both thread and fabric. The United States Military Office of Heraldry has specific guidelines regarding thread color. A book is available having a "Cable Color" chart which identifies all colors that are used for military insignia. Printers use the Pantone Color Matching System (PMS) to identify ink colors, and they can be cross-referenced to an embroidery company's thread colors. For an exact color match it is advisable to request a color chart from the embroidery company identifying the exact thread colors for your design, or they can provide a color swatch for your requested colors. The cost of such color charts varies from $30.00 for a basic chart to $200.00 for the military Cable Color chart.

DIGITIZING: Digitizing is the term used for the conversion of the design to a format which commands the computer of the embroidery machine. The digitizer, or technician, enlarges the design on a large tablet and uses a computer-style mouse device to re-draw the design and indicate the direction, pattern, and coloration to the computer. Digitizing is a skill which takes years to perfect, and the quality of the final product is directly related to the artistic skill and quality of the digitizer. Digitizing a design results in a calculation of the overall stitch count, which may vary from 10,000 to 50,000 stitches for the average-size law enforcement shoulder insignia (approximately 5" by 4"). The cost of digitizing a design can range between $10.00 to $20.00 per thousand stitches. The total stitch count depends on how much of the design is embroidered versus the area of the base fabric left visible, as well as the size of the design. After the design is digitized, a sample or "sew-out" can be produced on a single-head machine for the customer's approval. The cost of samples prior to production can range from $50.00 to $150.00, and it is advisable to have a sample made for complex patch designs, or for orders of 1,000 or more pieces.

MANUFACTURING MACHINERY: Multi-head embroidering machines were developed over twenty years ago. Prior to multi-head machines, emblems were manufactured on Schiffli machines, which are very large and use a thicker thread than multi-head machines. This can be seen by comparing pre-1970 vintage patches to today's finer-thread patches. Old-style patches do not have the definition and detail of those produced on modern multi-head machinery. The military still requires insignia to be manufactured on Schiffli machines, thus ensuring that they are made domestically. "Offshore" companies do not use the Schiffli machines, as they are generally outdated and primarily used today for embroidering on lace-type fabrices for drapery and linens. While there are many makers of multi-head machines, the leading manufacturers are Tajima and Baruden. Machines range in size from one to over twenty embroidery heads, and the average machine has the capacity of seven thread colors per head. If the design requires more than seven thread colors the machine must be rethreaded to complete all the colors. Some designs require fifteen or more thread colors, which takes extra time for the operator and adds to the cost of the emblem. The cost of the machines ranges between $30,000 for a single-head machine, to over $120,000 for a multi-head machine. Most large-volume embroidery companies use twenty or more head machines, which are run on three shifts, twenty-four hours a day. It takes only one operator to thread and monitor the machine during production.

FINISHING THE INSIGNIA: After the embroidery machine completes its process each individual design must be cut out of the large parent sheet. This is a very tedious and time-consuming procedure, but a skilled cutter can complete 1,200 or more pieces per hour. After the design is cut out it requires the additional procedure of finishing the edge. The most common is a merrowed edge, where the edge is oversewn from front to back. As the merrowing machine cannot follow certain curves and inside corners, irregular-shape designs may have to be laser-cut, which can follow even the most intricate shape. It is advised that laser-cut patches have plastic backing applied, to keep the edges from fraying.

PRICING: The cost of manufacturing patches is based on time and materials. The main elements of cost are machine time and the labor required to finish the patch after it is sewn, as the cost of the material is small. Most emblem embroiderers base their quotes on the size of the patch, its quality, number of thread colors, and percentage of embroidery coverage (partial to 100%). Prices may vary significantly depending on the digitizing time and the stitch count.

CAP PATCHES: Baseball or golf-style caps are becoming more popular as an adapted uniform piece for law enforcement. Recent studies have shown that they provide a high degree of sun-screening, which reduces the risk of skin cancer. Most commonly, a department's shoulder insignia is simply reduced in size for use as cap insignia, the standard height of which is 3", but which can be as tall as $3^1/_2$". The most comfortable styles are a polycotton blend; 100% wool caps are best suited for the winter months. The prostyle six-panel shape caps also will accept insignia. A special backing is applied to the patch, which allows it to be heat-sealed onto the cap without the need for sewing.
Examples: #0014, #0030

BADGE PATCHES: Today's computerized embroidery machines are able to very accurately produce a cloth version of traditional metal badges. No matter what the style: eagle-top, oval, five, six, or seven-point stars…silver, gold, or two-tone…and color center seals can be included. Badge patches are popular on jackets, and for such special units as emergency response teams and K-9. In certain applications they are preferable over metal badges as they have low reflectivity, don't catch on seatbelts or other obstructions, and often are more suitable for tactical responders. Lettering should be no less than 1/4-inch high for legibility. Cloth badges are significantly less expensive than metal.
Examples: #0013, #0018

ROUND-TOP: Round-top insignia are very distinctive for law enforcement, allowing for large, bold lettering used with a center area which can accomodate virtually any shape design. Center areas are being used to depict landmarks within the department's service area, and they can be very detailed to include state or local seals or a variety of other custom-designed graphic elements. Traditionally, a background color is used that matches the color of the uniform, with contrasting colors for the border and lettering. Originally, this shape was used extensively for sheriffs' departments, yet today it is common for both police and security uses.
Examples: #0238, #0269

SUBDUED TACTICAL: Over twenty years ago the first special response teams were activated. Today, even some of the smallest departments have designated teams for tactical response. Special unit patches are created in a style similar to the military subdued insignia. However, most law enforcement designs combine black and gray colors as opposed to black and olive drab, as the black and gray color combination is better suited to the urban environment. Often the standard shoulder insignia is simply the changed to this subdued coloration, although a great many departments choose to have a unique design produced for their team. Common designations are Emergency Response Team (ERT), or variations on that theme.
Examples: #0150, #0214

SHIELD: The most common shape for law enforcement shoulder insignia is the shield. It provides a large area for the most common design elements such as Police, Sheriff, Security, etc., along with identifying the location such as state or city, or a special unit. On the majority of shield patch designs the top line identifies the department, and the bottom line the location. The shield also provides a large center area for a star, state seal, or other graphic element such as a landmark or landscape.
Examples: #0206, #0310

3-POINT CASTLE: The 3-point castle shape has a military background. It may have originated during the Middle Ages as the symbol depicting a knight's name on his surcoat (a garment worn over the armor), which became known as the coat of arms. This vertical shape works well with a simple central design element such as an eagle, seal, or county or state shape, rather than a landscape. Commonly the 3-point castle has only two lines of lettering, the top being Police, Sheriff, etc., the bottom the location; however these are occasionally reversed.
Examples: #0254, #0281

3-POINT This design combines elements from both the 3-point castle and the shield. Its shape is not as militaristic as the 3-point castle, while having the vertical design of the standard shield. In general this design has a center insignia such as a five, six, or seven-point star, and may also include a state seal or a miniature version of the department's metal badge. Most are approximately 5" tall by 4" wide, and have a single rather than double border color, the latter being more common to the shield design. Variations on the 3-point design can include a round top.
Examples: #0384, #0490

TOMBSTONE: Shoulder insignia naturally lend themselves to vertical designs, and the tombstone shape allows for the most usable area of any of the standard shapes of law enforcement insignia. Tombstone patches may be as tall as 6", providing the greatest legibility of title, and allowing a large area for identifying the department and location. In general, lettering dominates the tombstone design, with any center graphic element being subordinate; however, its shape allows for a star or circle central design element, as well.
Examples: #0699, #1260

IRREGULAR: In recent years increasing numbers of insignia are breaking away from the conventional shapes, and often the most distinctive incorporate the shape of a state. As there are no boundaries or limitations to what an embroidery machine can produce, a skilled artist may combine the shape of a state with other elements, or create a large shoulder insignia in the shape of an eagle-top, oval, or star badge. Many round designs are associated with specialty units such as SWAT, ERT, and K9. Irregular-shaped designs are the fastest-growing segment of this market. They are visually appealing, and often reflect the new community policing policies.
Examples: #1257, #1385

HIGH-VISIBILITY: More and more law enforcement personnel are taking part, along with emergency medical and firefighters, in all types of incidents. While fire and EMS incorporate high-visibility in their basic uniform, law enforcement has adopted low-visibility for tactical situations. Thus one of the newest innovations is reflective patches, which reflect up to 500 candlepower and are visible from a distance of up to 3,000 feet. Reflective patches may be best suited for traffic officers or bike and motor details, and are available in a variety of colors which can be coordinated to match existing insignia. High visibility at night is extremely important in emergency situations involving traffic and crowd control.
Example: #2312

How To Collect

You have already taken the first step, which is to acquire a reference book! Now there are several other things you can do to become a successful collector.

Subscribe to *Police Collector News*. This is the Bible of the law enforcement insignia collecting hobby. It is the best way to keep up on what is happening in and to the hobby, to find out when and where swap meets are scheduled, to buy and sell all kinds of insignia, and to share your views and collection with the rest of the fraternity. *PCNews* is absolutely indispensible to the collector, and is just about the only bargain in the hobby today. See their ad on the inside front cover of this book.

Subscribe to other collecting publications, as well. If you collect FBI pins and patches, for instance, you'll want to take *The Bureau Trader* (see their ad also). It depicts FBI patches and pins in full color, and is very reasonably priced, too.

Buy any and all insignia reference books you can find. Many such books go out-of-print very quickly, so don't delay in getting a copy. See the section titled *Related Reading* in this volume for those books currently in print, and check *PCNews* for new books just coming out.

Attend local and national insignia swap meets. This is by far the single best way to meet and make friends with like-minded collectors, and to pick up the insignia needed for your collection. There, you'll find many people who will make note of what you're looking for, help you locate those items, and perhaps most importantly, steer you clear of the group of "schlockmeisters" who continue to infest this hobby. Here's a hint: At the first few meets you attend, do a lot of looking and listening, but go easy on the buying. Get a sense of who the honest players are, and who is to be avoided. Hobbyists love to gossip, so you'll pick up lots of useful information. Remember: New collectors are the crooks' preferred prey; let the buyer beware!

After you have acquired an overview of the collectibles that are available, decide what it is that you want to collect—pins, patches, old or current badges, commemoratives, model police cars, paper items—the list is virtually endless. You're limited only by your imagination, but if you don't settle on a single category (or two) pretty soon, after a while you'll end up with a large quantity of unrelated items that don't fit into a cohesive whole. If that is what you want, have at it. But most collectors find it more satisfying to concentrate on state highway patrol/state police patches, federal pins, presidential inaugural badges, or whatever captures their imagination and fits their pocketbook—they have a clear goal, an end in sight, and their collection reflects that focus.

Personally, I am not a computer guy, but a lot of collectors are now communicating with fellow collectors online. But be forewarned that a lot of repros and outright junk are being sold online—and that the buyer has little recourse if he gets stuck. An honest seller *always* allows the buyer an inspection/approval period during which he can satisfy himself that what he bought is what it was represented to be. These sellers will allow you to return the item for a refund with no questions asked, if you are not satisfied. Ask *before* you buy, and if they don't, go elsewhere.

Don't forget to get the word out to your fellow collectors, officers, family, and friends about what you now collect. You'll be surprised at how often you'll get leads on items that way.

Invest a mere three bucks, and put an ad in *PCNews*' "Bulletin Board" section. You'll get fifty words to advertise what you collect, or to dispose of what you no longer need. Every month, over 5,000 collectors will be exposed to your ad!

Don't waste your time writing to federal agencies asking for free patches. Most agencies immediately "round-file" such requests as they have no budget for give-aways, and they receive hundreds if not thousands of these inquiries each year. The head of the Chicago FBI Swat Team is not going to give you a patch, and the Secret Service isn't going to hand out a cloth badge, either. Once in a while a collector gets lucky, but don't count on it. If you do decide to write, offer to pay for your request and always enclose an SASE.

Finally, follow the Golden Rule. Treat other collectors as you want to be treated. Remember—What goes around, comes around!

Legal Aspects of Collecting Federal Law Enforcement Insignia

There is a great deal of apprehension concerning what is and what is not permissible with regards to possessing federal law enforcement insignia. Let us examine the controlling statutes and the one reported decision, and perhaps we can clear up some of the confusion.

Title 18 Section 701 United States Code, is a statute proscribing the possession of any "badge, identification card, or other insignia, of the design prescribed by the head of any department or agency of the United States for use by any officer or employee thereof, or any colorable imitation thereof...except as authorized under regulations made pursuant to law". This would seem to be a clear prohibition against even having a picture of a federal insignia—but, what is the intent of this law?

In the only reported case that I can find on this law, *United States v. Goeltz*, 513 F.2d 193 (1975) (which involved the unauthorized possession of some IRS seizure notices by members of a tax rebellion group), the Circuit Court held that the "Statute proscribing the unauthorized possession of any badge, identification card, or other insignia of the United States was intended to protect the public against the use of recognizable assertion of authority *with intent to deceive*." (my emphasis) This seems to me to be eminently reasonable—who wants some jerk passing himself off as a federal agent to harass citizens (the real agents can do that themselves) or to obtain entry to banks for nefarious purposes, ...you name it.

From my discussions with federal prosecutors and FBI and Secret Service agents, the consensus of opinion is that if you steal or counterfeit a federal credential, or use it to hold yourself out as a federal officer, or otherwise embarass the government with it (as with Mr. Goeltz), they will take action against you, and you could find yourself in hot water.

In addition, the Secret Service has been aggressive with regard to seizing unauthorized copies of their current badge. This seems reasonable, as no one wants a John Hinckley-type running around with an SS shield. I note that, in the case reported in a national collector's magazine, the Secret Service picked up their badge, then issued a receipt for contraband, in lieu of arresting the holder. From my conversations with representatives of the FBI and other federal agencies, they would also take steps to reclaim any of their current-issue shields unlawfully in private hands.

What about obsolete federal shields—can you possess them legally? Yes, in a word, many old shields are given to agents when a new design is adopted, and some of these find their way into private hands, legally. Retired agents are often given their shields (sometimes encased in lucite or attached to a plaque) and these occasionally turn up in circulation. Heads of agencies have been known to give one of their shields to a political figure, or to a foreign dignitary. With all of these shields around, it would be a prosecutor's nightmare to attempt to initiate proceedings for simple possession of obsolete federal badges. Again, if someone were to steal them, counterfeit them, or use them to falsely identify themself as a federal officer, the United States Attorney's office would consider prosecution on a case-by-case basis. You should also be aware that failure to turn over a federal insignia, if requested, is a separate offense.

Title 18, Section 713, United States Code, as amended by Public Law 91-651, (1971) details the prohibition of certain uses of the great seal of the U.S., the Presidential and Vice Presidential seals. Seals of the Federal Government departments, bureaus, and independent agencies are not in the public domain. No use may be made of any Government seal for other than official business without authorization of the agency involved.

The Secret Service informed the editor of the Police Insignia Collectors Assn. (PICA) newsletter that it is permissible to run pictures of federal shields, etc., if they are shown less than three-quarter size, or more than one and one-half times larger than actual size. (You will notice that the photos in this book meet that criteria).

Since federal patches are given out by many federal agents and agencies, and they do not bear the same potential for misuse as a badge or a commission, absent some embarassment to the government, you are probably all right in having them in your collection. Common sense would seem to be the watchword here, *i.e.*, if you start manufacturing federal patches, illegally, you can expect legal problems.

I hope this discussion has cleared up at least some of the misconceptions surrounding federal insignia. By the way, I am not an attorney, and what I have written is only the results of my research—if you have further questions, see your legal counsel.

Reproduction (Repro) Patches

Any time more than two collectors gather, the issue of reproduction insignia is bound to come up. Along with pricing, this seems to be the burning issue of the day.

"Repros" are patches that resemble legitimately-made emblems, but which don't come from the agency, or from the original source.

I have seen "commemoratives" (made up perhaps years after the event by someone with no connection to the case) being sold for big bucks, as well as patches made "on spec" by a dealer who will send some to, say, an FBI SWAT team with the hope of them being adopted by that unit. Even if they're not adopted, these patches then are sold to unwary buyers as authentic.

"Fantasy" patches also are fairly common, wherein some dealer decides that even if an agency doesn't have a particular patch, "they should," and so out comes another one.

Unscrupulous dealers also counterfeit issue patches, knowing that there always are more federal collectors than available patches. Some designers are copyrighting their designs and placing the copyright symbol under the backing, to identify the patch as an original. With the rise of computerized machines, it is now possible to duplicate even the most intricate designs almost perfectly. At the recent national meet in Texas, one dealer was forced to remove a stack of counterfeits from his table after the original designer saw them.

It is hard to protect yourself against a well-made repro, and I suspect that I have been victimized, along with may other collectors. With hundreds of dollars being asked for some extremely rare federal patches, it was just a matter of time before the "schlockmeisters" entered the hobby in a big way.

Types of Collectors

There are at least three schools of thought regarding repros, and each school of thought is closely associated with a particular type of collector:

1. THE PURIST: These collectors are absolutely opposed to the very existence of repros and consider those who sell or trade them as misled at best, or criminals at worst. Many insignia swap meets have notices posted which bear the legend "No Reproductions Allowed" or "Reproduction Items Must Be Labelled As Such." Purists question how some dealers can come by large quantities of scarce patches, and berate those who offer repros to hobby newcomers as legitimate issues.

Purists want police insignia collecting to remain a hobby and not a business. They prefer to trade for patches, rather than to buy and sell them.

2. THE ENTREPRENEUR: These are usually collector-dealers who acquire and offer for sale large stocks of patches from various sources. Some have the patches made up, some buy manufacturers overstocks or mistakes, and some won't reveal how they obtain them. Some emblem supply companies and their representatives attend insignia swap meets and/or advertise in police collector magazines.

Their point of view is that they supply a need in the hobby, and that the purists are those who got into the hobby years ago and acquired their patches when they were much easier to come by. They state that most beginning collectors cannot obtain access to a wide variety of patches, and that non-Police collectors start out at a considerable disadvantage, not having the type of job that enables them to make contacts for patches.

3. THE PRAGMATISTS: Neither as doctrinaire as the Purists, nor as *laissez-faire* as the Entrepreneurs, the Pragmatist is a middle-of-the-roader. He recognizes that every hobby has

counterfeits, and always will, and that the best defense against being "burned" is education. He will attempt to obtain as much provenance as possible, writing to other collectors, reading collector's publications, and seeking out agency sources, as well as buying insignia reference books. The Pragmatist knows that there are very few genuine "experts" in the field of police insignia collecting, and that everyone gets taken once in a while. He would like to possess only legitimate, issue patches, but will acquire a repro to help fill out a collection, until he can get the real thing.

I try to obtain a sample of every federal patch I encounter, both for self-protection and to show in my books. I note on the back of each patch the source and date I received it, for future reference. "Know your sources" are the watchwords. But it's not always possible, particularly when buying a large collection of patches gathered from many sources unknown to you.

PERSONAL OBSERVATIONS: From what I have seen during twenty-five years of police insignia collecting, many, if not most, collectors have a bit of each type in them. The Purist will gladly accept special-unit (SWAT, K-9) patches that are only used by a limited portion of the agency, and are not agency-issue. He will also buy and sell at times, in order to acquire needed items. Many Entrepreneurs want only legitimate-issue patches for their own collections, and will also swap as well as sell insignia with other collectors.

"Issue" Patches

Many of the patches illustrated in this book are not standard agency issue; that is, authorized cloth badges and shoulder patches specified by headquarters to be worn on raid jackets and ball caps. You'll notice hundreds of commemorative, anniversary, special unit, "giveaway," and local team patches, many of which are unknown or unapproved by headquarters.

Commemorative and other such patches often are used as tokens of appreciation for non-law enforcement officers who participate in task force investigations, or who, for instance, assist in helping federal agents make cases or otherwise do their jobs. The Secret Service and the FBI often use giveaway patches or pins for presentation to local or state officers or others as a sign of appreciation.

The Secret Service, for instance, relies heavily on local and state agencies to help provide protective support and to furnish investigative leads, and USSS field offices utilize any number of gifts such as patches and pins to express their thanks.

Patches are made up for a large number of task force members to commemorate the completion of a successful investigation. Commemorative patches also are used at the end of successful task force investigations, which typically involve multi-agency personnel and non-law enforcement support employees. Such patches are a relatively inexpensive way of expressing gratitude. Most never are worn, but are used in displays or sewn onto a baseball cap, or simply kept in binders. Some are very collectible.

Patch Prices

Price is a controversial topic in this hobby. Many collectors believe that federal patches cost too much today. While I'm no expert on *local* police patches, it has been my experience that in general they are fairly easy to come by. Many can be had for the time and expense of writing a letter to the department, or bought (with the exception of special unit patches) for less than five dollars each.

From my observations and experience with federal patches, it appears that with but a few exceptions (noted later) most of the more commonly-found federal patches run less than ten dollars each. Again, special unit patches will cost considerably more.

Why the difference in average prices? Consider several key factors:

1. There are far fewer federal agents nationwide than New York City Police officers. Obviously, fewer agents mean fewer patches are made or are available.
2. The most desirable federal patches seem to be the special unit patches, such as SWAT (Special Weapons And Tactics), HRT (Hostage Rescue Teams), SORT (Special Operations Response Teams), and similar small, elite unit emblems such as the U.S. secret Service Counter-Sniper and Counter-Assault (CAT) teams. Logically, small teams mean few patches.
3. Most federal agencies do not want their regular or special unit patches in the hands of non-team members. Thus, writing to them can be an exercise in futility. Management instructs the office heads and unit leaders to restrict the issue of their agency's insignia. Cost is a factor here, too.
4. Federal collectors take a back seat to no one when it comes to competing for the rare patches, and competition always drives prices upward. After all, there are several thousand federal insignia collectors and often only several hundred (or even fewer) patches available to an office or unit for their own use.
5. Patch contractors often are instructed to not sell over-runs to the public. Oftentimes there are NO spares, except perhaps a single patch allowed for the maker's sample book.

A contractor may receive an order for two hundred or fewer patches from a particular federal office. That office may, if the maker is lucky, allow him to sell or trade several dozen patches that the office will not need. The standard patch costs the dealer less than two dollars to make, unless it is specified that it be manufactured domestically, be fully embroidered, contain special threads (gold or silver mylar), have an elaborate design, or many colors, all of which drive up the cost. In addition, the contractor may have to pay to have the patch designed, to wine-and-dine or travel some distance to service the account, or to provide actual prototypes to land the contract in the first place, all the while feeling pressure to keep his prices low enough to remain in line with the competition.

So, faced with a very limited number of over-run patches that he can sell or trade to recover his costs, it is no surprise that the dealer will offer any spares to the highest bidders.

Remember, there may be several hundred collectors competing for those few dozen or less spares, so be prepared for sticker shock.

A while back I needed some rare FBI patches for my personal collection, and for several years offered up to two hundred dollars each to get them, *with no success*. Finally, I bought a large patch collection (the price was over *ten thousand* dollars), and thus was able to acquire them.

Writing books about federal patches does get my name out in front of collectors, but it generally doesn't give me access to dealer prices. In most instances, I am out there competing with you and many others for what I can get. I buy complete collections whenever possible, paying market prices or a bit below.

Finally, while some collectors feel that prices for federal patches are too high, I have done some research and have determined that the older state police and highway patrol patches regularly sell for many hundreds of dollars, and incredibly, that obsolete California police department patches often change hands for upwards of a thousand dollars. When I expressed surprise at my findings, fellow *PCNews* staff writer David Schulberg told me that an obsolete California city police patch (Alviso) recently sold on the Internet for $2,000.00! *Whew!* The highest price I have ever seen for a federal patch is $600.00, recently asked by a Boston dealer for an especially hard-to-get first issue FBI Hostage Rescue Team. He claims he got it, so apparently federal prices are on the way up, too. On my trade lists, I will list some rare patches as "trade only," or put a ridiculous price on them, hoping to draw out some rarities I can use in my own collection, and sometimes that works. One dealer in rare feds told me, "If you can't run with the big dogs, stay up on the porch...."

No matter how bad federal patch prices get, they can't hold a candle to those asked for federal *badges*. You can buy a fairly nice federal patch *collection* for the cost of a few federal badges, so it's all relative, I guess.

Abbreviations

Patch Description Abbreviations

R	Alleged reproduction
F	Fantasy patch
O/S	Obsolete
T	Twill
F/E	Fully embroidered
B	Bullion
SM	Silver mylar (thread)
GM	Gold mylar (thread)
C	Commemorative issue
A	Anniversary patch
SU	Special unit patch (SWAT, HRT, SORT, etc.)
P	Prop (used in movie or TV production)
PU	Provenance unknown; no background information now available
UID	Unsure if federal issue
C/S	Current style
C/B	Cloth badge
S/P	Shoulder patch

Agency Abbreviations

Large (and not-so-large) organizations are fond of using acronyms for their task forces, so here I'll show a few of the more common ones, particularly for the benefit of our foreign collectors.

SOG	Special Operations Group (U.S. Marshals, etc.)
OCDETF	Organized Crime Drug Enforcement Task Force
HIDTA	High-Intensity Drug Trafficking Area
FTF	Fugitive Task Force
SORT	Special Operations Response Team
SRT	Special Response Team
HRT	Hostage Rescue Team
FITF	Financial Investigative Task Force
JDIG	Joint Drug Investigative Group
EPIC	El Paso Intelligence Center
NDIC	National Drug Information Center
WETT	Warrant Entry and Tactical Team
HNT	Hostage Negotiation Team
CRT	Crisis Response Team
SWAT	Special Weapons And Tactics
SERT	Special Enforcement Response Team
CAT	Counter-Assault Team
DCT	Disturbance Control Team

Seal Heraldry

Lack of space and time precludes the listing of the heraldry of each federal seal, patch, etc., contained in this manual, but I will explain the FBI seal, which is an outstanding example of a well-made and colorful emblem.

Figures 1668 and 1669 show the FBI seal; it is made up in large and small editions. "Each symbol and color of the FBI seal has special significance, the dominant blue field of the seal and the scales on the shield represent justice. The endless circle of 13 stars denotes unity of purpose as exemplified by the 13 original states. The laurel leaf has, since early civilization, symbolized academic honors, distinction, and fame. There are exactly 46 leaves in the two branches, since there were 46 states in the Union when the FBI was founded in 1908. The significance of the red and white parallel stripes lies in their colors. Red traditionally stands for courage, valor and strength, while white conveys cleanliness, light, truth and peace. As in the American Flag, the red bars exceed the white by one. The motto, 'Fidelity, Bravery, Integrity,' succinctly describes the motivating force behind the men and women of the FBI. The peaked beveled edge which circumscribes the seal symbolizes the severe challenges confronting the FBI and the ruggedness of the organization. The gold color in the seal conveys its overall value."

Heraldry of the FBI Seal was published by the bureau itself; I am unable to find the name of the specific individual who wrote it.

The Institute of Heraldry— United States Army

The United States Armed Forces have used heraldic and other military symbols since the American Revolution, but it was not until 1919 that a coordinated military symbolism program was established. It was placed within the War Department General Staff, and moved to the Quartermaster General in 1924. In 1960, the Institute of Heraldry was established as a part of the Adjutant General's Office. It is situated in Alexandria, Virginia.

The Institute researches, designs, standardizes, approves, and controls the quality of emblems and insignia for the Executive Office of the President, the Armed Forces, and many other federal agencies.

How Many Federal Patches Are There?

The short, simple answer is that no one knows for sure. No central registry of federal patches exists, and many desirable special unit patches exist without the knowledge or official approval of the headquarters honchos—many of whom could care less about cloth insignia, unless they become a problem! I have somewhere around six thousand civilian federal law enforcement patches in my own collection, and I know there are very likely hundreds more that I don't have. My guess is that there are *well* over six thousand federal patches, not counting military base patches, Indian tribals, and Coast Guard ship patches.

I do know that their number keeps growing each day, and shows no sign of slowing down. Like the stock market, that number may top ten thousand in the not-too-distant future.

Future Editions

In a few years I probably will do an updated edition of this book. So, if you notice errors and/or omissions, please let me know. Also, as I am a serious collector myself and always looking for new patches to add to my collection, if you have a trade list I would appreciate receiving a copy. At the very least, I'd like either to borrow or get color scans (at my expense) of patches I don't have for the future edition, and you'll of course be given appropriate credit for them in the next book. My sincere thanks go to all of my fellow collectors who participated in the creation of this book.

Future Titles

The next book project I have scheduled for production is *Badges of the United States Treasury Department*. I already have thousands of photos, but am still seeking additional information and exhibits such as old pictures, credentials, dates badges were used, etc.

Please feel free to contact me at RHS Enterprises, Post Office Box 5779, Garden Grove, California 92846-0779. The telephone and fax number is 714-892-9012.

Organization of the Patch Exhibits

I used the *United States Government Manual* (see the section titled *Related Reading* in this volume) as a general guide to organizing the photos. You will find the Executive departments first (Agriculture, Commerce, Defense, etc.), and sections for the Congressional and Judicial branches, and also quasi-federal and independent agencies, trusts, territories, and U.S. possessions.

In some instances, for the sake of convenience, I have grouped together similarly-oriented organizations such as the Department of Energy/AEC/NRC/FEMA with private firms supplying nuclear security services, for instance.

Exhibit Numbering

At the request of many of you who are used to the exhibit numbers shown in Volumes One and Two of this series, I have listed those "old" exhibit numbers below the "new" exhibit numbers in this book. Because additional patches came in that I wanted to include even after the sections were already complete, you'll notice that the numbering in places is a bit strange. It does not go straight from 0001 to whatever, but may have an "A," "B," or "C" suffix after the same number.

I hope this doesn't throw you off, but I didn't want to hold up this already-overdue book by completely re-numbering the four thousand-plus exhibits!

Task Force Patches

Task forces (OCDETF, HIDTA, FTF, etc.) by their very nature are comprised of many agencies, some with overlapping jurisdictions. It's a situation that makes it difficult to decide into which agency chapter a particular task force patch should be included.

A separate chapter just for task force patches was initially considered, but the truth is that I ran out of space and time.

Generally, I assigned specific patches to a particular agency's section based on the nature of the task force. Thus, if it was drug enforcement-related it usually went into the DEA's chapter; if it involved anti-terrorist or violent gang cases, it went into the FBI chapter; fugitive task forces can be found in the U.S. Marshals section. While perhaps not the perfect solution, it was the best way I could come up with to handle this sensitive question. Normally, collectors of patches from a particular agency want any patch with the agency's name it.

Where a patch was not clearly related to a particular jurisdiction, I chose what I believed was "close enough for government work." Doubtless some collectors will be offended, and for that I apologize in advance. Your constructive criticism is always welcome.

United States Department of Agriculture

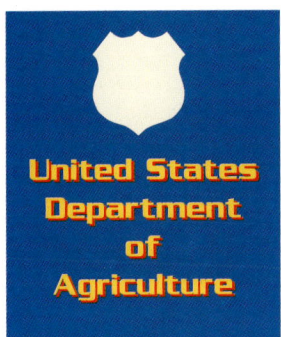

United States Department of Agriculture

0001

0002
Gold

0003
Blue

0004
V1/V2-290

0005

0006
V1/V2-299

0007
V1/V2-300

0008

0009
Brown border

0010
V1/V2-289
Gold border

0011
Script on bottom

0012
Rope-wreath border

0013

0014
V1/V2-297

0015
V1/V2-297a

0016

0017
Subdued

0018
F/E

0019
V1/V2-298a
Gold mylar thread

10 | The Encyclopedia of Federal Law Enforcement Patches

0020
Gold mylar thread

0021
Silver mylar thread
Variation has gold "OIG"

0022

0023
Gold mylar variation of #0022

0024

0025
Felt

0026
Gold bullion

0027

0028

0029
V1/V2-292

0030
V1/V2-293

0031
Subdued - green/black

0032
Subdued - green/black

0033
Subdued - green/black

0034
Subdued - green/black

0035
OD - Var.

0036
OD - Var.

0037

0038
V1/V2-291

0039
V1/V2-291
Green letter var.

United States Department of Agriculture

0040
Silver/green

0041
Silver/green

0042

0043
V1/V2-301
Rare

0044
V1/V2-295
Small - green

0045
V1/V2-1
Medium - green

0046
Large - black

0047
Brown "Forestry"

0048
V1/V2-296
White/orange

0049
V1/V2-2

0050
V1/V2-294
Large

0051
V1/V2-294v
Small

0052

0053
Red/gold var.

0054

0055

0056   **0057**

0058

0059

12   The Encyclopedia of Federal Law Enforcement Patches

0060
Silver mylar

0061

0062

0063

0064

0065

0066

0067

0068

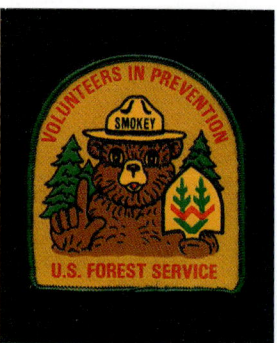
0069

0070

0071

0072

0073

0074

0075

0076

0077

0078

0079

United States Department of Agriculture

13

0080

0081

0082

0083

0084

0085

0086

0087

0088

0089

0090
Coronado

0091
Variation of #0090

0092

0093

0094
Variation of #0093

0095

0096

0097
Civilian Conservation
Corps - old - felt

0098
Civilian Conservation
Corps - old - felt

0099
Civilian Conservation
Corps - old - felt

The Encyclopedia of Federal Law Enforcement Patches

0100

0101

0102

0103

0104

0105

0106

0107

0108

0109
Old

United States Department of Commerce

0110
Bullion

0111
Large

0112
Medium

0113
V1/V2-306

0114
V1/V2-3

0115

0116

0117
New

0118
Silver mylar badge

United States Department of Commerce

15

0119
V1/V2-307
Gold mylar badge

0120
V1/V2-307
Tabs for SW, NE, NW and AK, too

0121
V1/V2-308

0122
V1/V2-305

0123

0124

0125

0126

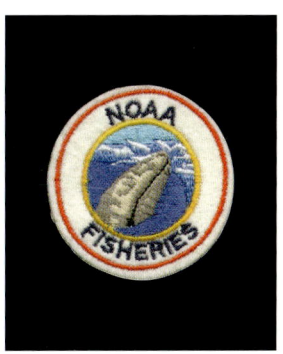
0127

0128

0129

0130
V1/V2-304
National Bureau of Standards

0131

0132

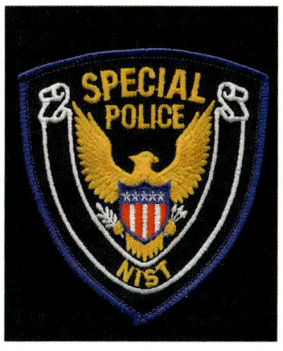
0133
Nat'l. Inst. Standards & Technology

0134
Nat'l. Inst. Standards & Technology

0135

0136

0137

0138

16 The Encyclopedia of Federal Law Enforcement Patches

0139

Central Intelligence Agency/ National Security Agency

0140
V1/V2-327
Gold border

0141
Black border

0142
One star

0143
V1/V2-328
S/P Blue Border

0144
S/P Black border

0145
Set

0145a
Extremely rare

0146
C/B - CIA Police

0147
C/B - CIA Police
Subdued

0148
S/P - CIA Police
First issue - this style

0149
S/P - CIA Police
Second issue - this style
Fake or variation

0149a
S/P - CIA Police
Current issue - more detail

0150
S/P - CIA Police
Subdued; Current issue
- BDU K-9/EOD

0151
S/P - CIA Police
Current issue - EOD

0152
S/P - CIA K-9
Old issue

0153
Fake

0154
V1/V2-666
WW2 - OSS

0155
Proposed (unused)
retirement item

Central Intelligence Agency/National Security Agency

0156
Blazer use - before uniforms

0157
CIA Police Cadet patch

0158
CIA Police Current issue

0159
CIC

0160
CIA Spl. unit?

0161
Possible fantasy

0162
V1/V2-229 Large seal

0163
V1/V2-665 Small seal

0164
Small seal - var.

0165
Old seal

0166
50th anniversary

0167
Bullion - black border

0168
Bullion - gold border

0169
Third issue

0170
Task force

0171
Bike Patrol

0172
Current K-9

0172a

0173
Spy plane - Blackbird

0174
Spy plane - U-2

18 The Encyclopedia of Federal Law Enforcement Patches

0175
Color version of #0151
Issued - never worn

0176
CIA - Range 33

0177
CIA-SPS-Midnights
Famous "Alert" patch

0178
CIA Armory Staff
First issue

0178a
Rare - First issue
"Office of Security"

0178b
Bullion

0178c
Movie prop - "Mission Impossible" film

0178d
Issued - not worn

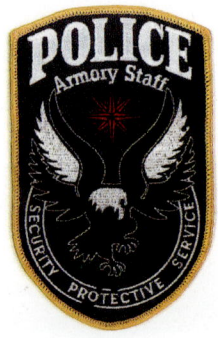
0178e
Issued - not worn

0178f
Special unit

0178g
Color error

0178h
Second issue
Unused

0178i
New Prototype

United States Department of Defense

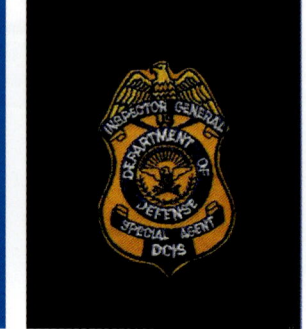
0179
Defense Criminal Inv.
Service - small

0180
Defense Criminal Inv.
Service - large

0181
V1/V2-323

0182
V1/V2-322

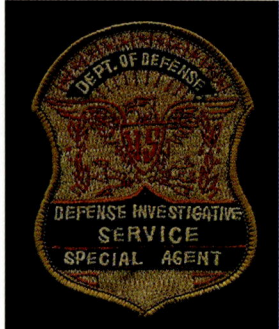
0183
V1/V2-12

0184

United States Department of Defense

0185
Defense Investigative Service

0186
Variation

0187
No information
Possibly not federal

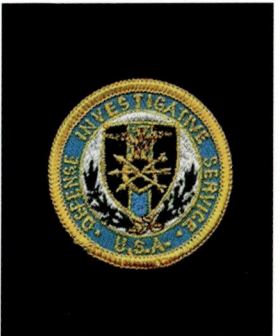
0188
V1/V2-13

0189
Small

0190
Large

0191
Variation of #0188
Small

0192
Variation of #0188
Large

0193

0194

0195

0196

0197
V1/V2-11

0198
Bullion

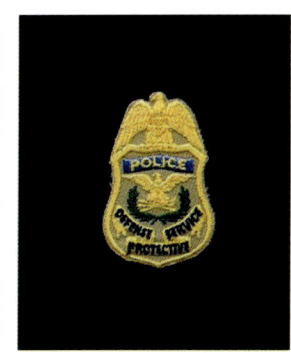
0199
Small C/B

0200
Large C/B

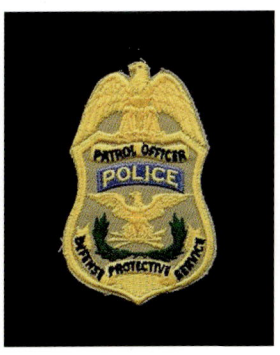
0201
Var. C/B

0202
C/B

0203
C/B

0204
S/P

20   The Encyclopedia of Federal Law Enforcement Patches

0205
Black S/P (one var. has gold border)

0206
S/P Def. Prot. Srvc.

0207

0208
V1/V2-324
Defense Nuclear Agency

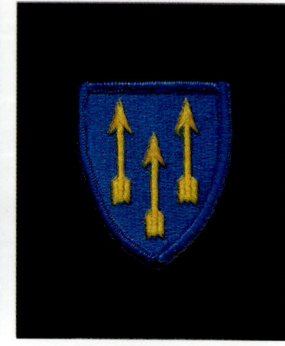

0209
V1/V2-325
Defense Nuclear Agency

0210
Defense Nuclear Agency
Johnston Atoll

0211
Defense Nuclear Agency
Johnston Atoll

0212
Nuclear Weapons
Storage

0213
Anti-terrorism TF

0214
Anti-terrorism TF
Subdued

0215

0216
Drug Task Force

0217
Drug Task Force

0218
"Star Wars" Missile
Defense

0219
Gold mylar

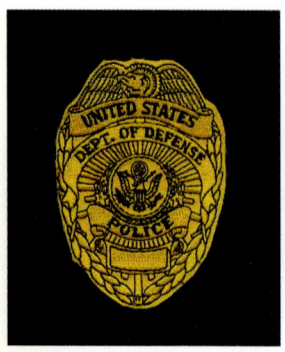

0220

0221

0222

0223

0224
Medium

United States Department of Defense

0225
Large

0226

0227

0228

0229

0230

0231
Variation of #0230

0232
V1/V2-319

0233
Fort Ord - silver

0234
Fort Ord - gold

0235
Camp Parks,
Alameda, CA

0236
Ft. Ord, CA

0237
Original Ft. Ord

0238
Original Ft. Ord

0239
Special Response Team

0240

0241
Nat'l. Ground Intell.
Center, VA

0242
Philippine Islands
Mid 70s

0243

0244
Utah

21

22 The Encyclopedia of Federal Law Enforcement Patches

0245   0246   0247   0248   0249
                           V1/V2-321   V1/V2-320
                           Gold and silver   Old
                           versions used

0250   0251   0252   0253   0254
Silk-screen   Variation of #0251   Sub base   Large

0255   0256   0257   0258   0259
         SRT   SRT

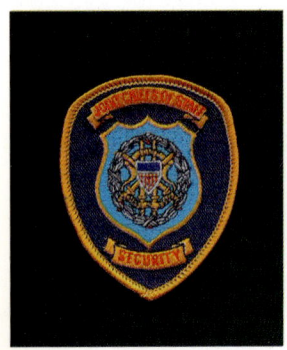

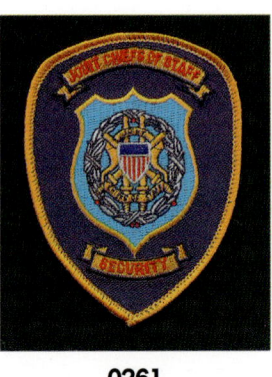
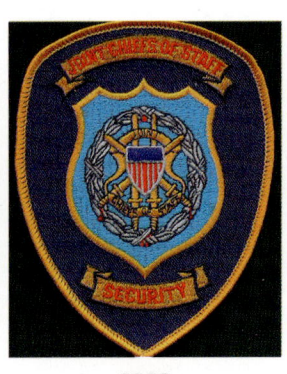

0260   0261   0262   0263   0264
Small   Medium   Large   DOD - Joint Activities
                                    Pentagon

United States Department of Defense

0265
Pentagon

0268
Defense Logistics Agency

0269
V1/V2-10
Defense Logistics Agy.

0270
DOD Housing Police California

0271

0272
Olive drab Courier (OD)

0273
Color version Courier

0274
Armed Forces Courier

0275
Armed Forces Police NYC - prior to 1976

0276

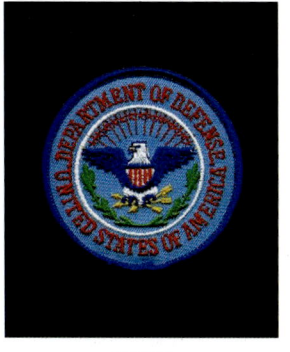
0277
Seal

0278
Pearl Harbor

0279
Plural "Guards"

0280
Medium

0281
Large

0282
Eagle faces left

0283
V1/V2-6
Eagle faces right

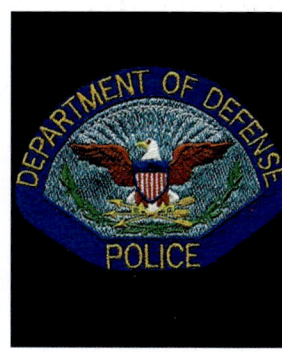
0284
One of many variations

0285

0286

24 The Encyclopedia of Federal Law Enforcement Patches

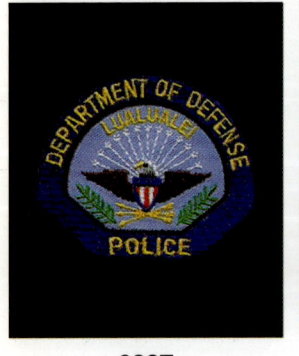 0287

 0288

 0289

 0290
V1/V2-316

 0291

 0292

 0293

 0294
V1/V2-5

 0295

 0296

 0297

 0298

 0299

 0300
V1/V2-4

 0301

 0302

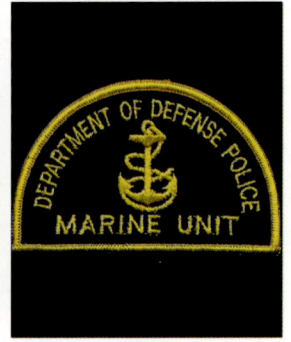 0303

 0304

 0305
Rank set

 0306

United States Department of Defense

0307

0308
V1/V2-310

0309

0310
V1/V2-8

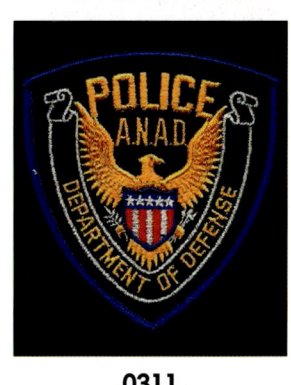
0311
Army Depot

0312
V1/V2-311
Army Depot

0313

0314
V1/V2-7

0315

0316

0317

0318

0319

0320

0321

0322
V1/V2-312
Lexington Bluegrass
Army Depot

0323

0324

0325

0326

26 The Encyclopedia of Federal Law Enforcement Patches

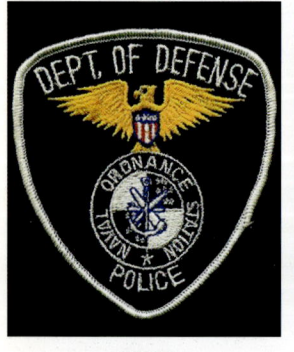
0327

0328

0329

0330

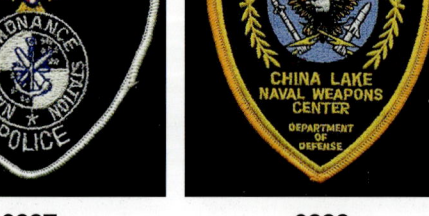
0331

0332
Mare Island
Var. reads "Guard"

0333

0334
Naval Supply Center

0335
V1/V2-313

0336
V1/V2-314
AR National Guard

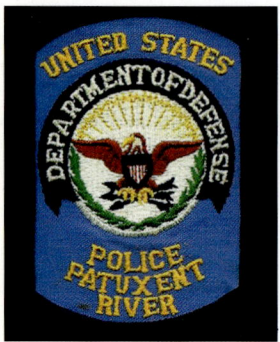
0337
V1/V2-315

0338
V1/V2-9

0339
V1/V2-317

0340

0341
OD version of #0340

0342
V1/V2-318

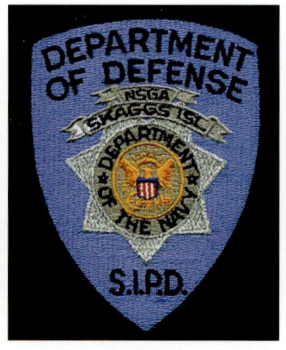
0343

0344

0345

0346

United States Department of Defense

27

0347

0348

0349

0350
EMT
Counter Narcotics
Tact. Ops.

0351
EMT-OD

0352
Large C/B

0353
Small C/B

0354
50th Anniversary C/B

0355
Two sizes:
5" & 7"

0356

0357

0358
3"

0359
4"

0360
Office of Special Invest.
Counter Espionage

0361
Office of Special Invest.
Counter Espionage
Variation

0362

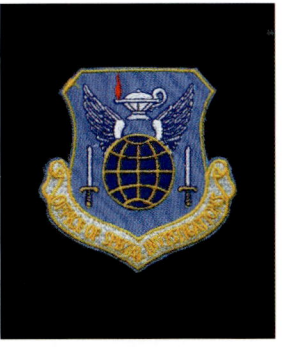
0363
V1/V2-330
Several variations -
Gold border/gold globe

0364
V1/V2-331
Subdued version

0365

0366

28   The Encyclopedia of Federal Law Enforcement Patches

0367

0368

0369

0370
V1/V2-334
Intelligence Service -
Reserve

0371
Intelligence Service -
Reserve

0372
V1/V2-20
Security service - 4"

0373
Variation - red border
4"

0374
Variation - 3"

0375
Variation - 2½"

0376

0377
380th Sec. Pol.
1980 Olympics

0378
Alaska Wildlife Agent

0379
Alaska Wildlife Agent
Variation

0380
"Doomsday" plane

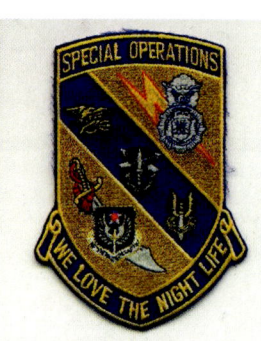
0381

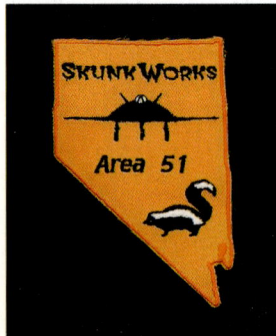
0382
Probably a fantasy?

0383
Probably a fantasy?

0384
Drug Task Force 6

0385
Drug Task Force 3

0386
Drug Task Force
Subdued

United States Department of Defense

29

0387 Spy satellite agency Subdued	**0388** Spy satellite agency Color	**0389** Presidential squadron Color	**0390** Presidential squadron Subdued	**0392** Pres. Squadron
0393 89th Military Airlift Wing	**0394** 89th Military Airlift Wing - variation	**0395** 89th Military Airlift Special Missions - AF/1	**0396** Elite Guard	**0397** AF-One/California
0398 89th K-9 Team	**0399** V1/V2-337	**0400** Kirtland AFB-NM	**0401** Academy - Sec. Pol.	**0402** K-9
0403 Silver lettering	**0404** Novelty Lackland AFB	**0405**	**0406**	**0407** 5½"

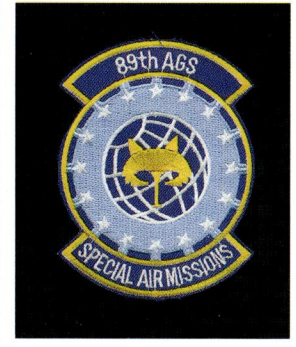

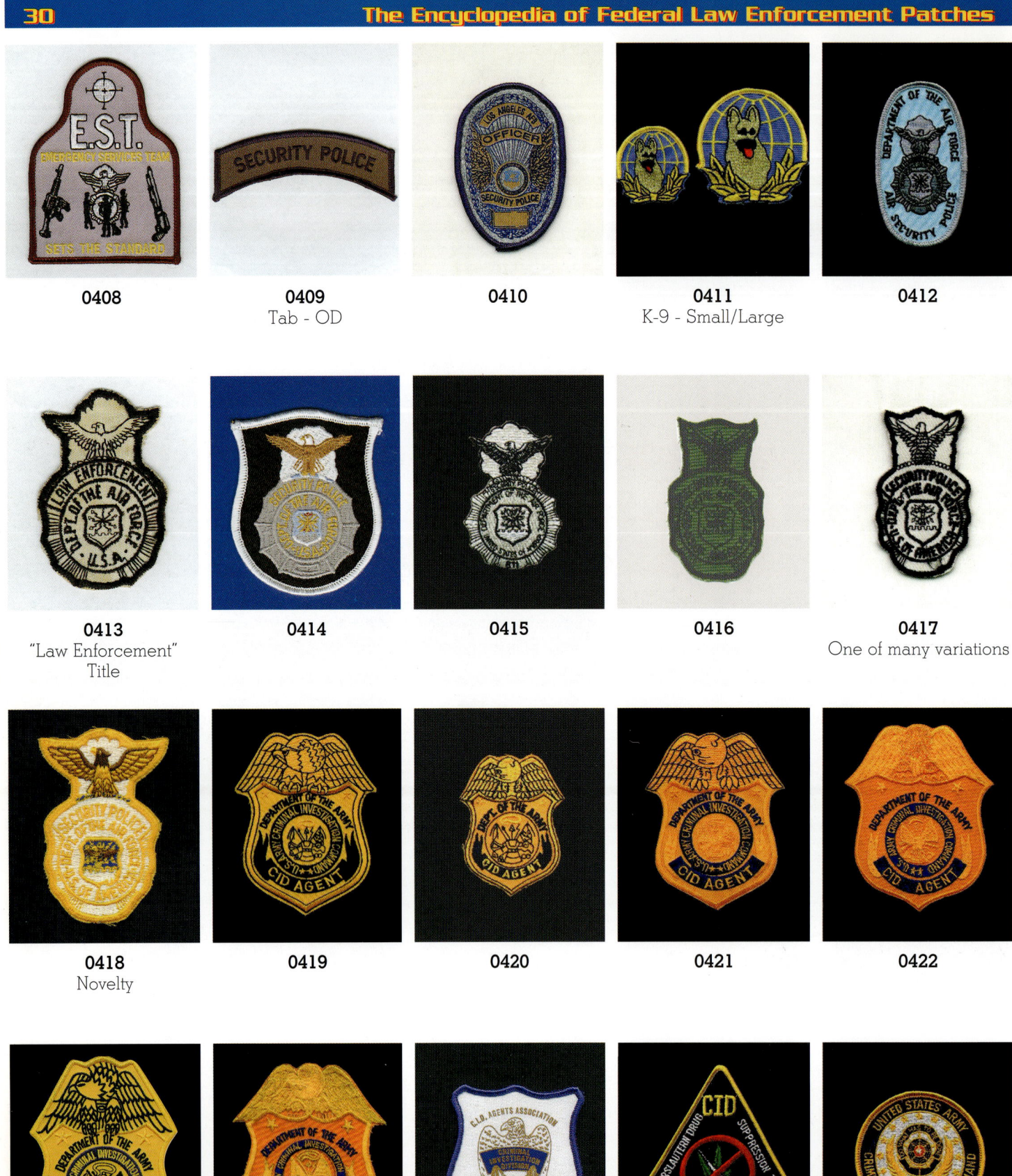

The Encyclopedia of Federal Law Enforcement Patches

0408

0409
Tab - OD

0410

0411
K-9 - Small/Large

0412

0413
"Law Enforcement"
Title

0414

0415

0416

0417
One of many variations

0418
Novelty

0419

0420

0421

0422

0423

0424
V1/V2-339

0425

0426

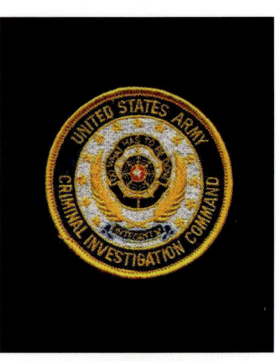

0427
V1/V2-26
Small

United States Department of Defense

0428
Medium

0429
Large

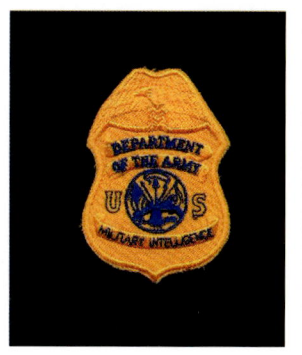

0430
V1/V2-344 (var.)

0431
Variation

0433
V1/V2-34
U.S. Army Intelligence Cmd.

0434
V1/V2-35
U.S. Army Intelligence Subdued

0435
V1/V2-343
Gold mylar

0436
V1/V2-342

0437
MP Black border

0438

0439
V1/V2-37

0440
V1/V2-36

0441
Small and large versions

0442

0443
Gold version

0444
V1/V2-345

0445

0446

0447

0448
V1/V2-39

The Encyclopedia of Federal Law Enforcement Patches

0449
V1/V2-40

0450

0451

0452

0453

0454

0455

0456

0457

0458
V1/V2-346
Ft. Hood

0459

0460

0461

0462
V1/V2-38
Several variations 5"

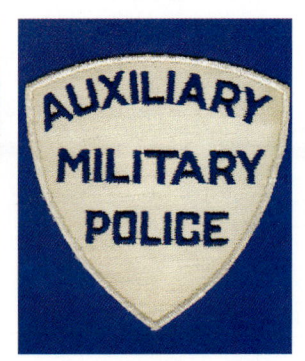

0463
White/blue letters 5"

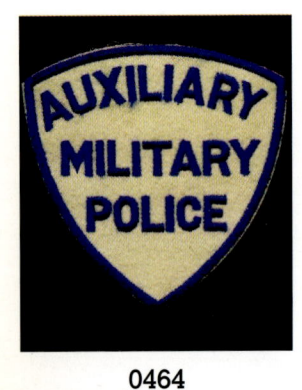

0464
5", 4", 3", 2½" versions

0465

0466
Very old

0467

0468
Old

United States Department of Defense

33

0469 "Mean Streets" design

0470 Camp Roberts, CA

0471

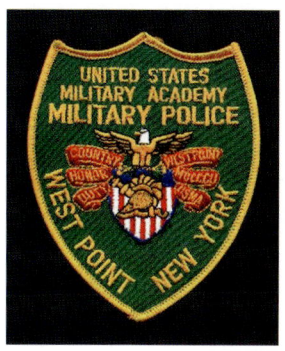

0472 4" & 3" versions exist

0473

0474 West Point Police

0475 Military Academy - West Point

0476

0477

0478 Desert Shield - Iraq Novelty

0479 Desert Storm - Iraq Novelty

0480 Joint Services K-9

0481 Philippines Old patch

0482 V1/V2-51

0483

0484

0485

0486 Disciplinary barracks

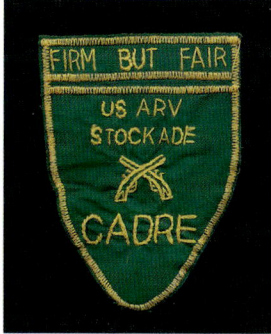

0487

0488

The Encyclopedia of Federal Law Enforcement Patches

0489

0490 Inspector

0491 Old and rare

0492 Mil. assist. cmd. Vietnam

0493 V1/V2-341 Dignitary travel unit Army I - like Marine I

0494 V1/V2-340 President's helicopter Army I - like Marine I

0495 Drug unit

0496 Drug unit

0497 Army customs Bullion

0498 Vietnam MP Pleiku

0499 Special Response Team MP

0500 Security - Supreme Allied Command

0501 Note clock hands

0502 Note clock hands

0503 MP Sniper School

0504 MP Invest.

0505 Armband

0506 New Jersey

0507 Army Ammo Depot SRT

0508 Very few Federal fire patches

United States Department of Defense

35

| 0509 | 0510
Marine
Counterintelligence | 0511
Two versions –
Yellow, gold | 0512 | 0513
Special Response Team |

| 0514 | 0515
"1775" | 0516
Two versions –
Silver, gold | 0517 | 0518 |

| 0519
OD | 0520 | 0521 | 0522
"MCBH" | 0523 |

| 0524 | 0525
V1/V2-55 | 0526
V1/V2-57 (var.) | 0527 | 0528 |

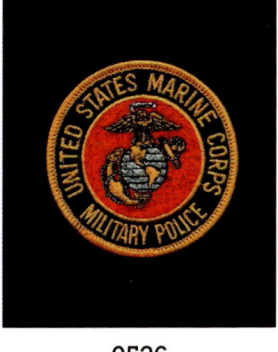

The Encyclopedia of Federal Law Enforcement Patches

0529

0530

0531
3"

0532
V1/V2-351
4"

0533

0534

0535

0536

0537

0538

0539

0540
"War Dogs"

0541

0542
(Japan)

0543

0544

0545

0546

0547
Special Response
Color

0548
Special Response
Subdued

United States Department of Defense

0549 Intelligence Training

0550

0551 Sub base

0552 Marine Corps Air Station - CA

0553 Marine I

0554 V1/V2-56 Four+ versions

0555 Bullion version

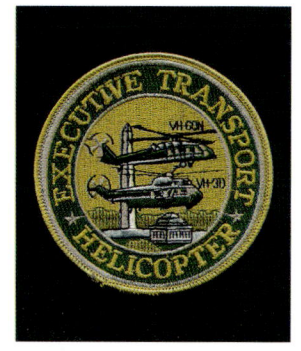

0556

0557

0558

0559 Two versions: 3½" & 3"

0560

0561 Two versions: 3½" & 4½" Authorized version

0562 Variation

0563

0564 Probably a fantasy

0565

0566 Silk-screen version

0567 V1/V2-352 F/E

0568 Embassy security

The Encyclopedia of Federal Law Enforcement Patches

0569

0570
(Liberia)

0571
(Pakistan)

0572

0573
Variation of #0568

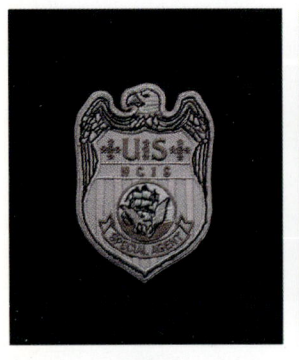

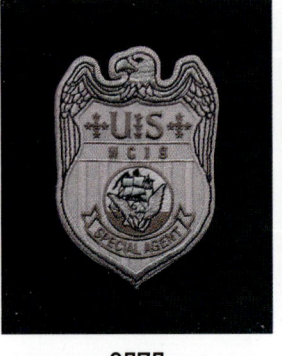

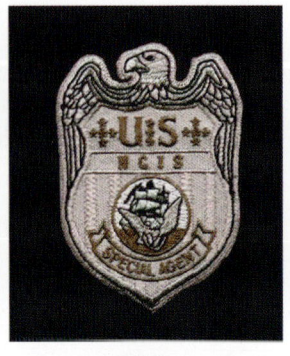

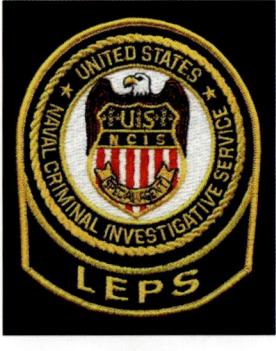

0574
3"

0575
4"

0576

0577

0578
Variation

0579

0580

0581
Law Enf. Physical Sec.

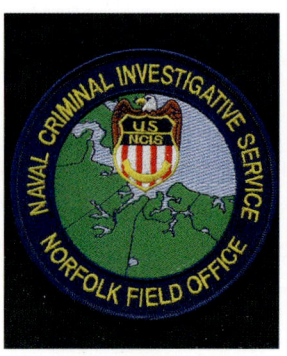

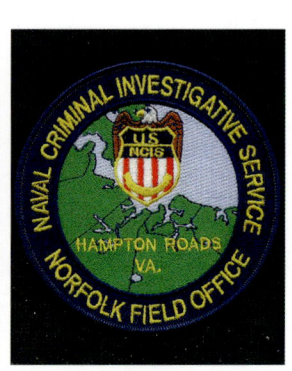

0582
OD

0583

0584

0585

0586

0587

0588
Reads
"Hampton Roads, VA"

United States Department of Defense

0589 Foreign Counter Intell. SFO

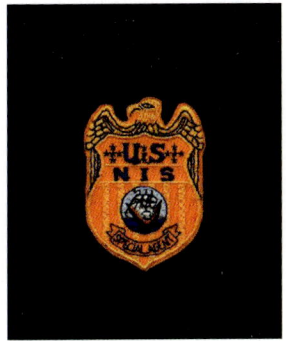

0590 2¾"

0591 V1/V2-356 4¼"; several var. incl. 4"

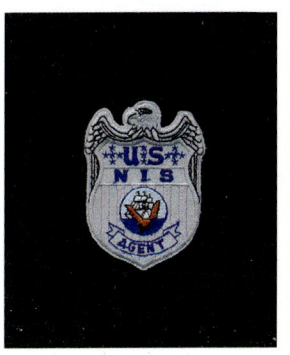

0592 2¾" silver

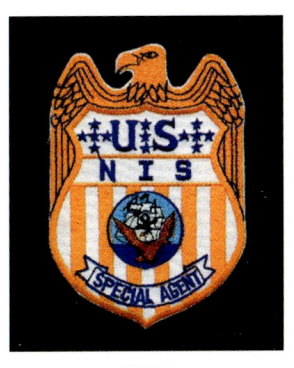

0593 4¼" silver

0594 White stripes

0595 V1/V2-357

0596 Gold border; Variation has black border

0597 Bullion

0598 V1/V2-60

0599 Variation with green lettering

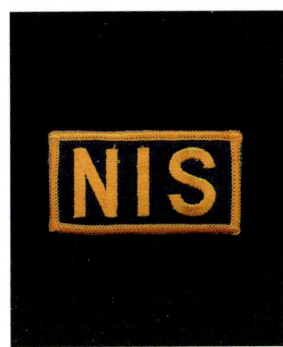

0600 V1/V2-358 Tab

0601 Large tab

0602 Felt; old

0603 Rare

0604

0605 Foreign Counter Intell.

0606

0607

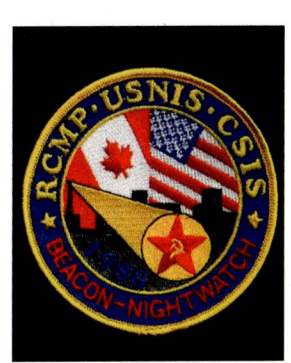

0608 U.S./Canada task force (Spy)

39

The Encyclopedia of Federal Law Enforcement Patches

0609
Completely unauthorized!

0610

0611
Two versions: red shield/blue shield

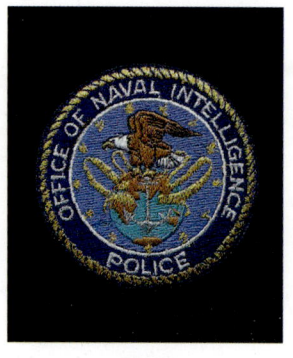

0612

0613

0614

0615

0616

0617

0618

0619
V1/V2-59

0620

0621

0622

0623

0624
Drug task force with USCS

0625
V1/V2-329
Naval Support Activity Vietnam

0626

0627
Panama Canal Security

0628
Guam

United States Department of Defense

41

0629	0630	0631	0632	0633
Master At Arms Ship's Police	Maine	Ship's Police		

0634	0635 V1/V2-58	0636	0637	0638

0639	0640	0641 ROTA	0642	0643 Special School

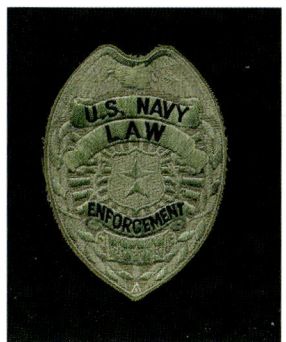

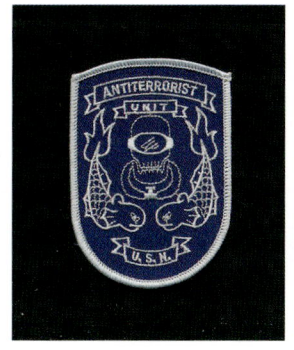

0644 Anti-Terrorist Unit	0645	0646	0647	0648

The Encyclopedia of Federal Law Enforcement Patches

0649

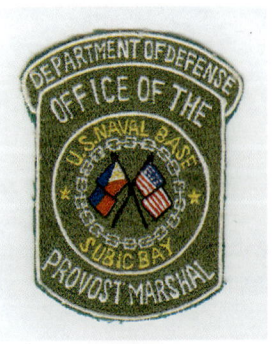

0650
V1/V2-62
Philippines

0651
Philippines

0652
Two variations:
Dog left/dog right

0653
Jail!

0654
Tac Team

0655

0656

0657

0658

United States Department of Education

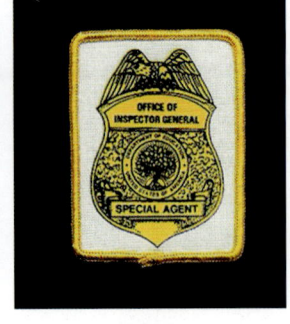

0659

0660

United States Department of Energy

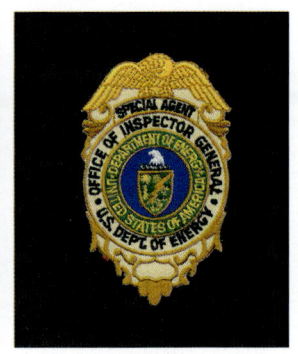

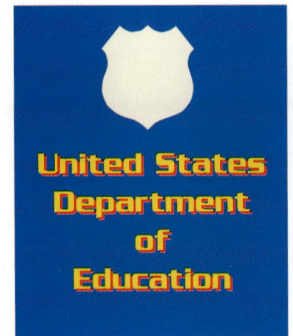

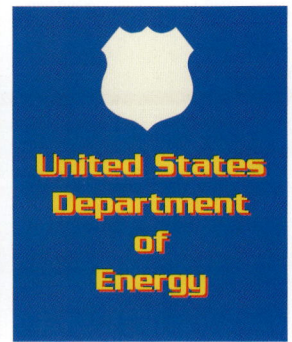

0661

0662

0663

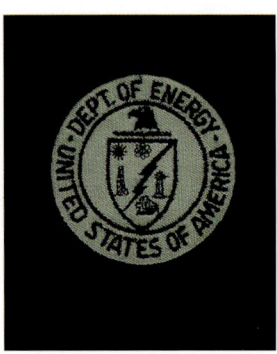

0664

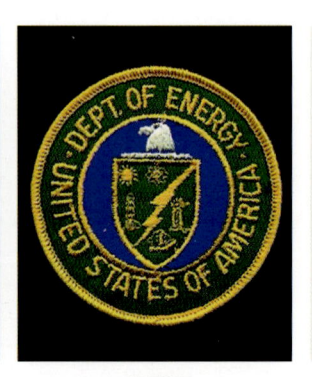

0665
V1/V2-362
Dark blue version also exists

0666

United States Department of Energy

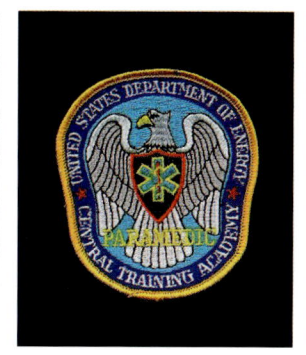

43

0667

0668
V1/V2-379

0669

0670
N.M SWAT Trng. Fac.

0671
2 3/4" Training Academy

0672
V1/V2-363
6" Training Academy

0673
Transp. Safeguard
Security Div. Acad.

0674

0675

0676
V1/V2-372
Nuclear Emergency
Search Team

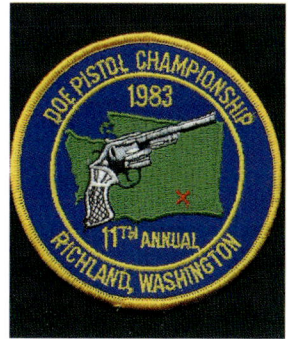

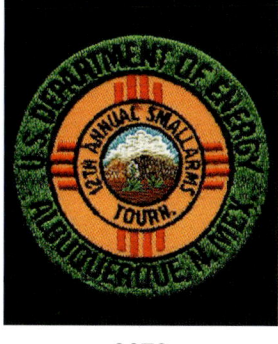

0677
V1/V2-374

0678

0679
V1/V2-375

0680

0681

0682

0683

0684
Ever Faithful
Special Resp. Team

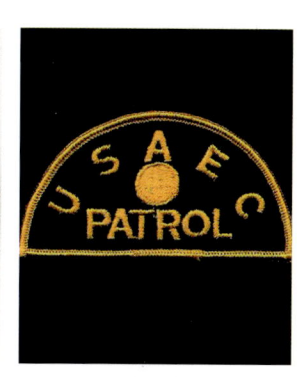

0685

0686
V1/V2-383
Atomic Energy Comm.

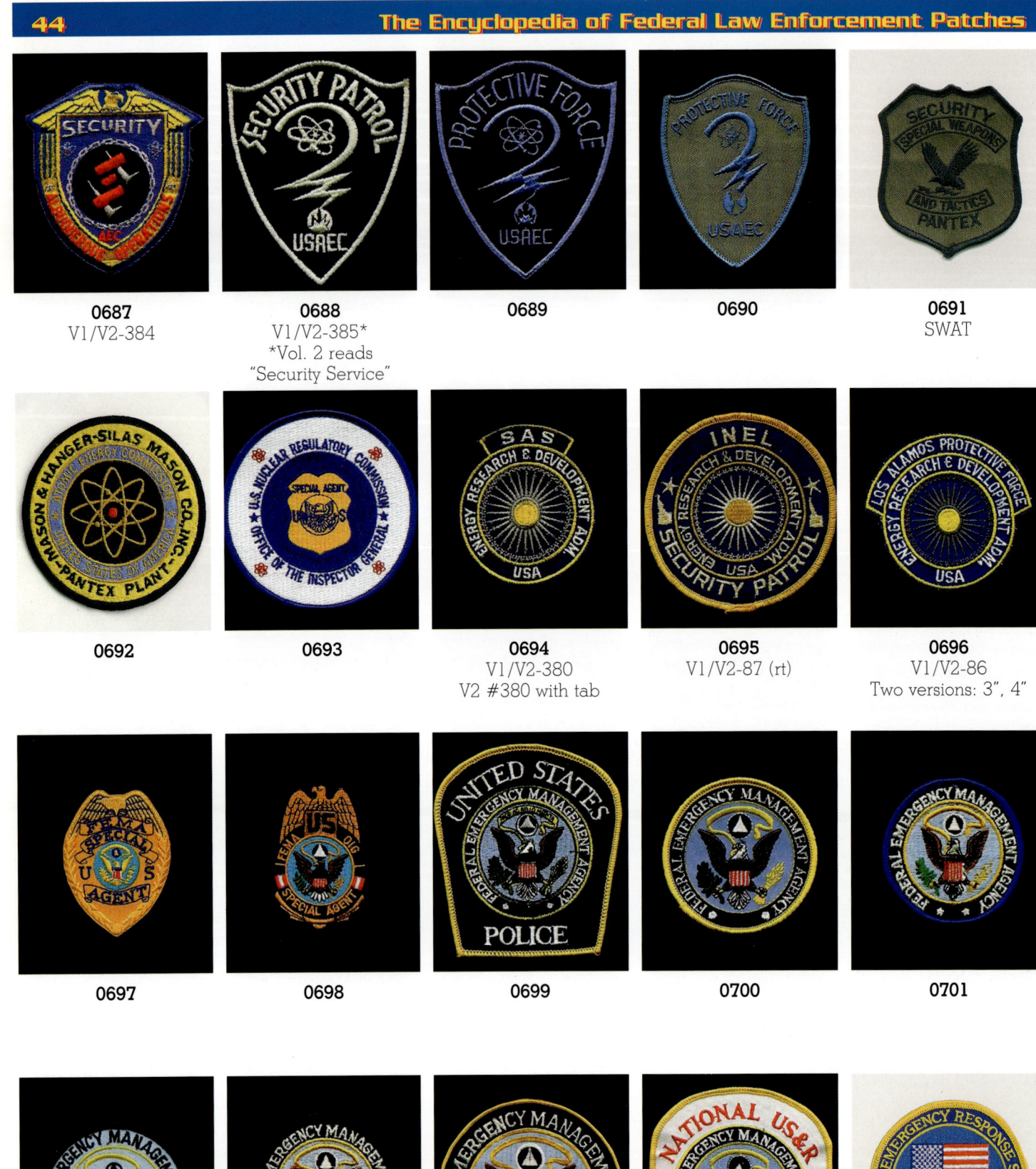

The Encyclopedia of Federal Law Enforcement Patches

0687 V1/V2-384	0688 V1/V2-385* *Vol. 2 reads "Security Service"	0689	0690	0691 SWAT
0692	0693	0694 V1/V2-380 V2 #380 with tab	0695 V1/V2-87 (rt)	0696 V1/V2-86 Two versions: 3", 4"
0697	0698	0699	0700	0701
0702	0703	0704 7½"	0705	0706

United States Department of Energy

0707

0707a
FEMA
Washington, D.C.

0708

0708a
Old

0709
Federal Fire Academy
Original

0710
Federal Fire Academy
2nd version

0711

0712
Cruder version of
#0711

0713
Heavily armed nuclear
transport

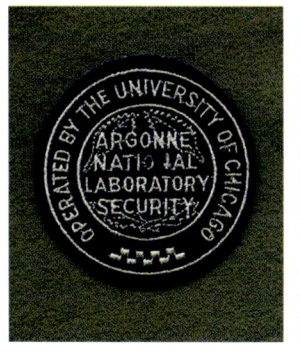

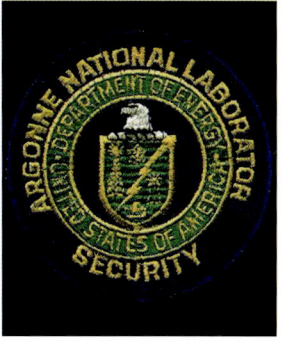

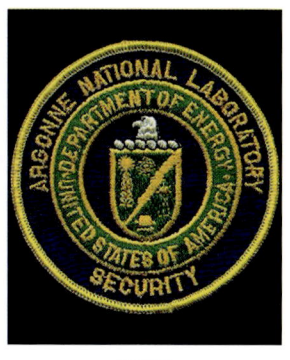

0714

0715

0716

0717
V1/V2-364

0718

0719

0720
V1/V2-368
Two versions:
gold/blue; silver/black

0721
V1/V2-367
Two versions:
gold/blue; silver/black

0722
V1/V2-370
Richland, WA O/S

0723
var.

0724
var.

The Encyclopedia of Federal Law Enforcement Patches

0725 Three versions: Subdued/OD/silver

0726 V1/V2-369

0727

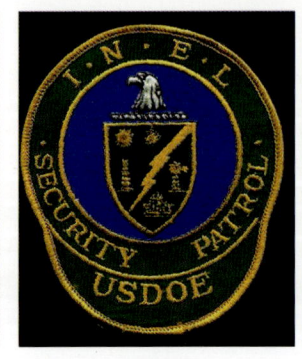

0728 V1/V2-87 (L)

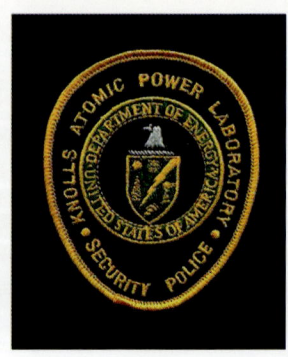

0729

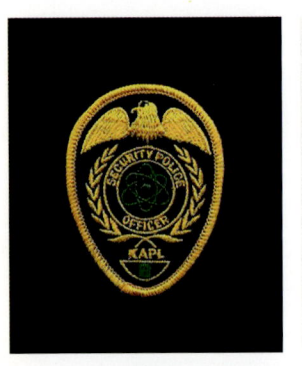

0730

0731

0732

0733 Rapid Response Team

0734 Old

0735 V1/V2-371

0736

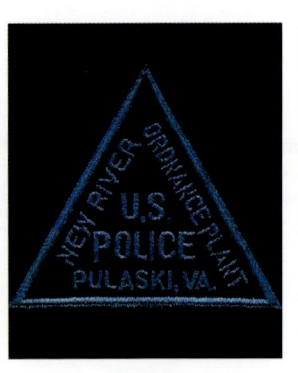

0737

0738

0739 Three versions: FLA., SLA., SRT

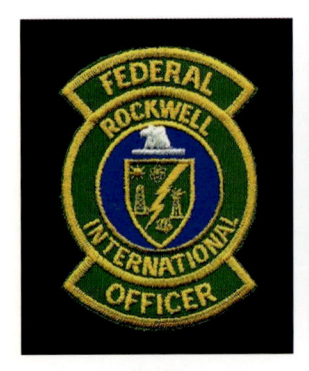

0740 V1/V2-377

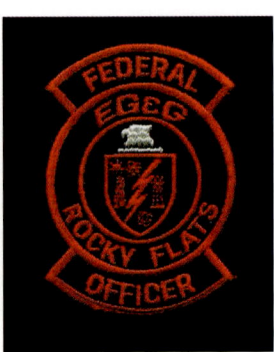

0741

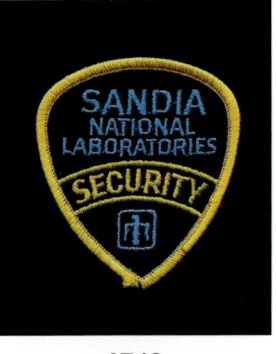

0742 Used until 1995 Two versions: 3", 4"

0742a 1st issue (Energy) NM

0742b 1st issue S/P NM

United States Department of Energy

47

0742c 3rd issue	0743 Rare	0744 12+ years old	0745 V1/V2-378 (also see #0774)	0746
0747	0748 V1/V2-373	0749	0750	0751
0752	0753	0754	0755	0756
0757	0758	0759 Old	0760	0761

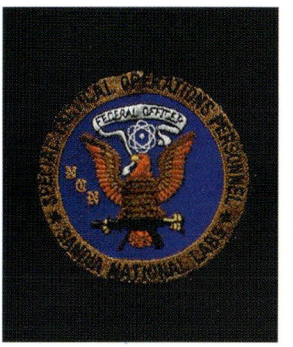

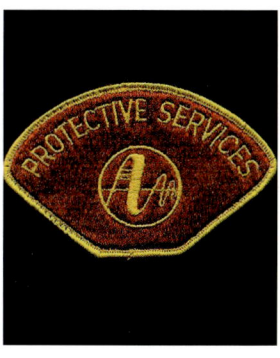

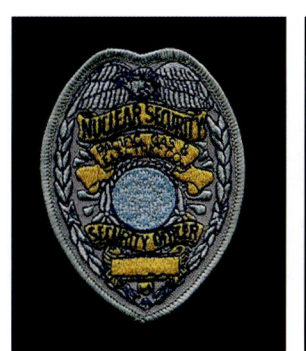

The Encyclopedia of Federal Law Enforcement Patches

0762

0762a
(Energy)

0763

0764

0765

0766

0766a
5" & 4" versions

0767

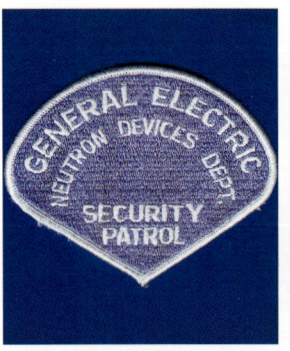

0768

0768a
(Energy)

0769

0770

0770a
Nuclear security

0771

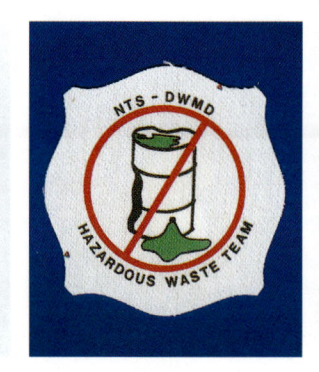

0772
Nevada Test Site

0773
Nevada Police/
Federal Auth.

0774
V1/V2-382

0774x

0774y

0774z

Environmental Protection Agency

49

Environmental Protection Agency

0775

0776

0777

0778

0779

0780

0781
V1/V2-695

0782

0783

0784
V1/V2-697
Several variations exist

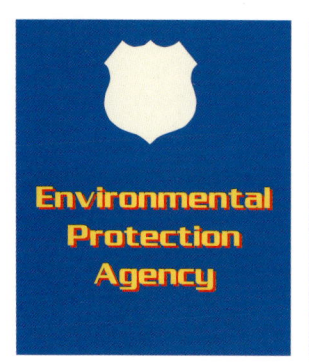

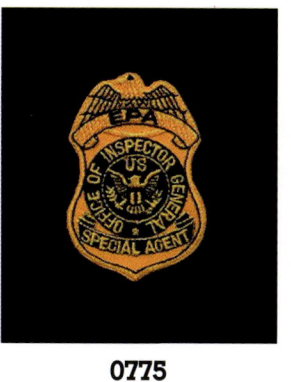

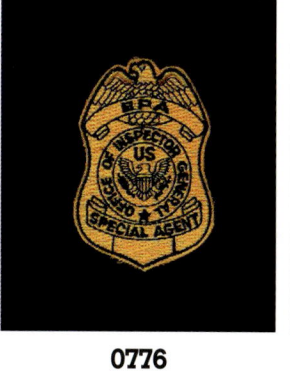

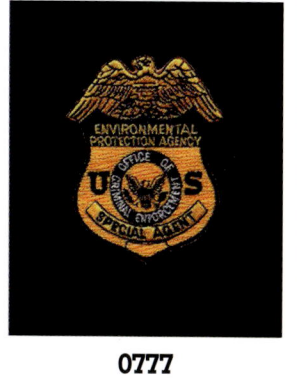

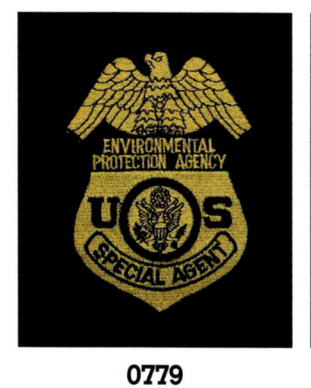

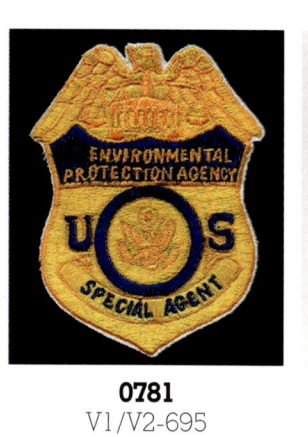

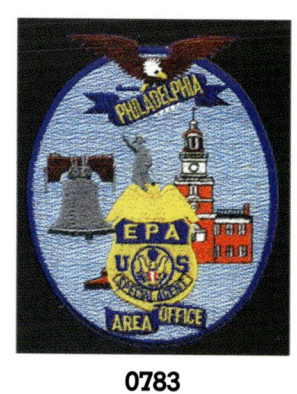

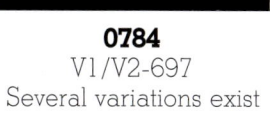

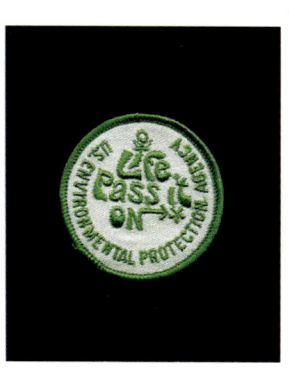

0785

0786
V1/V2-693

0787

0788

0789

0790

0791
V1/V2-696

0792

0793
V1/V2-692

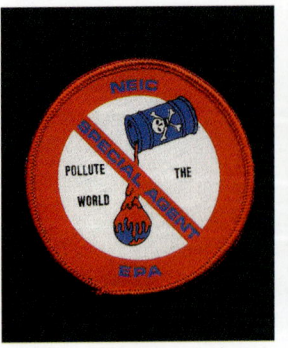

The Encyclopedia of Federal Law Enforcement Patches

0794

0795

0796

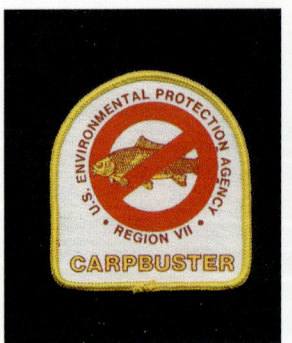

0797

0798

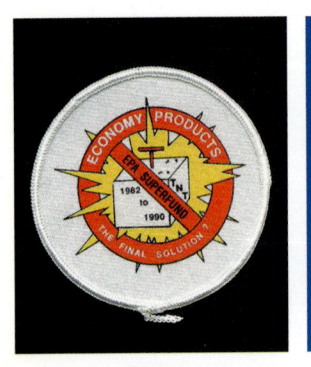

0799

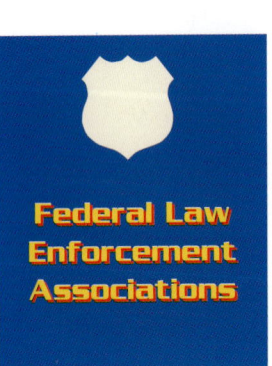

Federal Law Enforcement Associations

0800
Federal/State/Local

0801
Association of Federal Investigators

0802

0803
V1/V2-88
AFI Seal

0804
V1/V2-89
Federal Crim. Invest.
Assn. - small

0805
Federal Crim. Invest.
Assn. - large

0806

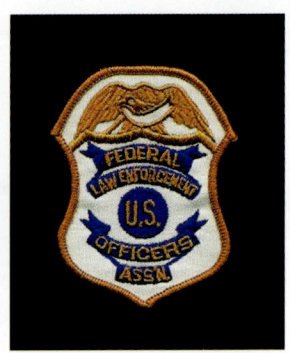

0807
V1/V2-90
3½" blue

0808
3" black

0809
V1/V2-387
Prototype - red

0810
V1/V2-386

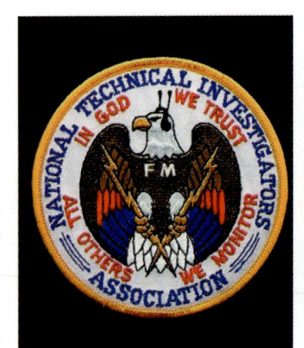

0811
Wires and pliers

0812
Color variation

Federal Law Enforcement Associations

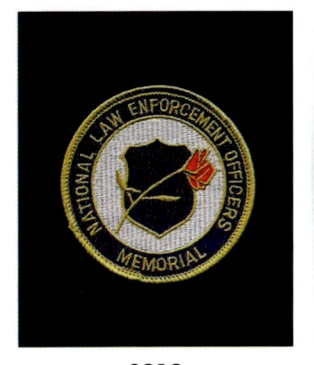

51

0813 Federal/State/Local

0814 International Police Association

0815 National Federation of Federal Employees

0816

0817

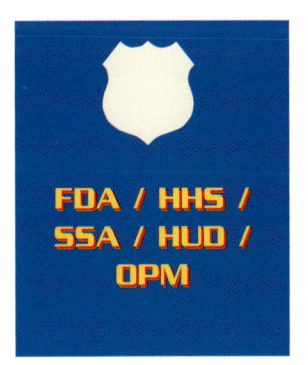

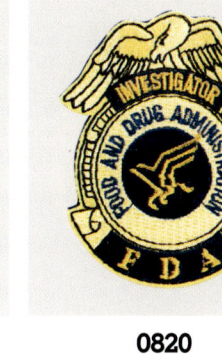

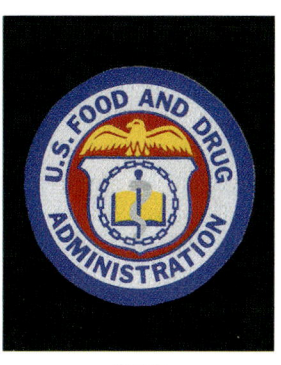

FDA / HHS / SSA / HUD / OPM

0818

0819

0820

0821

0822

0823

0824

0825

0826

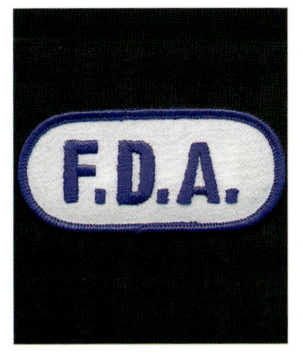

0827 V1/V2-392

0828 Public Health Service

0829 V1/V2-390 3"

0830 V1/V2-391 2¾"

0831

The Encyclopedia of Federal Law Enforcement Patches

0832

0832a

0833

0834
Gold bullion

0835

0836
Blue

0837
Black

0838

0839

0840

0842

0843
Gold bullion

0844

0845

0846

0847

0848

0849

0850

0851

FDA / HHS / SSA / HUD / OPM

0852

0853

0854

0855
Security Team

0856

0857

0858

0859

0860

0861

0862
V1/V2-91
Maryland

0863
Maryland

0864
V1/V2-393
Destination for bogus
White House "guests"

0865
4½"

0866

0867

0868

0869

0870

0871

The Encyclopedia of Federal Law Enforcement Patches

0872

0873
Six border colors

0874

0874a
New

0875

0876
V1/V2-394

0877
Special Police - SFO
HUD Housing
1989-1993

0878
Special Police - SFO
HUD Housing
1989-1993

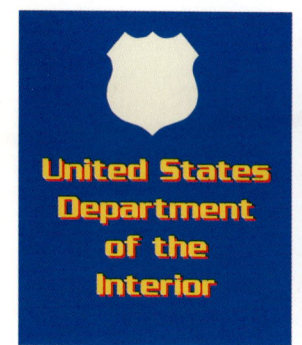

0879

0880

United States Department of the Interior

0881

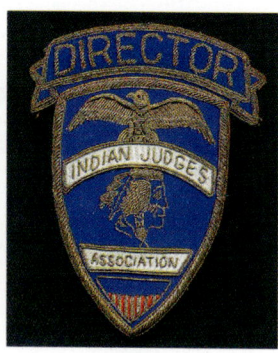

0882
Gold bullion

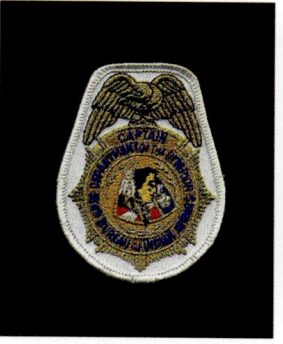

0883

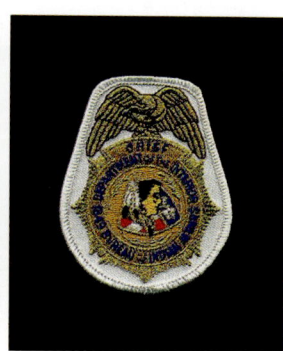

0884

0885

0886

0887

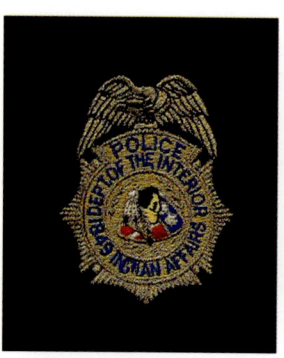

0888

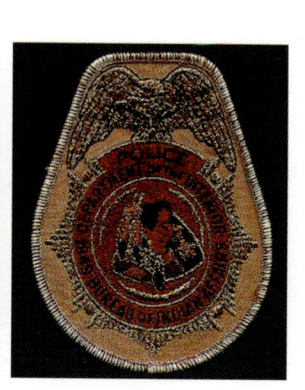

0889
Brown version

United States Department of the Interior

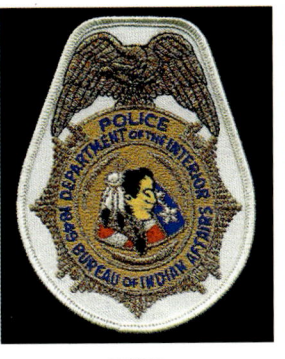

0890

0891

0892
V1/V2-403

0893
V1/V2-402
Cap and utility patch

0894
Black "Police"

0895
Red "Police"

0896

0897

0898
Bullion

0899
Commemorative
Oklahoma bombing

0900

0901
V1/V2-396

0902
V1/V2-98

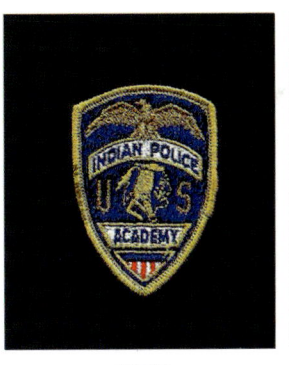

0903
V1/V2-395
3" version

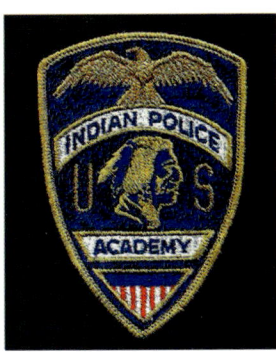

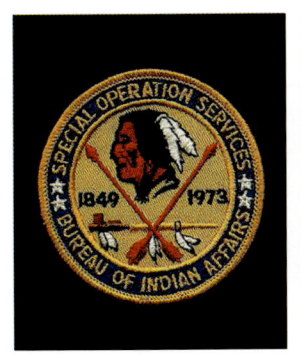

0904
4¼" version

0905
V1/V2-96

0906

0907

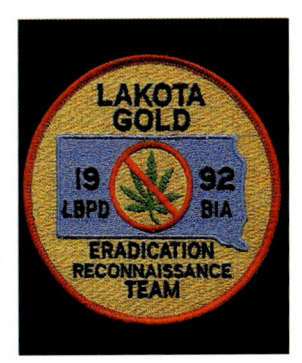

0908
3" & 4" versions

0909
3" & 4" versions

55

The Encyclopedia of Federal Law Enforcement Patches

0910
V1/V2-406

0911

0912
V1/V2-401
Several versions

0913
V1/V2-97
Many versions - brown, blue

0914
Green - two versions

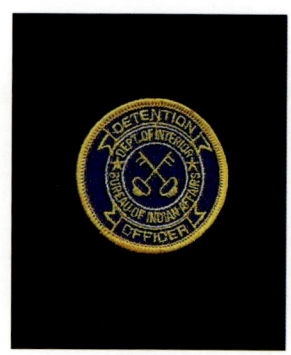

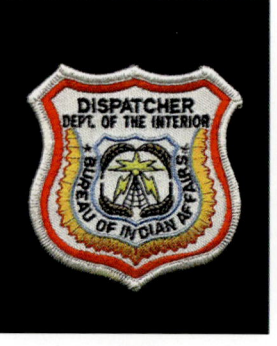

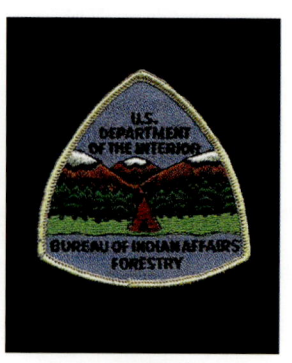

0915

0916

0917

0918

0919
V1/V2-95

0920

0921
V1/V2-400

0922

0923

0924

0925

0926

0927

0928
V1/V2-399
Var. has black border

0929
V1/V2-398

United States Department of the Interior

| 0930
11" | 0930a | 0930b | 0931
V1/V2-397 | 0932 |

| 0934 | 0934a | 934b
Bureau of Indian Affairs | 0935
V1/V2-411 | 0936 |

| 0937
V1/V2-414 | 0938 | 0939 | 0940 | 0941
Dark blue |

| 0942
Light blue | 0943
Bullion | 0944 | 0945 | 0946
V1/V2-413 |

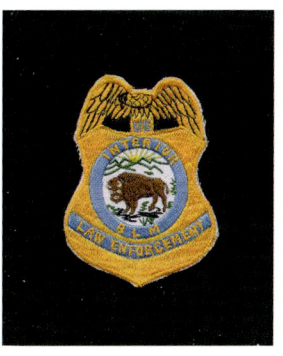

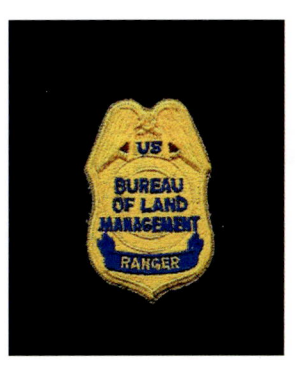

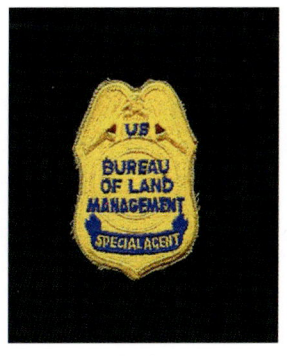

The Encyclopedia of Federal Law Enforcement Patches

| 0947 | 0948 | 0949 | 0950 | 0951 |

| 0952 V1/V2-409 | 0953 V1/V2-415 | 0954 | 0955 V1/V2-118 | 0956 V1/V2-407 |

| 0957 | 0958 Silver mylar border | 0959 | 0960 V1/V2-408 | 0961 |

| 0962 UID BLM | 0962a 1984-1991 FLETC Raid Patch - NPS | 962a Interior - BLM | 0963 | 0964 V1/V2-119 |

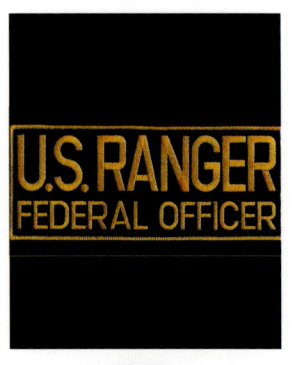

United States Department of the Interior

| 0965 | 0966 Bullion | 0967 V1/V2-93 | 0968 | 0969 |

| 0970 V1/V2-417 | 0971 V1/V2-416 | 0972 V1/V2-418 | 0974 | 0975 Black |

| 0976 Blue | 0977 Bullion | 0978 Felt backing | 0979 V1/V2-120 Old | 0980 Several variations |

| 0981 Includes tab | 0982 Tab alone | 0983 Used at Hoover Dam | 0984 Used at Hoover Dam | 0985 |

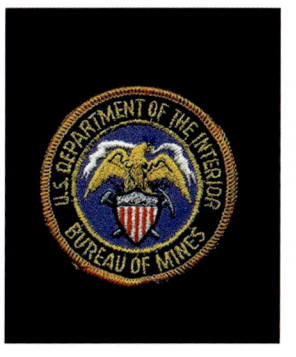

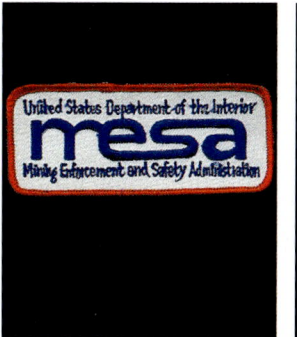

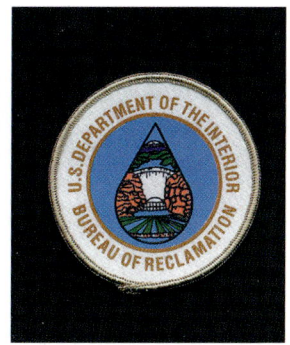

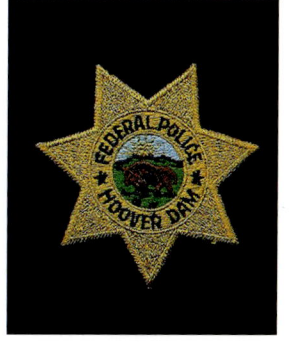

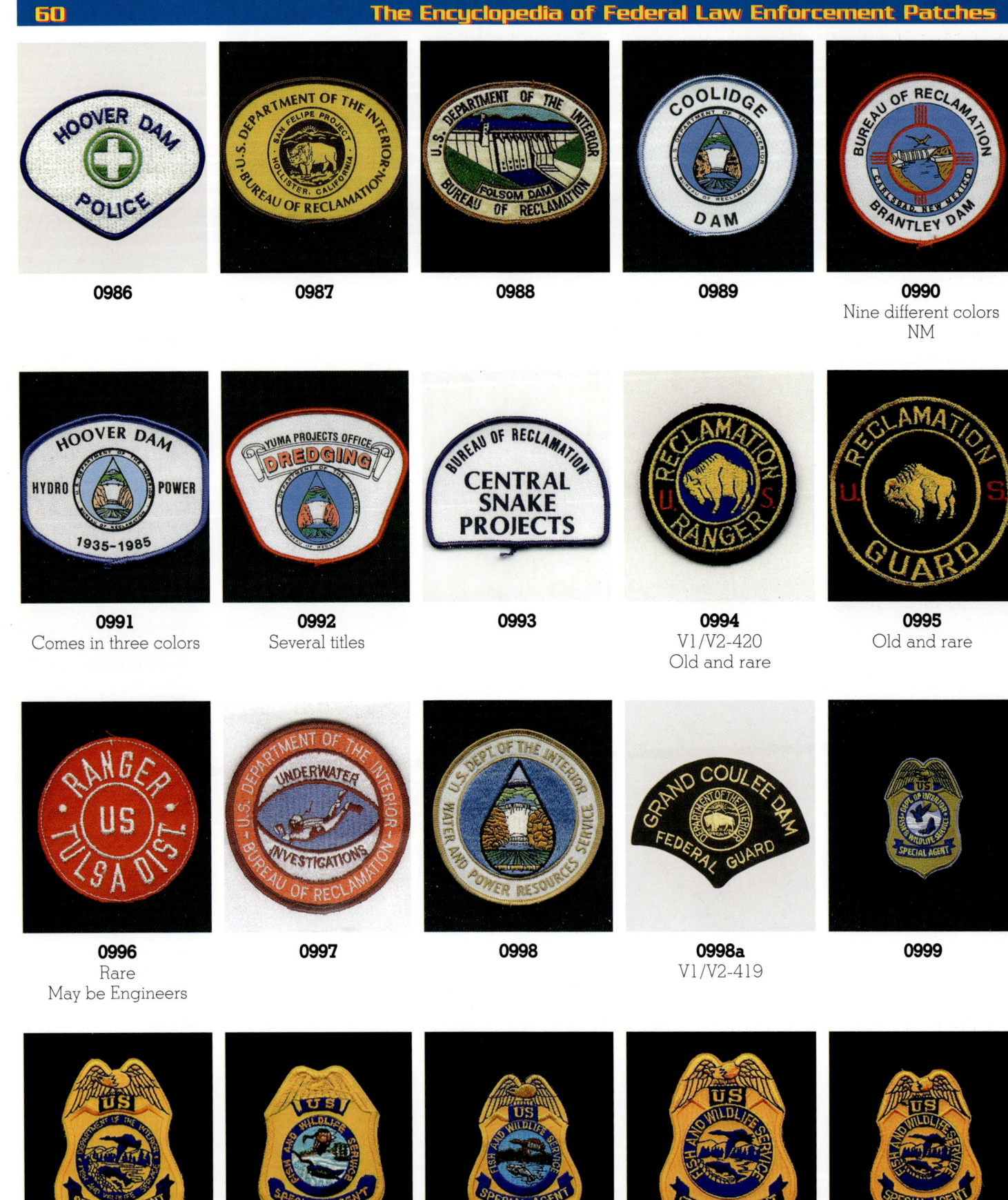

The Encyclopedia of Federal Law Enforcement Patches

0986

0987

0988

0989

0990
Nine different colors
NM

0991
Comes in three colors

0992
Several titles

0993

0994
V1/V2-420
Old and rare

0995
Old and rare

0996
Rare
May be Engineers

0997

0998

0998a
V1/V2-419

0999

1000

1001

1002

1003

1004

United States Department of the Interior

1005
V1/V2-425

1006
V1/V2-424

1007

1008
Brown thread - top
Variation

1009
Yellow thread - top
Variation

1010
Blue thread - top
Variation

1011
Very old

1012
Gold mylar top thread

1013
Red color

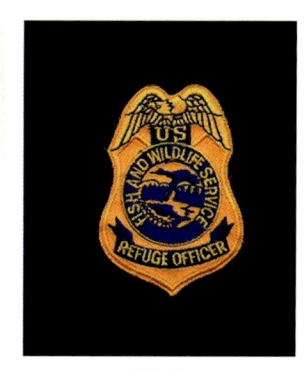

1014
3" version

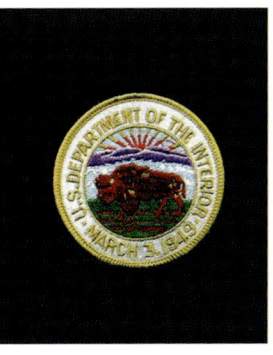

1015
seal

1016
Bullion seal

1017
District patch

1018
1st off. issue
1961-1966 - 4"

1019
V1/V2-122
2nd issue, 1967-1978
3½"

1020
1967-73 crescent tab
for #1019

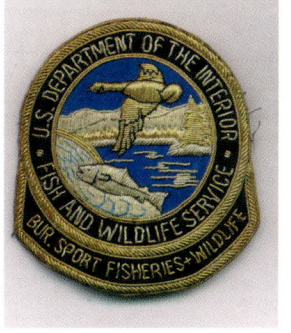

1021
V1/V2-421
Bullion version -
Crescent dropped 1974

1022
1978 - new seal

1023
V1/V2-427
Two versions: regular &
mylar

1024
Variation with red
border

The Encyclopedia of Federal Law Enforcement Patches

1025
Numbers 1025-1030 are color prototypes

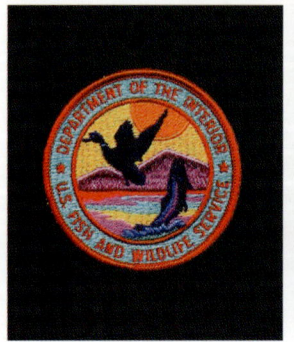

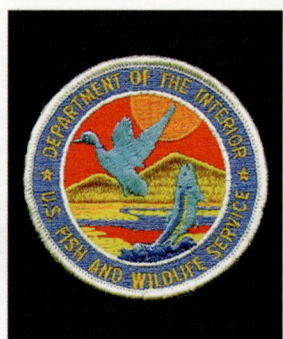

1026

1027

1028

1029

1030

1031
3" version
1978 issue

1032
V1/V2-121
4" version

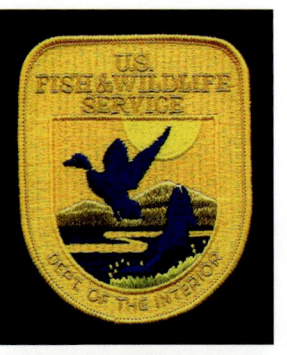

1033
Numbers 1033-1053 are prototypes/color variations

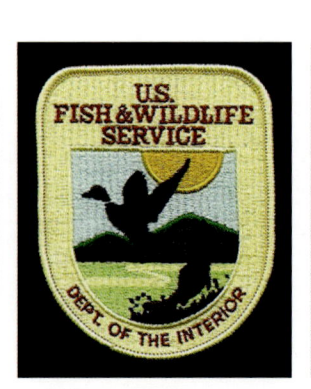

1034

1035

1036

1037

1038

1039

1040

1041

1042

1043

1044

United States Department of the Interior

1045  1046 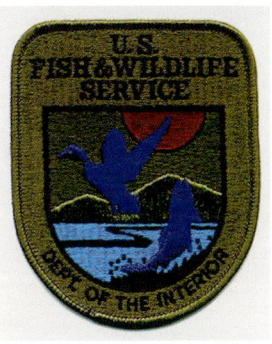 1047  1048  1049

1050  1051  1052  1053  1054

1055  1056 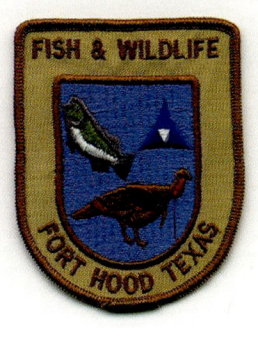 1057  1058  1059

1060

1061
V1/V2-428

1062
Var. has gold letters

1063
Twill 3¾"

1064
Twill 3"

The Encyclopedia of Federal Law Enforcement Patches

1065
F/E 4"

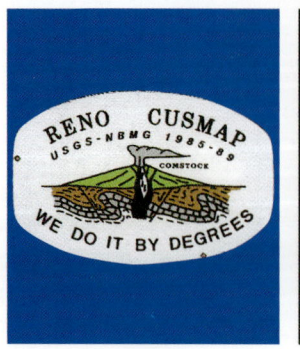

1066

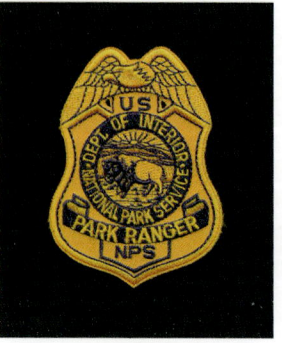

1067

1068

1069
Law Enf. Rgrs. C/B
authorized in 1991

1069a
Subdued version
1990 - Delaware
NPS Investigator var.

1070
1983
Western region

1071
FLETC var.
1984-1991

1072
V1/V2-436v
FLETC var.
1984-1991

1073
Bullion

1074
Crepe back version

1075
F/E - black

1076
V1/V2-435
Gold mylar

1077
Gold letters

1078
V1/V2-431
Reproduction

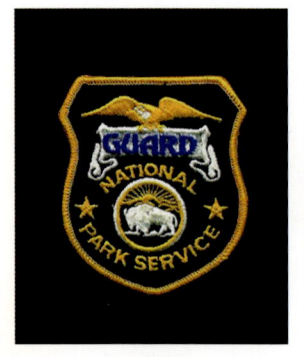

1078a

1079

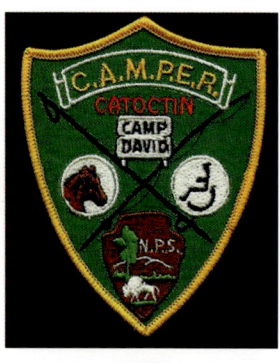

1080
Presidential retreat

1081

1082

United States Department of the Interior

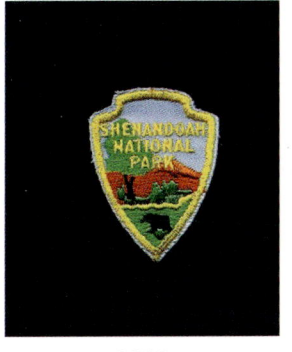

1083

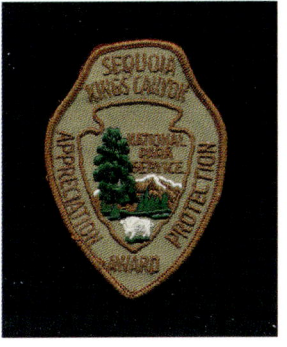

1084

1085
V1/V2-126
Arrowhead design
Adopted 1952 - Twill 3½"

1086
V1/V2-125
2½" hat patch
1962-present

1087
F/E var.

1088
Variation

1089
Variation

1090
V1/V2-432
Variation

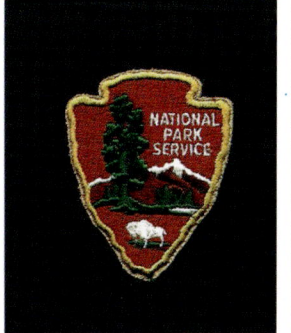

1091
Variation

1092
V1/V2-124
Variation - rounded top
variation exists

1093
Gold mylar border

1094
Bullion

1095
Bullion

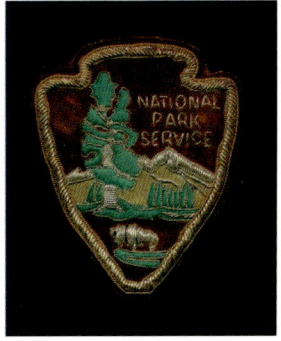

1096
Bullion

1097
Bullion

1098
Bullion

1099
2¾"

1100
V1/V2-441
3"

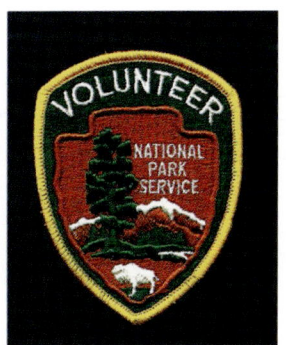

1101
V1/V2-129
3¾"

1102
Mylar version of #1101

65

The Encyclopedia of Federal Law Enforcement Patches

1103
Volunteer variation

1104
1953 to present
6"

1105
1953-1983
4" version

1106
1937-1953 issue

1107
Subdued cap patch
2½"

1108
V1/V2-433
Subdued - 3½"

1109
2½"

1110
3½"

1111
Utah

1112
V1/V2-440
Wisconsin
Two sizes

1113
V1/V2-430

1114

1115

1116

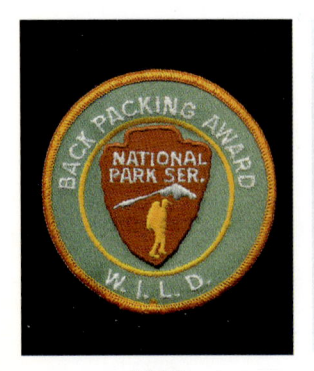

1117
4"

1118
3½"

1119
V1/V2-429

1120
Maine

1121
North Carolina

1122

United States Department of the Interior

1123

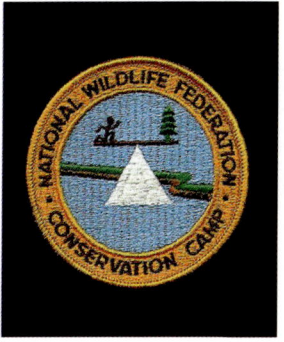

1124

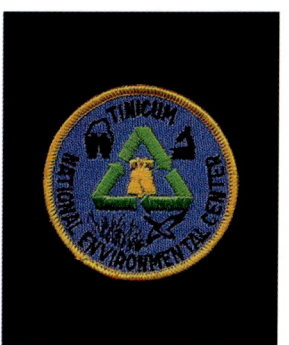

1125

1125a

1125b
V1/V2-434
1920 Ranger
Sleeve brassard

1125c
V1/V2-437
1920 Superintendent
Sleeve brassard

1125d
V1/V2-438
Tab

1126
V1/V2-444
Felt

1127

1128

1129
Gold mylar

1130
V1/V2-445
Gold mylar

1131

1132

1133
V1/V2-443

1134
V1/V2-442

1135
2½"

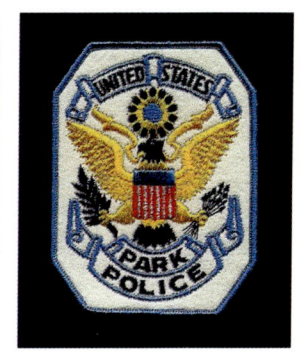

1136
4½"

1137
10"

1138
V1/V2-450

67

The Encyclopedia of Federal Law Enforcement Patches

1139 V1/V2-451

1140 V1/V2-130

1141 Leather!

1142 Variation

1143 Variation

1144 Variation

1145 V1/V2-131 Felt

1146 Gold mylar

1147 Early and rare

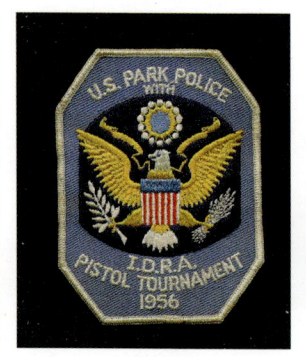

1148

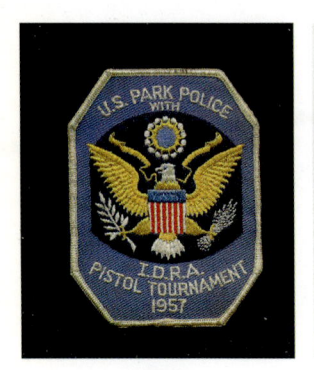

1149

1150 V1/V2-446

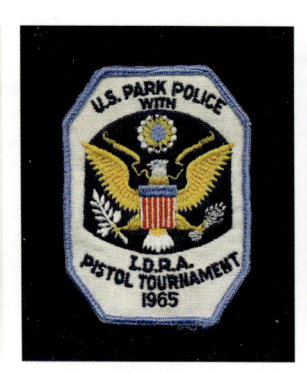

1151

1152

1153 V1/V2-447

1154 V1/V2-448

1155 V1/V2-449

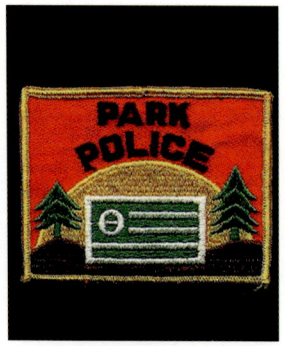

1157 Federal?

1158 V1/V2-133

1159 V1/V2-452

United States Department of Justice

United States Department of Justice

1160

1161
Bullion

1162
V1/V2-134v
Bullion

1163

1164

1165
V1/V2-135

1166

1166a
El Paso Response Team

1167

1167a

1168

1169

1170
Bullion

1171

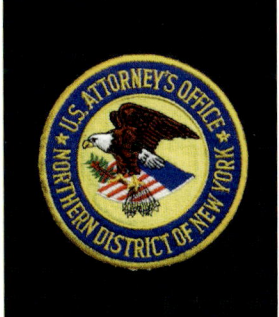

1172

1173

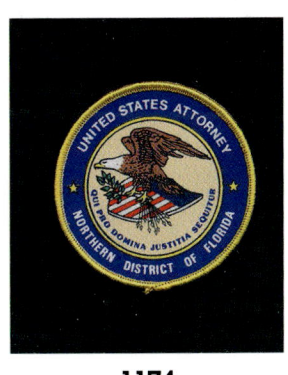

1174

1175
Old patch - UID

1176

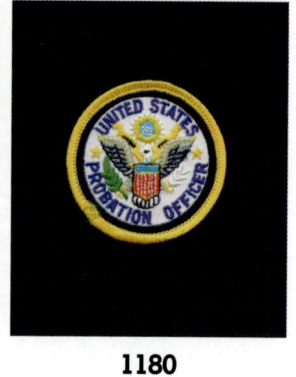

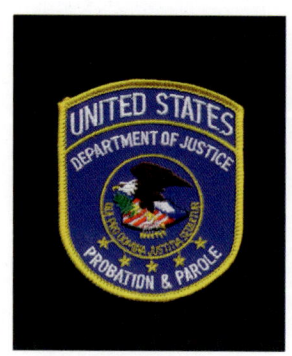

The Encyclopedia of Federal Law Enforcement Patches

1177

1178

1179

1180

1181

1182

1183

1184

1185

1186
Jt. Spl. Resp. Team
Color

1187
Blue (subdued) version

1188
Raid jacket patch

1189
Raid jacket patch

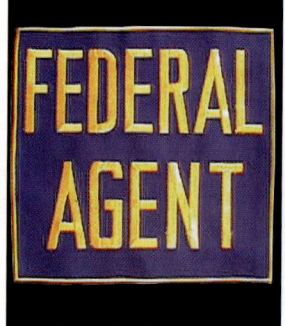

1190
Raid jacket patch

1191
1st issue
Bureau of Prisons

1192
V1/V2-149
2nd issue Bureau of
Prisons - diamond

1193
V1/V2-148
2nd issue Bureau of
Prisons - round/1972

1194
V1/V2-147
3rd issue - 1976

1195
V1/V2-470
4th issue

1196
Larger version

United States Department of Justice

1197 Variation

1198 Variation - light wings

1199 Repro./Fantasy

1200 No info.

1201 FLETC strip

1202 FLETC strip

1203 FLETC strip

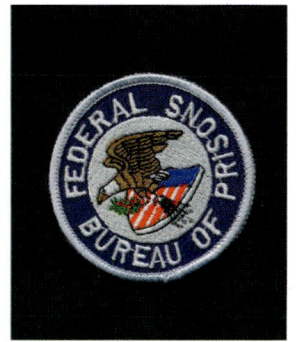

1204 Cap patch

1205 Bullion presentation

1206 Bullion presentation

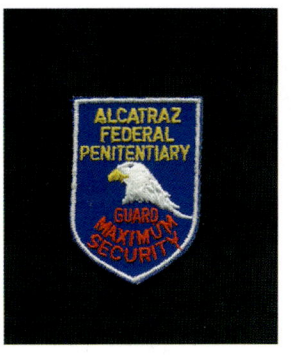

1207 Novelty

1208 Novelty

1209 V1/V2-475 Movie Prop - "Escape from New York"

1210 Novelty

1212

1213

1214

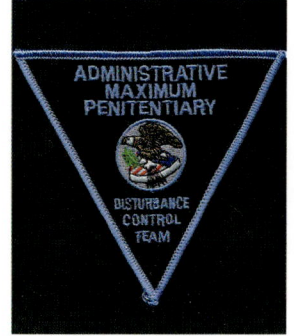

1215

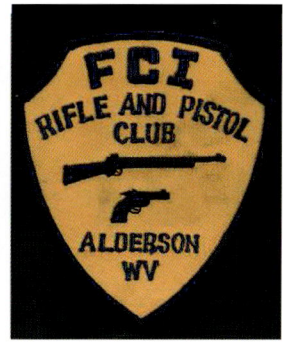

1216 West Virginia

1217 West Virginia

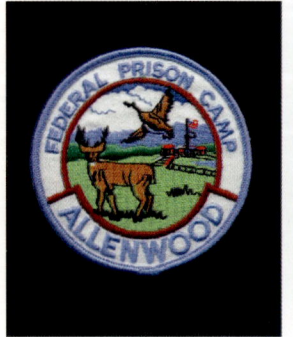

The Encyclopedia of Federal Law Enforcement Patches

1218
Pennsylvania

1219
Pennsylvania

1220

1221
1st issue - Atlanta

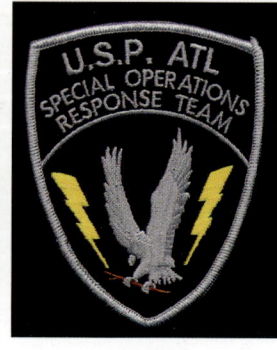

1222
2nd issue - Atlanta

1223

1224

1224a
Texas

1225
California

1226
California

1227
Disturbance Control Team

1228
2nd issue
another variation is
"FCC" Butner

1229
1st issue

1230
Texas

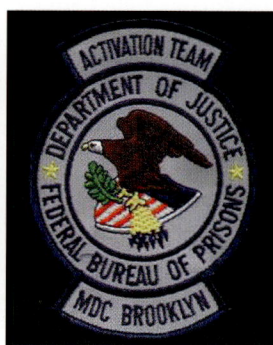

1231

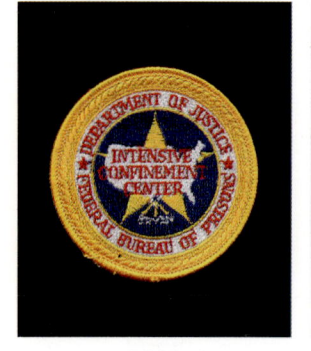

1232
Bryan, Texas

1233
Safford, Arizona
Current

1234
Current

1235
Current

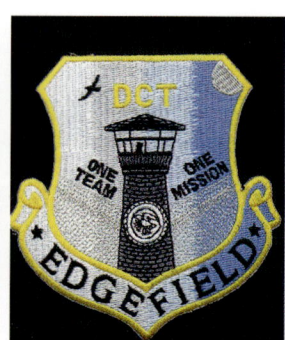

1236
Current

United States Department of Justice

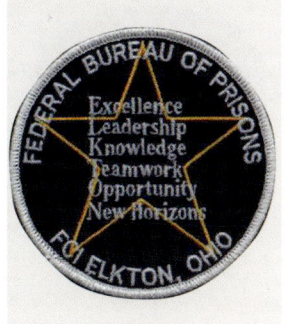

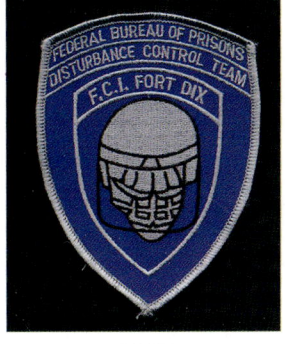

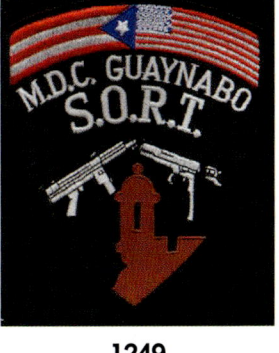

1237

1238

1239

1240

1241

1242

1243

1244

1245

1246

1247

1248
Current

1249

1250

1251
Jessup, Georgia

1252
Texas

1253

1254
Leavenworth SORT

1255

1256
Current

The Encyclopedia of Federal Law Enforcement Patches

1257

1258

1259

1260

1261

1262

1262a
Bureau of Prisons

1263
V1/V2-472
1st issue

1264
V1/V2-473
3rd issue

1265
Current

1266
Current horse patrol

1267
1st issue

1268
Current

1269

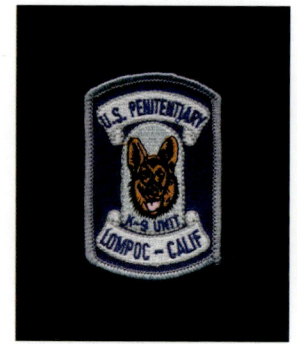

1270
1st issue

1271
Current

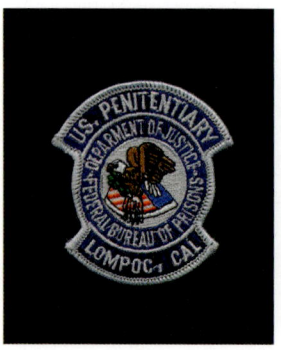

1272

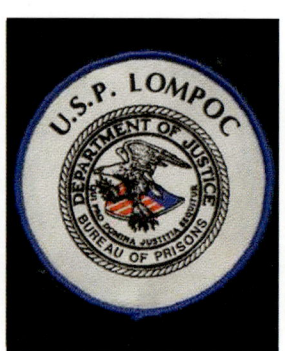

1273

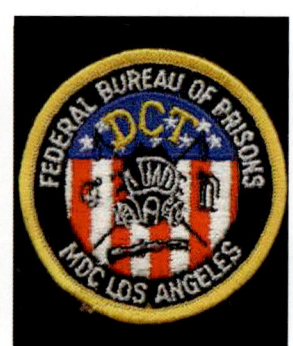

1274

1275
Kentucky

United States Department of Justice

1276 Illinois 1st issue

1277 2nd issue

1278 3rd issue

1279 Marion, IL SORT

1280 1st issue

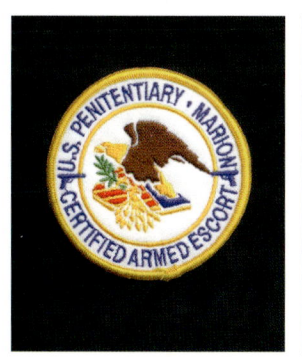

1281 Issued after training

1282 Memphis 2nd issue

1283 Memphis 1st issue

1284 Memphis Current issue

1285 Michigan

1286

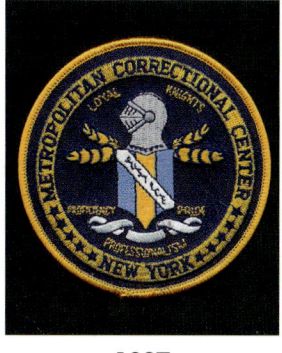

1287

1288 Oakdale, LA

1289 Oakdale, LA

1290

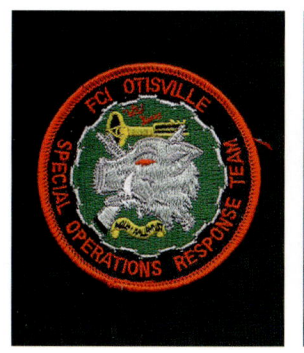

1291 Current

1292 Wisconsin

1293 Wisconsin

1294 Virginia

1295 1st issue

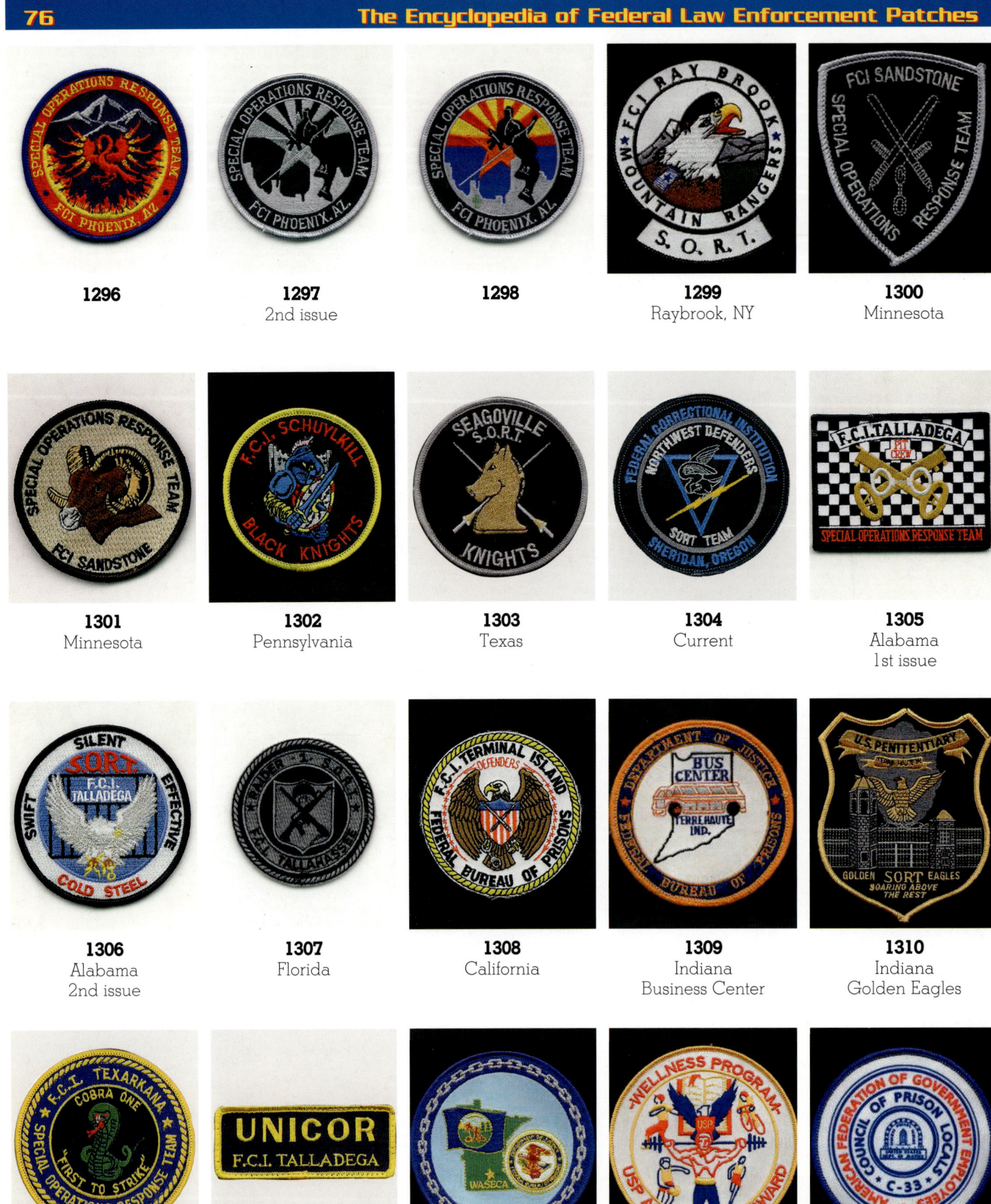

The Encyclopedia of Federal Law Enforcement Patches

1296

1297
2nd issue

1298

1299
Raybrook, NY

1300
Minnesota

1301
Minnesota

1302
Pennsylvania

1303
Texas

1304
Current

1305
Alabama
1st issue

1306
Alabama
2nd issue

1307
Florida

1308
California

1309
Indiana
Business Center

1310
Indiana
Golden Eagles

1311

1312
Prison Industries
Current

1313
Wisconsin

1314
Award - Lewisburg, PA

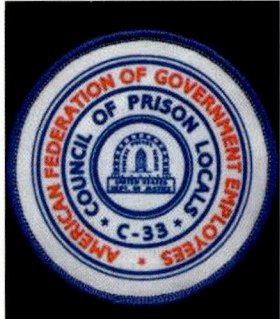

1315
Prison Union

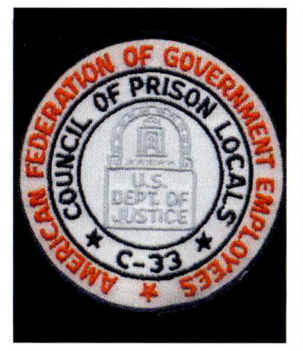

United States Department of Justice

1316
Prison Union

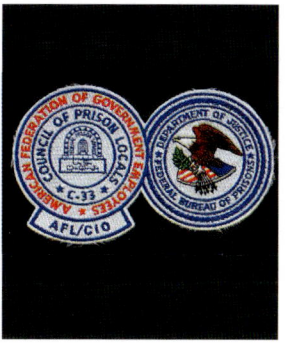

1317
Prison Union

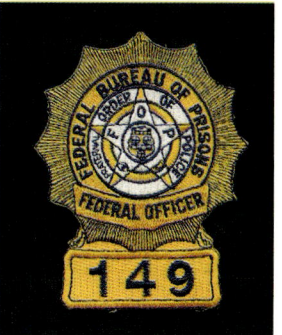

1318
Possibly NY MCC

1318a
Just closed

1319

1319a
Hat patch

1320
Novelty

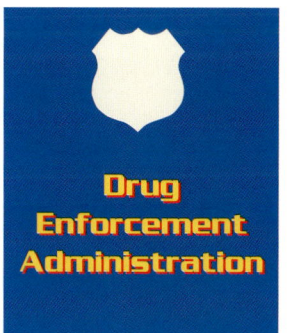

Drug Enforcement Administration

1321
V1/V2-137v
4½"

1322
4.4"

1323
4 3/16"

1324
4"

1325
3¼"

1326
3½"

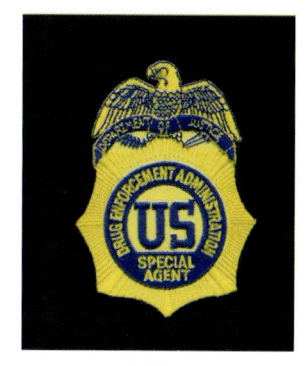

1327
3"

1328
4½"
Not DEA production

1329
Current raid jacket strip
Velcro

1330

1331

1332

The Encyclopedia of Federal Law Enforcement Patches

1333

1334
3½"

1335
V1/V2-138
3"

1336
3¾"

1337
3"

1338
2¾"

1339
4½"

1340
4"
Detroit

1341
3¾"

1342
3½"

1343
6" bullion

1344
4" bullion

1345
4" bullion

1346
3¾" bullion

1347
Bullion

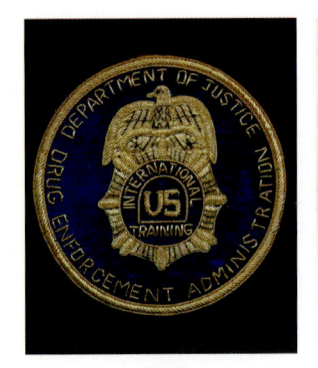

1348
Bullion

1349
Bullion

1350
Bullion

1351

1352
Bullion

Drug Enforcement Administration

1353 Bullion 
1354 Bullion 
1355 
1356 
1357

1358 V1/V2-139 
1359 3" 
1360 4" 
1361 
1362 New version

1363 1st issue Subdued var., too 
1364 2nd issue 
1365 
1366 
1367

1368 Two versions: 4" & 3"
1369 
1370 
1371 
1372

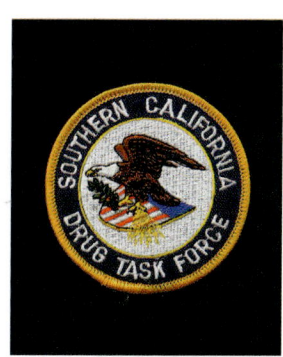

The Encyclopedia of Federal Law Enforcement Patches

1373
4"
Beware of poorly-made repro.

1374
3"

1375
Back of real patch = "D. Haynes"

1376

1377
Slightly smaller Variation

1378
JDIG - Los Angeles
FBI funding

1378a
JDIG - Houston

1379
L.A.-NV OCDETF

1380

1381

1382

1383

1384

1385
2nd version
1st had no states

1386
Tulsa, OK

1387

1388

1389
4½"

1390
3"

1391
WV added
3"

Drug Enforcement Administration

1392
3¾"

1393

1394
5"

1395
4"

1396

1397

1398

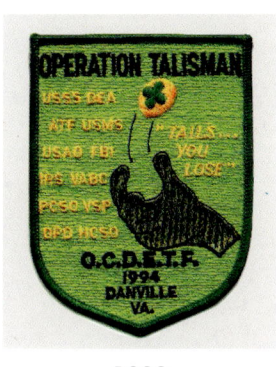

1399

1399a

1399b
Old

1399c
Variation
Old

1399d
Key West TF -
DEA/USC/USN

1399e
Old

1400

1401

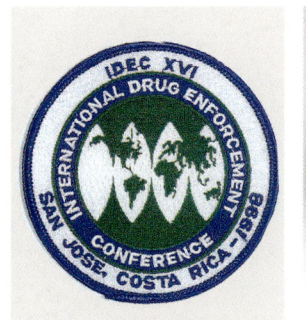

1402

1403
Roanoke, VA patch

1404
Later version - Texas

1404a
Multi-agency Federal
Drug TF

1405
Redrum = murder

82 The Encyclopedia of Federal Law Enforcement Patches

1406

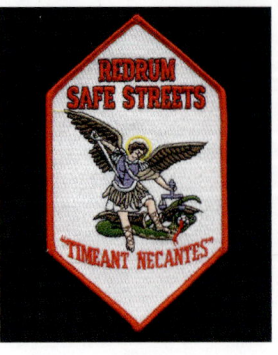

1407

1408

1409

1410

1411

1412
Officer Survival Course

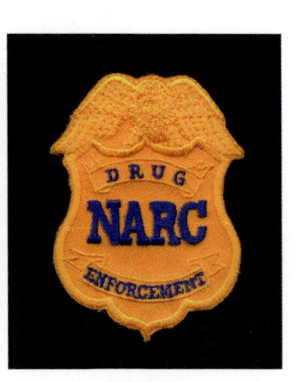

1413
Novelty?

1414
LAX DEA
1984 Olympics

1415
Dulles-National
Airports

1416
Anniversary

1417
Joint DEA-U.S. Customs

1418
Hawaii

1419

1420
Joint DEA-USC
New York

1421
Cleveland, OH

1422
Authorized wings

1423
Authorized wings

1424
Aerial observer wings

1425
Unauthorized but worn

Drug Enforcement Administration

1426 Latest version

1427 Earlier version

1428

1429

1429a

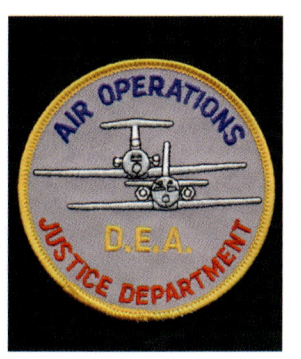

1430 Fake/Fantasy

1431 Two versions Two sizes: 3³⁄₄" & 3¹⁄₄"

1433 5¹⁄₂" bullion

1434 4" bullion

1435 3" bullion

1436 V1/V2-136 Official seal 4"

1437 3³⁄₄"

1438 Variation 4"

1439 4" subdued

1440 3"

1441 3" variation

1442

1443 No info.

1444 6" x 11" Velcro back Patch

1445 1" x 4"

The Encyclopedia of Federal Law Enforcement Patches

1446
Velcro back
Clan. Lab. vest front

1447
2" H x 4½" W

1448
2" H x 2½" W

1449
2½" H x 2½" W

1450
OD

1451
Silver "DEA"

1452
Gold "DEA"

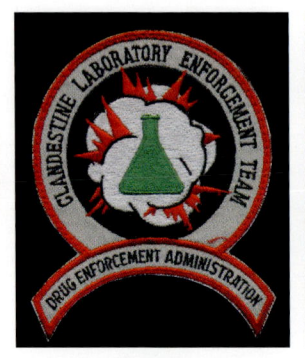

1453
Velcro back - original "CLET" has gray cloud behind flask

1454
Good variation

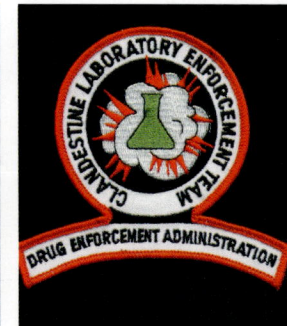

1455
No info.

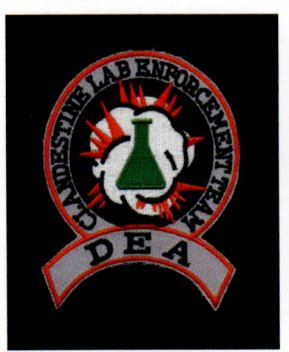

1456
3"
San Diego

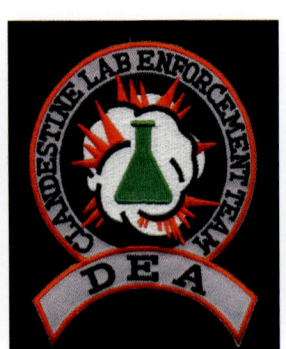

1457
3½"
San Diego?

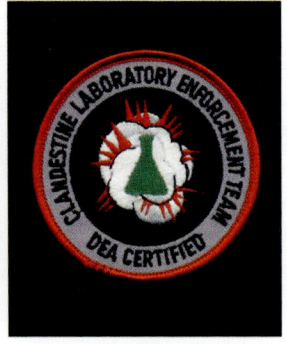

1458
Given to police attendees

1459
Original cap patch

1460
Fake

1461
Was at USCS HQ

1462
Bullion

1463
Was at USCS HQ

1464
SW Border TF

1465

Drug Enforcement Administration

1466

1467
Early issue

1468
Early issue variation

1469
Current style - black border

1470
Current style - gold border

1471
Arizona border

1472
Arizona border

1473
3"
Johnstown, PA

1474
5"
Johnstown, PA

1475
Produced by Mexico DEA

1476
Produced by Mexico DEA

1477

1478

1479
USN-USCG

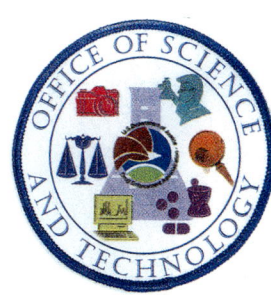

1480
DEA-OST

1481
Inside joke

1482
Washington, D.C. unit
Unofficial

1483
Washington, D.C. unit
Unofficial

1484
20th anniversary

1485
20th anniversary
Variation

The Encyclopedia of Federal Law Enforcement Patches

1486
NY office produced
Agency approved

1487
V1/V2-457
FLETC

1488
FLETC

1489
One of a kind
Intell. Analyst school

1490
Darth Narc?

1491

1492

1493
Made by HQ
Demand Reduction Ofc.

1494

1495
Official - FLETC
Certified boat handlers
1994

1496

1497

1498

1499
5" H

1500

1501

1502

1503

1504

1505

Drug Enforcement Administration

1506

1507
HQ radio section

1508
1st issue

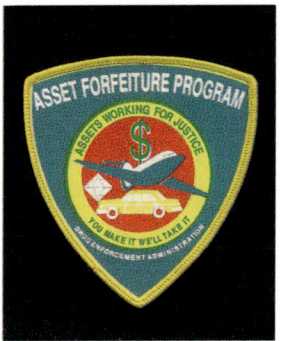

1509
Latest version
Produced by HQ

1510
Prototype

1511
Unofficial

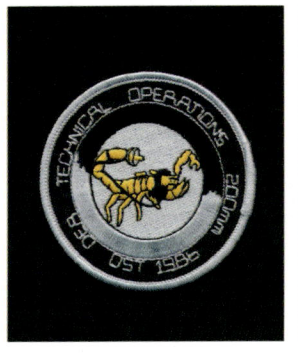

1512
1st issue
1986

1513
2nd issue

1514
Chicago office

1515
Texas

1516

1517

1518
DEA Conference patch

1519
Missouri

1520
Tennessee

1521
California (Campaign
Against Marijuana Plant)

1522

1523

1524
New Jersey

1525

87

The Encyclopedia of Federal Law Enforcement Patches

1526 No info. Appears old

1527 Coast Guard involved

1528

1529 Bahamas interdiction

1530

1531 Ball cap patch

1532

1533

1534

1535

1536

1537

1538

1539

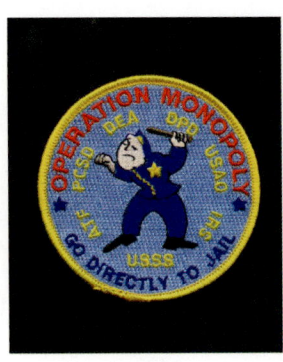

1540 3¼"

1541 3¾"

1542

1543

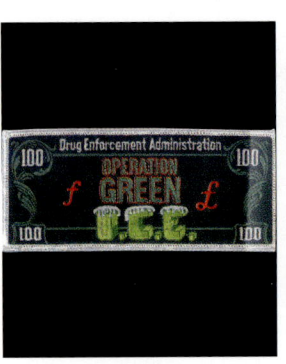

1544

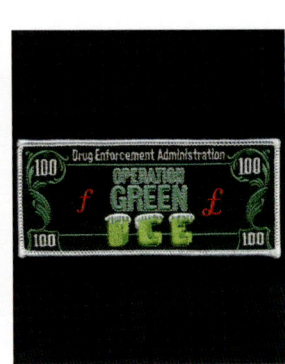

1545

Drug Enforcement Administration

1546

1547
South America ops.

1548
South America ops.

1549
3"
California TF

1550
5½"
California TF

1551
California TF

1552
California TF

1553

1554
Georgia

1555

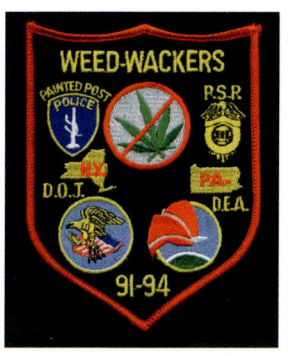

1556

1557
Hawaii

1558
Hawaii

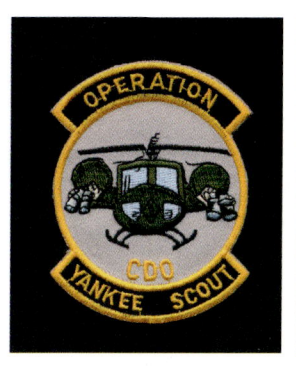

1559
Counter-Drug
Operation

1560
Counter-Narcotic
Operation

1561

1562

1563

1564

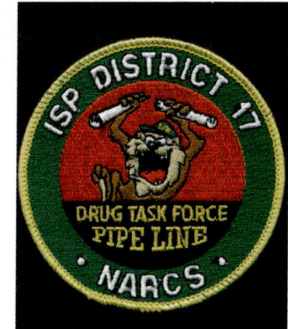

1565

89

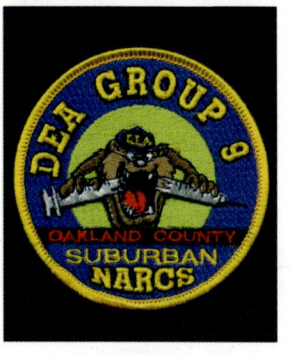

The Encyclopedia of Federal Law Enforcement Patches

1566

1567

1568

1569
DEA-Postal inspection
Current

1570
DEA-Postal inspection
Prior issue

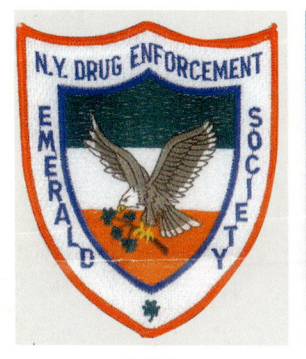

1571
Irish Society

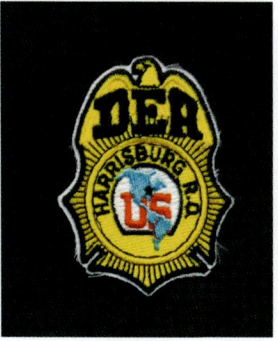

1572
3"

1573
5"

1574

1575

1576
Thailand

1577

1579

1580

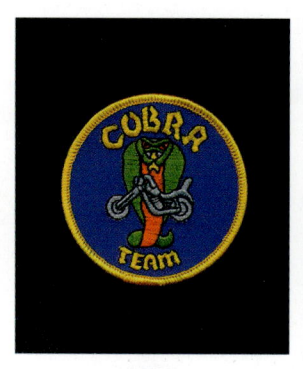

1581
Col. Outlaw Biker Res.
Attack team

1582
Connecticut

1583

1584

1585
Georgia

Drug Enforcement Administration

1586 4"

1587 3"

1588

1590

1591

1592 Maryland

1593

1594

1595

1596

1597

1598 New Jersey

1599

1600 "Federal" replaces "DEA"

1601

1602 "Fed" replaces "DEA"

1603

1604

1605

91

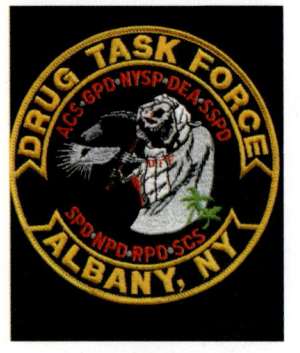

The Encyclopedia of Federal Law Enforcement Patches

1606
5"

1607
Southeast Asian Task Force

1608
Gray/red version

1609
Liberty lady also in green

1610
Liberty lady also in blue

1611

1612
No color

1613
Color center

1614

1615

1616

1617

1618
1980s - Texas

1619

1620

1621
Washington

1622
Elvis in DEA raid jacket

1623

1624
5½" & 3½" versions

1625
2nd version 5½"

Drug Enforcement Administration

1626
3" version

1627
V1/V2-455
DEA Los Angeles
"Little Bad Guys"

1628
DEA participates

1629
Inside joke
"Cocaine"

1630
No info.

1631
V1/V2-453
Ex-Fed. Narc. Assn.

Federal Bureau of Investigation

1632
Gold mylar

1633
Bullion, not issue

1634

1635
Subdued SWAT C/B

1636
3" new Raid jacket
patch - 1995

1637
4" new Raid jacket
patch - 1995

1638
FBI Police - HQ
Uniformed

1639
V1/V2-459
FBI Police Seal

1640
Officer C/B

1641
Sergeant C/B

1642
Lieutenant C/B

1643
Captain C/B

1644
Colonel C/B

The Encyclopedia of Federal Law Enforcement Patches

1645
V1/V2-458
Early armband, circa 1960s

1646
Later armband

1647
Twill version of #1640

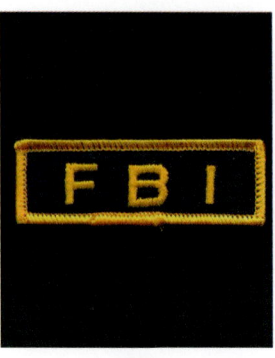

1648

1649

1650
V1/V2-463

1651

1652

1653

1654
V1/V2-142
Hat patch
Blue & black versions

1655
3" x 6"

1656
V1/V2-146
3" x 6" light blue

1657
4" x 9¾" back patch

1658

1659

1660

1661

1662

1663

1664

Federal Bureau of Investigation

1665

1666
4"

1667
4"

1668
V1/V2-140
4"

1669
V1/V2-141
3½" black & blue versions

1670
3½"

1671
3"

1672
3"

1673
3" gold mylar

1674
V1/V2-460
3" yellow

1675
3"

1676

1677
3" bullion

1678
4" bullion

1679

1680
5½"

1681
7" new raid jacket back patch

1682

1683
Novelty - cap

1684

The Encyclopedia of Federal Law Enforcement Patches

1685
3"

1686
4"

1687

1688

1689

1690
V1/V2-466

1691
V1/V2-143
4½"

1692

1693
4½"

1694
3"

1695
3"

1696

1697

1698
3" bullion

1699
3½" bullion

1700
3"

1701

1702
V1/V2-464, 465
4½" & 3¼" variations

1703

1704

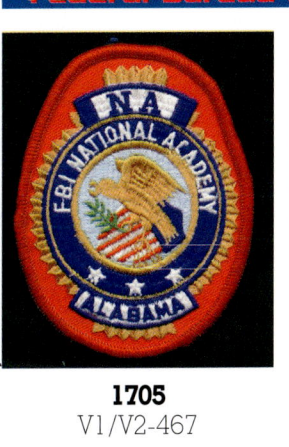

Federal Bureau of Investigation

97

1705 V1/V2-467	**1706** Australia	**1707** V1/V2-468	**1708**	**1709**
1710	**1711** Sweden	**1712**	**1713**	**1714**
1715	**1716**	**1717**	**1717a**	**1717b**
1718	**1719**	**1720**	**1721**	**1722**

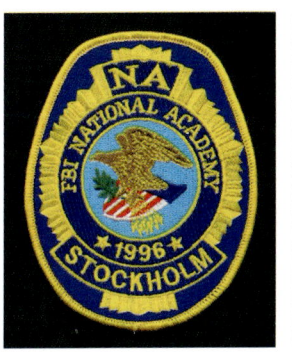

The Encyclopedia of Federal Law Enforcement Patches

1723

1724

1725

1726

1727

1728

1729

1730

1731
Inside Joke

1732
Agent's association

1733
V1/V2-145

1734
Variation

1735
Ex-agent's association
Twill

1736
Silk-screened version
Old - 50th

1737
Bullion
Cut out 3"

1738
Bullion
Circle

1739

1740

1741
Bullion

1742
25th anniversary

Federal Bureau of Investigation

99

1743

1744 New Jersey

1745

1746

1747 Blue border

1748 Gold border

1749

1750 Subdued Washington

1751 Color

1752

1753 Real FBI Pilot wings - RT

1754 Foreign-made fake

1755 Foreign-made fake

1756 FBI chopper pilot patch

1757 1940-1950 FBI baseball team

1758

1759 Bomb data center

1760

1761 Certified FBI bomb tech

1761a FBI

The Encyclopedia of Federal Law Enforcement Patches

1762 Redstone Arsenal trained tech - Variation reads "HDS" at top

1763 FBI a member

1764

1765 Spy hunters

1766

1767 Nickname for FBI agents

1768

1769 Some have Velcro backing

1770 "Silence of the Lambs" motif

1771

1772

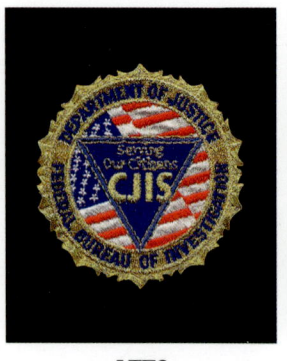

1773

1774

1775 2 3/4"

1776 4"

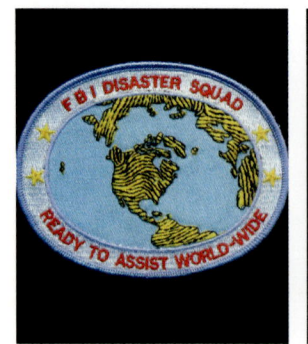

1777

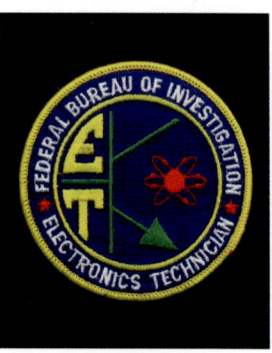

1778

1779 "Descendants of Irish Kings"

1780 Early 1980s FBI HQ

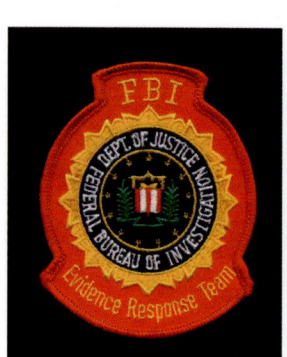

1781 Comes in twill and F/E

Federal Bureau of Investigation

1782

1783

1784
60th anniversary

1785

1786
Combat range

1787
4" felt

1788
4½" felt

1789
Recreation association

1790
Los Angeles office

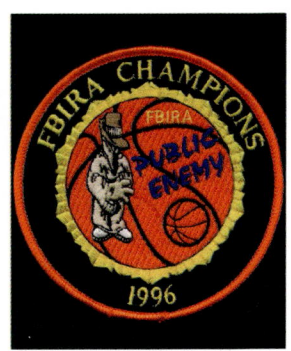

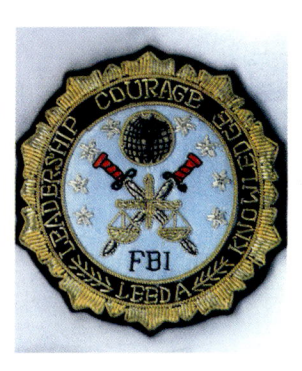

1791

1792

1793

1794

1795

1796
Rare patch

1797

1798

1799

1800

1801
Bullion version

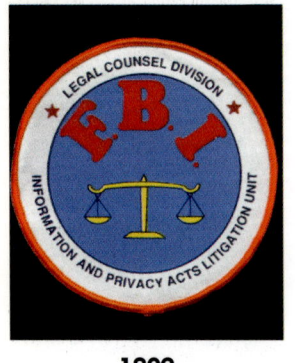

The Encyclopedia of Federal Law Enforcement Patches

1802
Var. has "Class Action Task Force" on bottom

1803

1804
Rejected prototype

1805

1806
3"

1807
3¾"

1808

1809

1809a
FBI

1809b
Medical Rescue School

1810
FBI agents were the investigators

1811

1812

1813

1814
Variation has "95" on bottom left

1815

1816

1817

1818

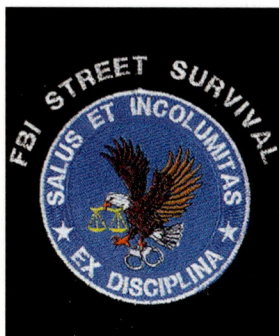

1819

Federal Bureau of Investigation 103

| 1820 | 1821 | 1821a
"Don't lose them, don't get caught" | 1822 | 1823 |

| 1824 | 1825
FBI a member | 1826 | 1827 | 1828 |

| 1829 | 1830
Silk-screened (old) | 1831
"WWP" = Wonderful World of Police | 1832 | 1833 |

| 1834 | 1835 | 1836 | 1837 | 1838 |

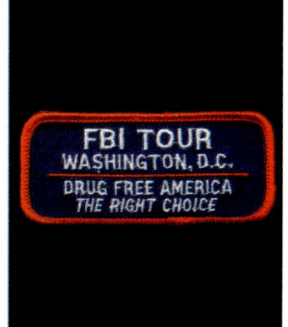

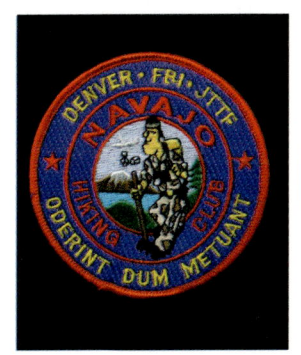

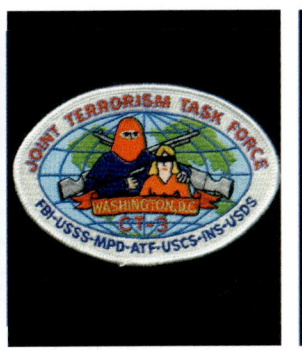

104 The Encyclopedia of Federal Law Enforcement Patches

| 1839 Made for FPS Police | 1840 | 1841 | 1842 | 1843 |

| 1844 | 1845 Texas | 1846 | 1847 | 1848 |

| 1849 NA patch | 1850 FBI a member | 1851 FBI a member | 1852 FBI a member | 1853 |

| 1853a New | 1854 | 1855 FBI a member | 1856 FBI a member | 1857 FBI a member |

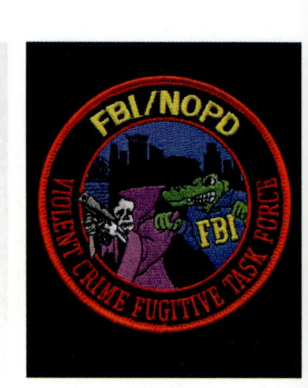

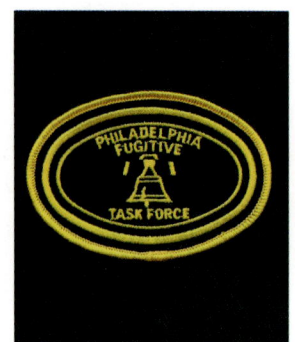

Federal Bureau of Investigation

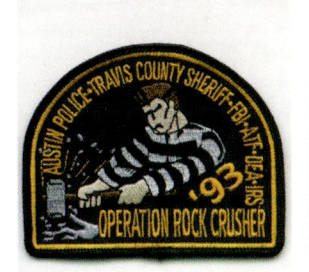

1858
FBI a member

1859
FBI a member
(Asian org. crime)

1860
FBI a member

1861
FBI a member
3" & 5" versions

1862

1863
3" & 4" versions

1864

1865

1866

1867
Note the initials

1868

1869

1870

1871

1872

1873
Texas

1874
Texas

1875
Massachusetts

1876

1877
5"

The Encyclopedia of Federal Law Enforcement Patches

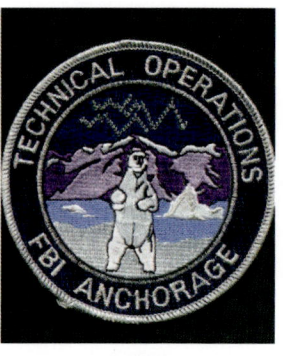

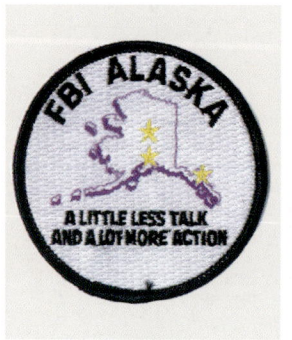

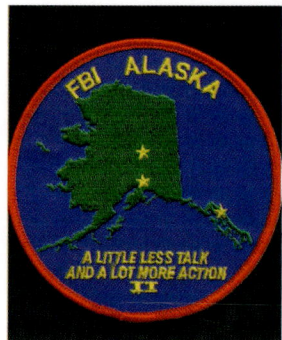

1878

1879

1880

1881

1882

1883

1884

1885

1886

1887

1888

1889

1889a
FBI L.A./Hollywood

1890

1891

1892
"I came, I saw, I swept up"

1893

1894

1895

1896
D.C. - Washington metro field office

Federal Bureau of Investigation

1897
Bank of Credit & Commerce Int'l.

1898

1899

1900
"Technician" misspelled - Corrected later

1901
Saudi Arabian bombing

1902
Saudi Arabian bombing

1903

1903a
"Art Deco" FBI

1904

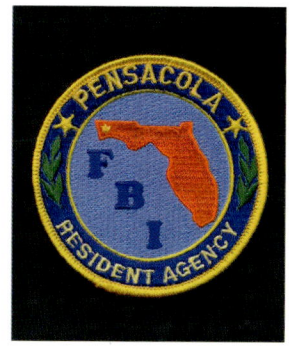

1905

1906

1907
"ITC" = Information Technology Center (FBI)

1908

1909

1910

1911

1912
Chicago Pilot - medium

1913
Chicago Pilot - large

1914
Chicago team

1915

The Encyclopedia of Federal Law Enforcement Patches

1916

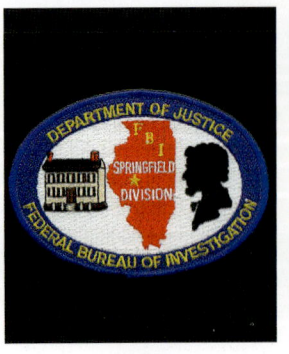

1917

1918

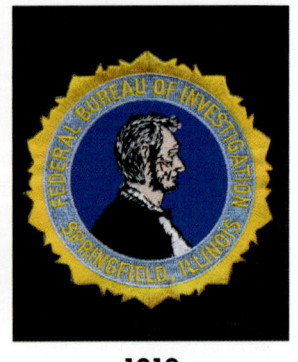

1919

1920

1921

1922
Has been reproduced often

1923

1924

1925

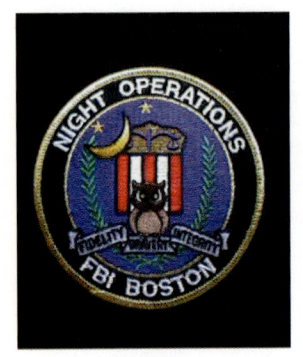

1926

1927
Detroit, MI

1928

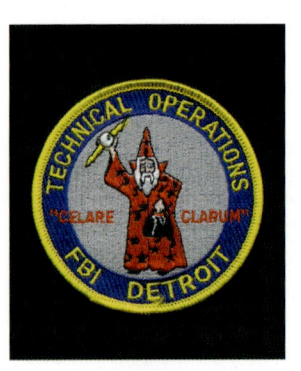

1929

1930

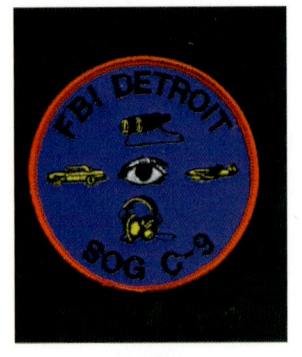

1931

1932
"UCO" = Undercover Operations

1933

1934

1935

Federal Bureau of Investigation

1936
Nebraska

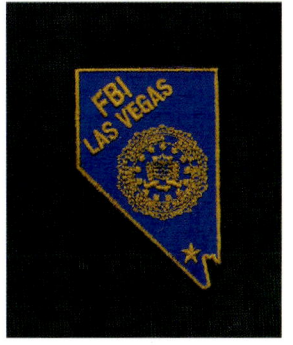

1937

1938

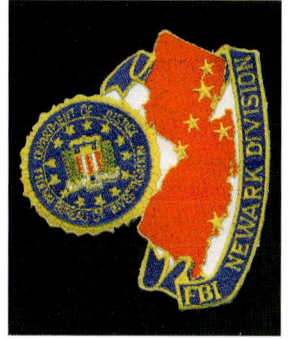

1939

1940

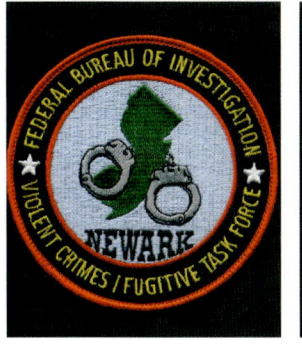

1941

1942

1943

1944

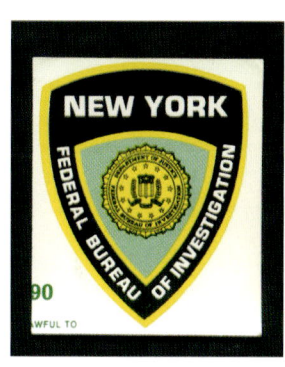

1945
Window plaque

1946
1987

1947

1948

1949

1950

1951

1952

1953

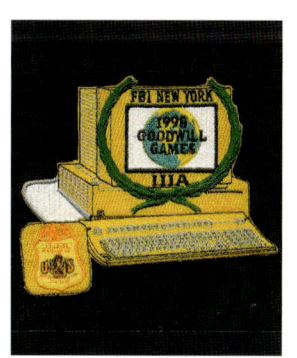

1954

1955

The Encyclopedia of Federal Law Enforcement Patches

1956 Old patch

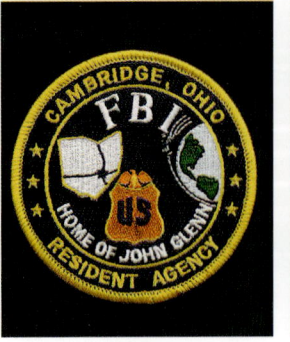

1957

1958

1959

1960

1961 "PFM" = Patrick Francis Murphy (Murphy's Law)

1962 5"

1963 Variation omits "U.S." in shield

1964 Gold mylar

1965

1966

1967 Puerto Rico

1968 Puerto Rico

1969

1970

1971

1972

1972a New

1973

1974

Federal Bureau of Investigation

111

1975
HRT - 1983
Gray twill

1976
HRT - 1983
Blue pinpoint

1977
HRT - color version

1978
1994- twill

1979
1995 - F/E

1980
1996 Olympics
OD - Velcro

1981
Possible fantasy

1982

1983
HRT - Maritime squad

1984
Foreign-made bullion
Fantasy

1985
Early 1970s SWAT
Rare

1986

1987

1988

1989
Rare SWAT-HRT School

1990
20th Anniversary

1991
Novelty

1992
OD sniper

1992a
Seal of FBI 2-piece
SWAT set

1992b
Square badge of
2-piece set

The Encyclopedia of Federal Law Enforcement Patches

1993

1994
Off-color

1995
4th version

1996

1997
2nd issue

1998
2nd issue

1999
Two versions

2000
Prior issue

2001
3rd version

2002

2003

2004

2005

2006

2007

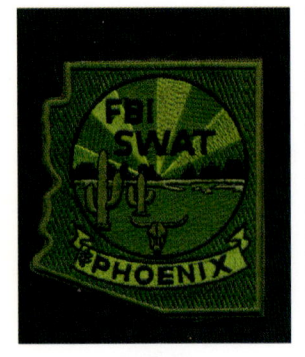

2008

2009

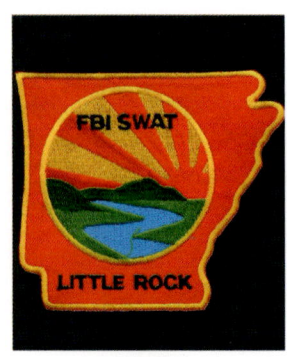

2010
1st issue/current

2011

2012
1984 Olympics
2nd issue

Federal Bureau of Investigation 113

2013
1984 Olympics
1st issue

2014

2015

2016

2017
Current/1st issue

2018

2019
1st issue

2020
Current

2021
Red "SWAT" = 1st issue
Green "SWAT" exists, too

2022
Current

2023
1st issue/current

2024
2nd issue

2025

2026
3rd issue/current

2027

2028
Fantasy

2029

2030

2031
Washington, D.C.
1st issue
"Buzzard Point"

2032
2nd issue

The Encyclopedia of Federal Law Enforcement Patches

2033
3rd issue

2034
1st issue
Often reproduced

2035
Reproductions have thinner daggers

2036
Tampa or Miami SWAT

2037

2038

2039
Conflicting information
1st issue or prototype

2040
1996 Olympics

2041

2042

2043
Norfolk, VA
Olympic patch

2044
Actually used

2045
Given as gifts

2046
Fantasy

2047
Real

2048
Reproduction
Plastic backing

2049
Twill - has been reproduced

2050
Twill - has been reproduced

2051
V1/V2-469
F/E

2052
Rare camo version

Federal Bureau of Investigation

2053 Current OD version

2054 3" version

2055 Current

2056 O/S

2057

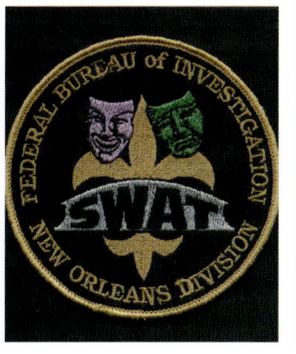

2058 Darker 4"

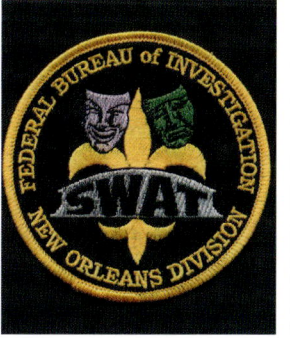

2059 Lighter 4"

2060 3½"

2061 1st issue/current

2062

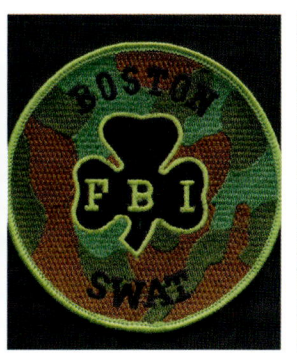

2063 4" camo

2064 4" OD

2065 4" color

2066 3" 1st issue

2067 Kentucky

2068 Kentucky

2069 Detroit SWAT

2070 Small letters

2071 Large letters

2072 Michigan

The Encyclopedia of Federal Law Enforcement Patches

2073 Michigan

2074 "Slash" 1st version

2075 "Slash" 1st version

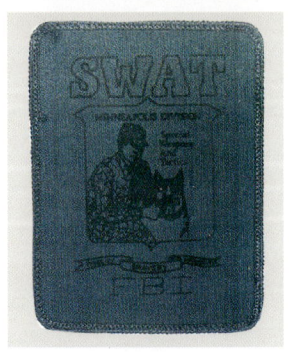

2076 Minnesota

2077 Minnesota

2078 Minnesota

2079 #1658 goes with this

2080 #1658 goes with this

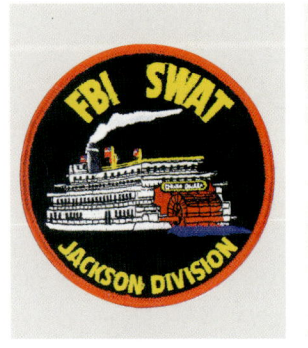

2081 Current

2082 Current

2083 1st issue

2084 1st issue

2085 2nd issue - current

2086 2nd issue - current

2087 "Poker Chip"

2088 Rarest FBI SWAT patch

2089

2090 Blue - 2nd version

2091 Black - 2nd version

2092 1st version

Federal Bureau of Investigation

2093 1st version

2094 Adopted in 1997

2095

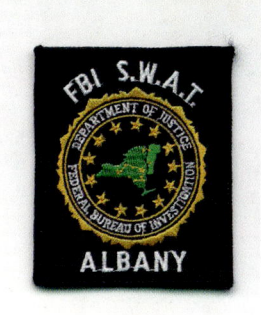

2096 2nd issue - current

2097 1st issue

2098 Current

2099

2100

2101

2102

2103

2104

2105 North Carolina

2106 Rare!

2107 1st issue

2108 2nd issue - current

2109

2110 Oregon 1st issue - current

2111 1st issue - current

2112 Bullion version also exists

The Encyclopedia of Federal Law Enforcement Patches

2113
4"
1st issue

2114
3"
1st issue

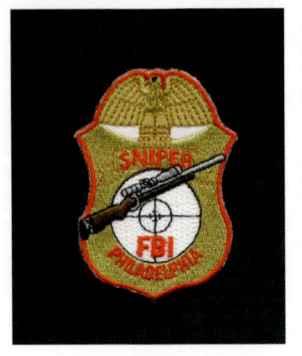

2115

2116

2117

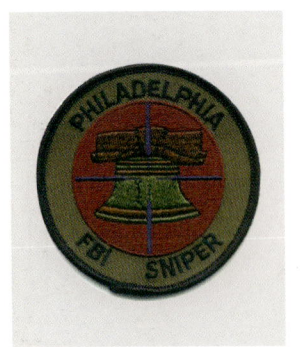

2118

2119
Very rare "Coqui" frog
Puerto Rico

2120
Puerto Rico
2nd issue

2121

2122

2123
Tennessee
Several variations

2124
Tennessee

2124a
Tennessee SWAT

2125
Current

2126
Need additional info.

2127
Not team authorized

2128
Original - <u>red</u> star on top, black ring inner circle

2129
Original - dark gray letters - silver inside

2130
Reproduction - <u>blue</u> star on top

2131
Reproduction

Federal Bureau of Investigation

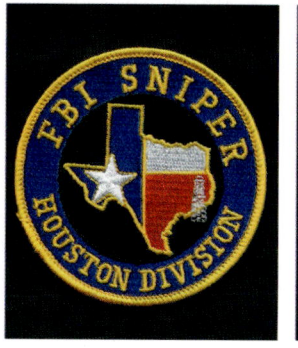

2132

2133
Current
Special Ops. Group

2134
3½" - Two versions
silver or gold oil wells

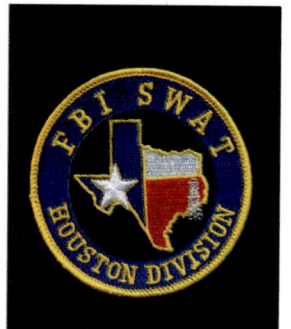

2135
3"
Note well color

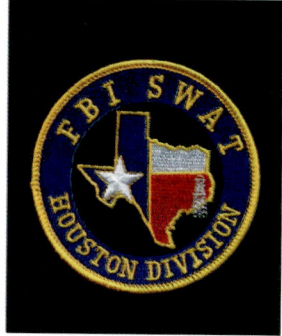

2136
3"
Note well color

2137
1st issue

2138

2139

2140

2141

2142
Under 50 made
8 years old

2143
Salt Lake City SWAT
(+ Phoenix)

2144
1st issue - current

2145
1st issue

2146
2nd issue

2147
2nd issue

2148
Washington, D.C.

2149

2150
1st issue
Reproductions have
thicker letters

2151
1st issue

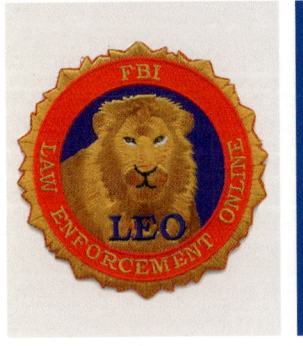

The Encyclopedia of Federal Law Enforcement Patches

2151a
FBI - 4 versions
Blue, black, white, green

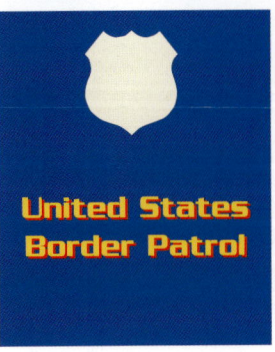

United States Border Patrol

2152
3"

2153
V1/V2-479
3½"

2154

2155
3"

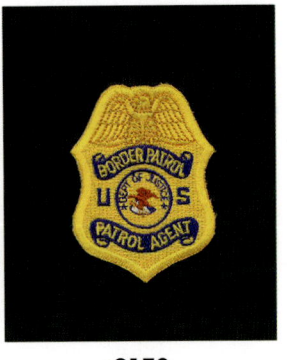

2156
2¾"

2157
O/S ERT
2¾"

2158
2½"

2159
V1/V2-478
2½"

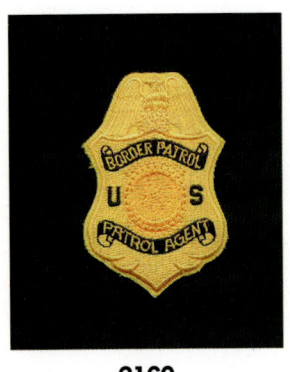

2160
3"

2161
3¼"

2162
5"

2163
3¼"

2164
3½"

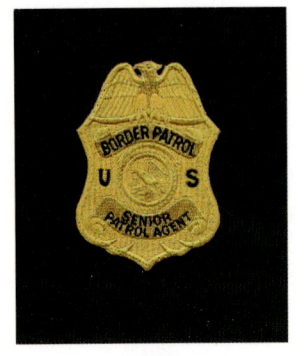

2165

2166

2167

2168

2169

United States Border Patrol

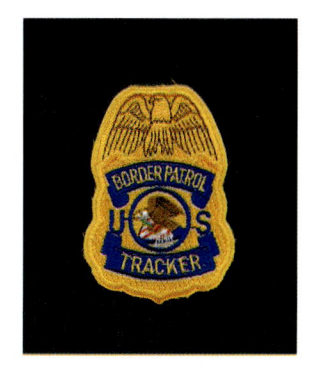

121

2170

2171

2172

2173

2174

2175

2176

2177

2178

2179

2180
5"
Tucson sector

2181
3¼"
San Diego area

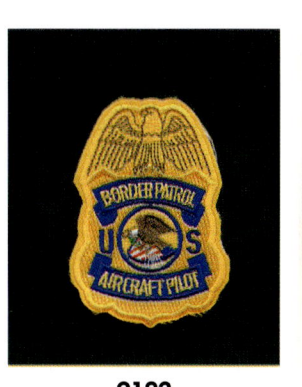

2182
4"

2183
3"
Has been reproduced

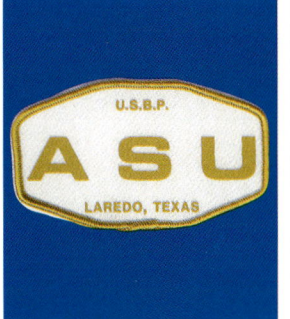

2184
3" Velcro back

2185
Anti-Smuggling Unit
Texas

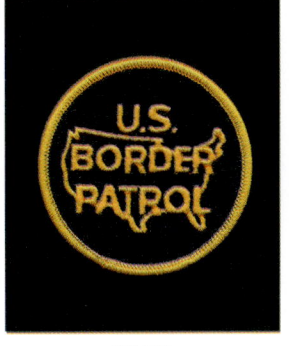

2186
V1/V2-151
New style F/E - 3"

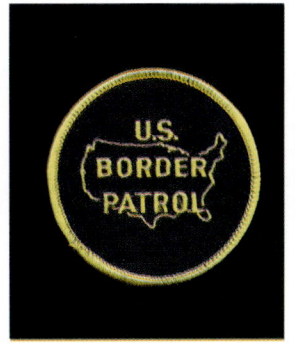

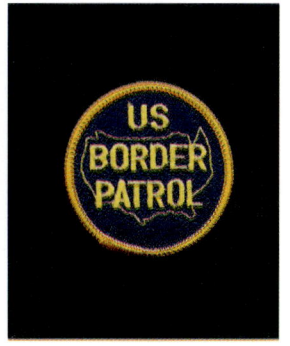

2187
Twill 3"

2188
2½" twill

2189
V1/V2-477
3" twill

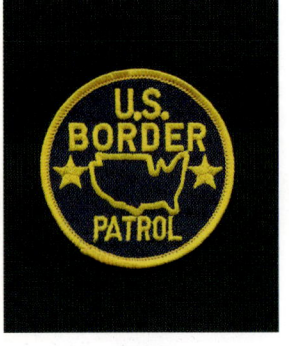

The Encyclopedia of Federal Law Enforcement Patches

2190

2191
3" Twill
Black border

2192
3" F/E
Olive border

2193
3" F/E
Blue border

2194
3" F/E
Black border

2195
4" Twill
Black border

2196
Rare 3½" F/E
Border Tactical Unit

2197
Bullion

2198

2199
3½"

2200
Rare

2201
El Paso area

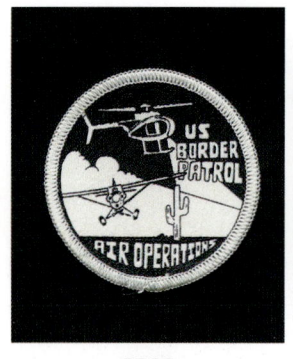

2202
Silk-screened
3" - black & white

2203
3½" F/E color

2204

2205
V1/V2-480

2206
Silk-screened
50 made 1988/89

2207

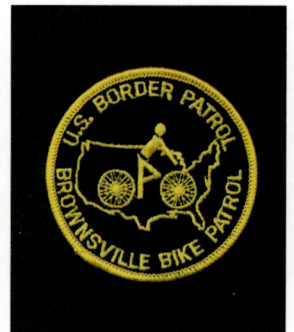

2208

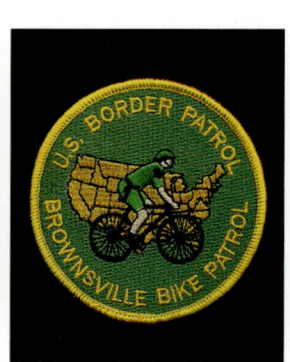

2209

United States Border Patrol

123

2210
No info.

2211

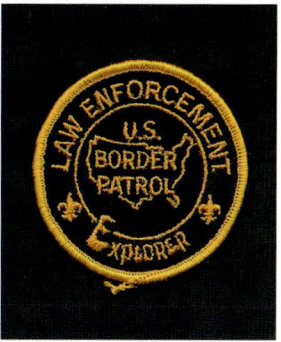

2212
Tucson sector
1988

2213
3½" F/E

2214
Texas

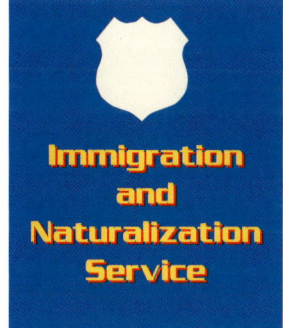

Immigration and Naturalization Service

2216
4¾"

2217
3"

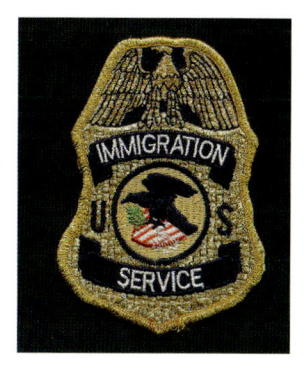

2218
5" gold border

2219
V1/V2-483
5" black border

2220
3"

2221
3½" reproduction

2222
3" reproduction

2223
1¾" - old
Need info.

2224
Union

2225
4¼"

2226
Bullion - 1996

2227
Dark letters

2228
White letters

The Encyclopedia of Federal Law Enforcement Patches

2229
Crew patch - 1997

2230
5" Crew patch - 1992

2231
4" - 30 made
W/TX 1997

2232

2233
Spl. Prot. Ofcr.
New & official

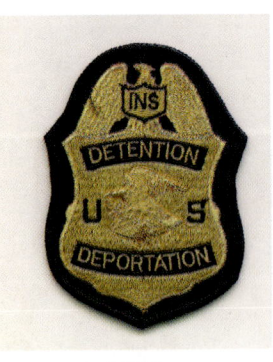

2234

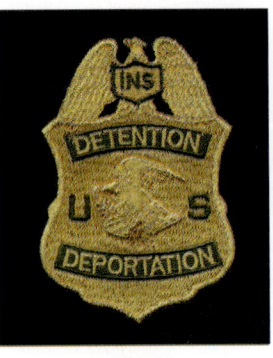

2235

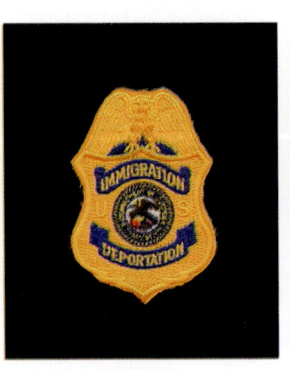

2236

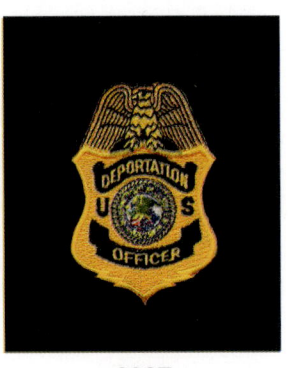

2237

2238
V1/V2-485
5"

2239
V1/V2-484
3"

2240
3"

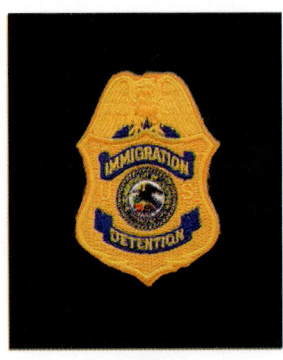

2241
3"

2242
5"

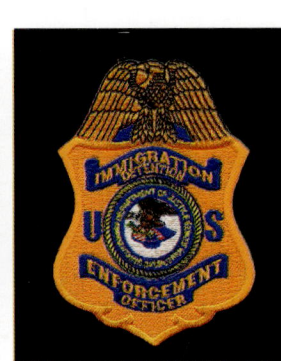

2243
4"

2244
V1/V2-153

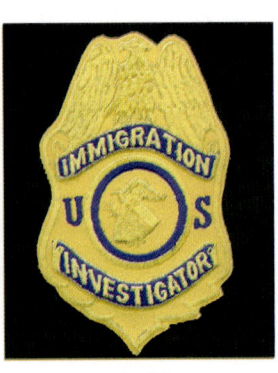

2245
V1/V2-489
4½"

2246
3"

2247
4"

2248
Prototype

Immigration and Naturalization Service

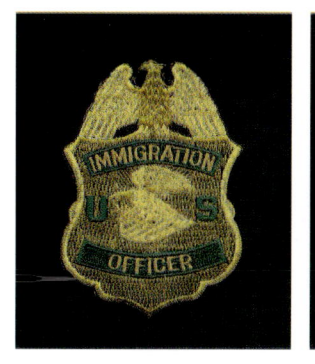

2249
4"

2250
4"

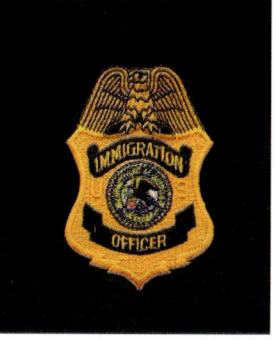

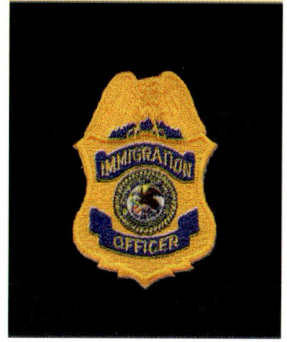

2251
3"

2252
Two sizes: 3 3/4" & 2 3/4"

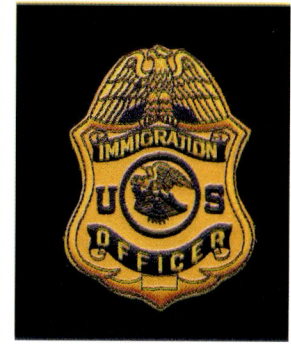

2253
Two sizes: 3 3/4" & 3"

2254
3 3/4"
El Paso office - 1997

2255
5"

2256
3 1/4" - Variation has brown eagle

2257
3"

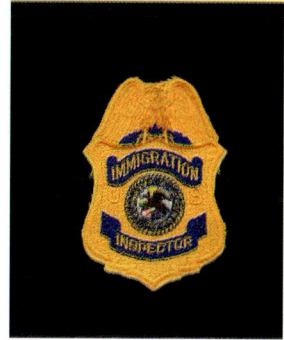

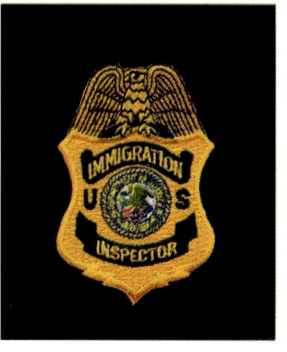

2258
2 3/4"

2259
3"

2260
Bullion

2261
Old

2262
Old
Silk-screened

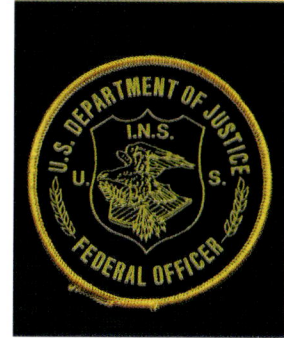

2263
Old

2264
Old

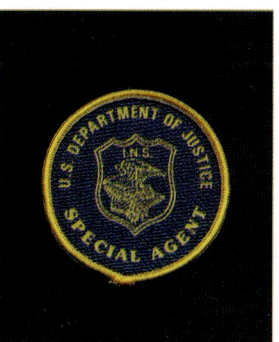

2265
Old

2266
V1/V2-490a
5"

2267
V1/V2-490
3"

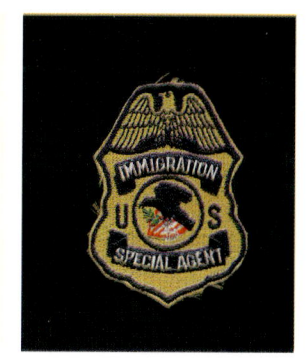

2268
3"

126 — The Encyclopedia of Federal Law Enforcement Patches

#	Size/Notes
2269	4 3/4"
2270	3"
2271	3 3/4"
2271a	Real?
2272	3"
2273	4"
2274	3 3/4"
2275	3"
2276	
2277	5"
2278	5"
2279	V1/V2-481, 3 1/4"
2280	4" silk-screened, Old
2281	
2282	3 1/4"
2283	3 1/2", Plastic-foam back
2284	3 1/4" F/E
2285	3" bullion
2286	V1/V2-482, 2 1/4"
2287	Two sizes: 2 1/8" & 2 3/8"

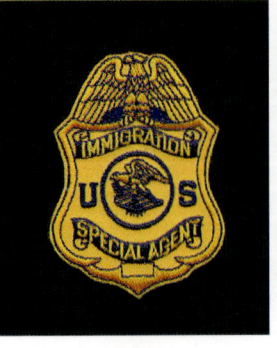

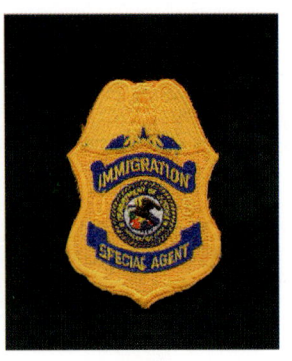

Immigration and Naturalization Service

2288
3"

2289
Port Isabel ERT-INS
20 made - 1992

2290
INS Miami
1994

2291
INS/FBI/FEMA
Tactical Medics

2292
INS Task Force

2293
SFO Airport

2294

2295
California

2296
Texas

2297
Texas - 1997

2298
New York

2298a
INS-BOP Joint operation

2298b
Texas

2298c
Texas

2299

2300
Final version - 1989

2301

2302

2303
V1/V2-152
Many variations

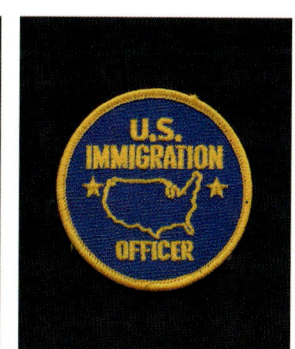

2304

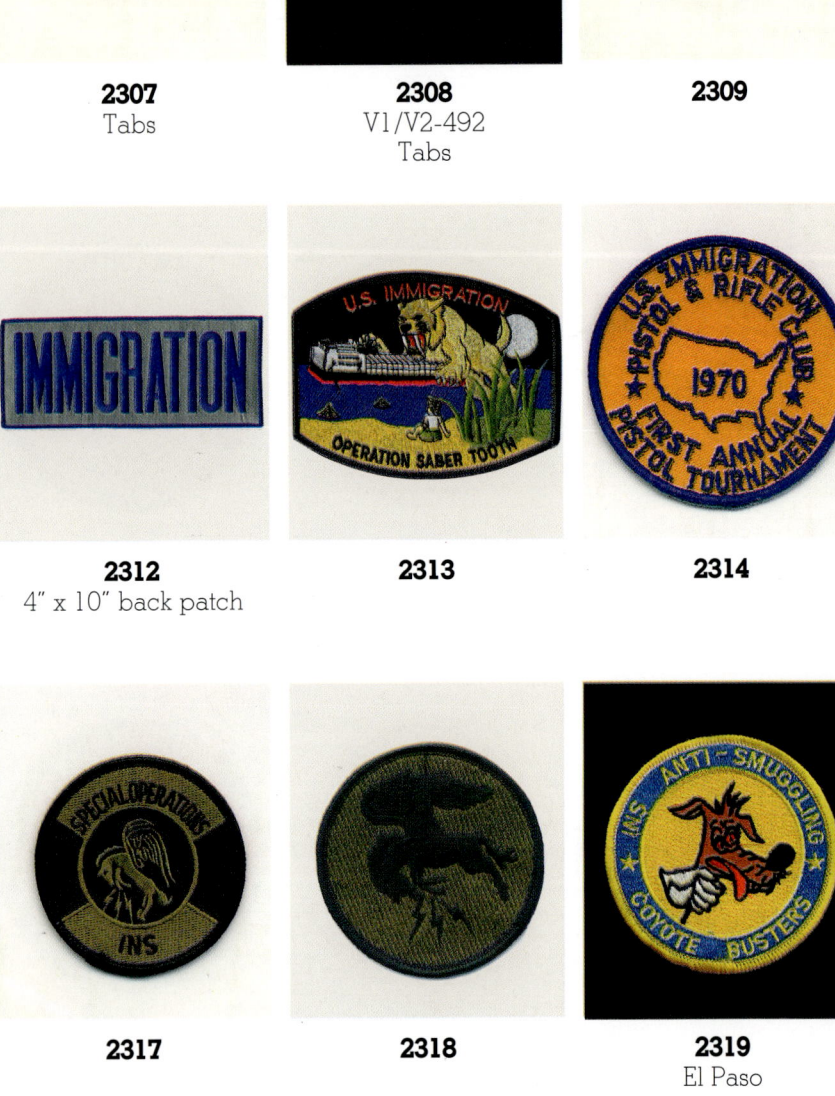

128 The Encyclopedia of Federal Law Enforcement Patches

2305
V1/V2-491
Tabs

2306
Tabs

2307
Tabs

2308
V1/V2-492
Tabs

2309

2310
V1/V2-154

2311
1" x 4"

2312
4" x 10" back patch

2313

2314

2315

2316
West Texas - 1996

2317

2318

2319
El Paso

2319a
Operation Gatekeeper
250 made

2320
New patch

2321

2322

2323

Immigration and Naturalization Service

2324
Variation has white letters

2325

2326

2327
White letters

2328
Gold mylar

2329
Prototype

2330
V1/V2-487

2331
V1/V2-486

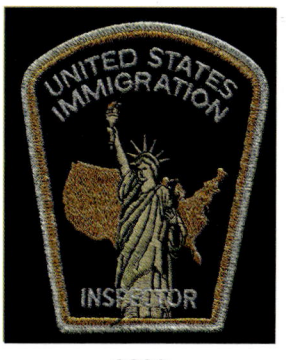

2332
Gold/silver mylar

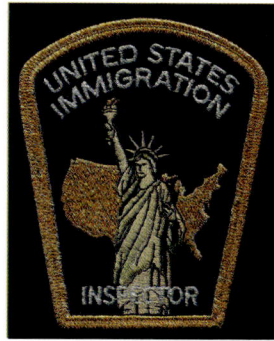

2333
Gold mylar border

2334
Gold mylar

2335
Gold/silver mylar

2336
V1/V2-488

2337

2338
Red & yellow flame variations

2339

2340

2341

2342

2343

The Encyclopedia of Federal Law Enforcement Patches

2344

2345

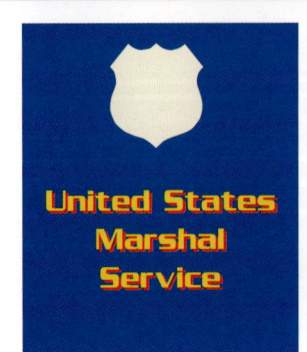

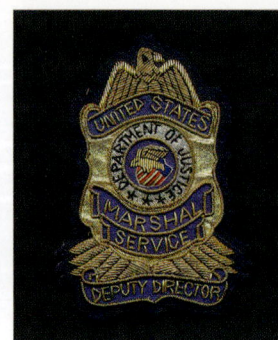

United States Marshal Service

2347
Bullion

2348
V1/V2-155
"Ike" badge

2349

2350
3"

2351
V1/V2-156
3 3/4" - variation omits "Service"

2352
4" silver

2353
3" silver

2354
3" silver variation

2355
4" gold

2356
3" gold

2357
Alaska

2358
Utah

2359
Utah

2360

2361

2362

United States Marshal Service

2363

2364
2¾"

2365
3"

2366
V1/V2-497
3"

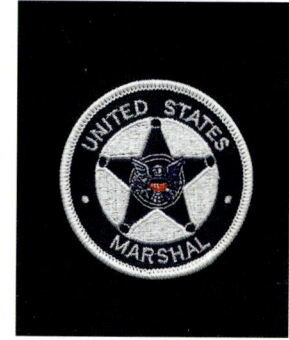

2367
2¾"

2368
Bullion

2369
3¾"

2370
4"

2371
4¼" bullion

2372
4"

2373
V1/V2-160
4" gold/brown

2375
Rare

2376
Deputized Insp. Gen'l.

2376a
Very old bullion

2377
Unofficial

2378

2379

2380

2381
Original patch
4"

The Encyclopedia of Federal Law Enforcement Patches

2382
5" Air ops pilots
1995

2383
2¾" bullion seal

2384
V1/V2-158
Many variations - 4"

2385
<u>Pink</u> eagle!
4"

2386
3"

2387
3"
Many variations

2388
3¼" variation

2389
2½" variation

2390
V1/V2-157
3" variation

2391
V1/V2-495
4"

2392
3"

2393
2½"

2394
1½"

2395

2396
3"

2397
V1/V2-496
4"

2397a
Real?

2398
3"

2399
4¼" & 7½" versions

2400
7½"

United States Marshal Service

2401 3¾" & 7½" versions

2402 Bicentennial patch

2403 Bicentennial patch

2404 Wings

2405

2406

2407 Variation

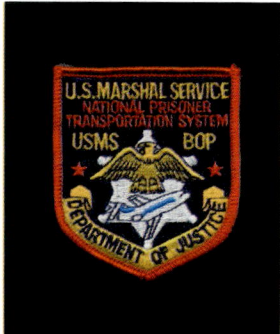

2408 3"

2409 4¼ & 4½" versions

2410 Rare

2410a Real ones from Worldwide Co.

2411

2412

2413

2414

2415 Witness Security Rare

2416

2417

2418

2419 Bullion

134   The Encyclopedia of Federal Law Enforcement Patches

2420 Movie prop - "Die Hard" series

2421 Prop

2422 TV series "Crime Story"

2423 V1/V2-159 Movie prop - "Outland"

2424

2425 4¼" 1996 - 3rd trial

2426 4¼" 1995 - 2nd trial

2427 4½" 1994 - 1st trial

2428 4¼" 1997 - final trial

2429 6" 1997 - final trial

2430

2431

2432

2433

2434

2435 V1/V2-503 Armband 4" x 6½"

2436 Armband 4" x 12"

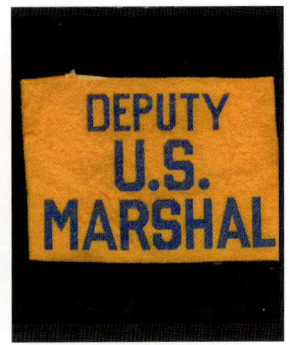

2437 V1/V2-504 Armband 4" x 12" 1960s, "Ole Miss" - James Meredith

2438 Armband 4½" x 7"

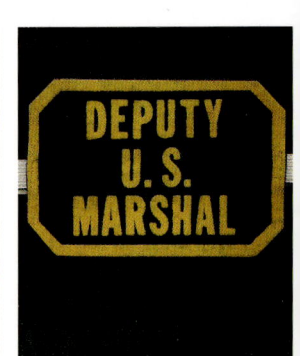

2439 Old armband Felt - 3" x 4½"

United States Marshal Service

2440
Back patch
4" x 10"

2441
Back patch
6" x 12"

2442
Back patch
4" x 10½"

2443
1996 Olympic Games

2444
Possible reproduction

2445
Original

2446

2447

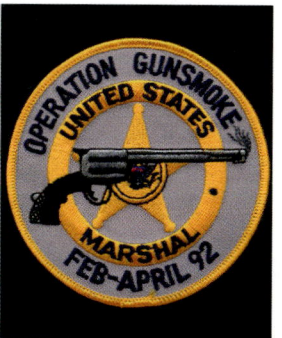

2448

2449
Sony "Fist"

2450
Kansas abortion protests

2451

2451a
4½" & 4" versions

2452
Houston, Texas 1995

2454

2455

2456
Baltimore

2457
3½" - 1996

2458
3" - 1996

2459
3"

2460
3½" - 1996

2461
V1/V2-501
3½"

2462
3"

2463
Alleged repro. var. has red letter dates

2464

2465

2466

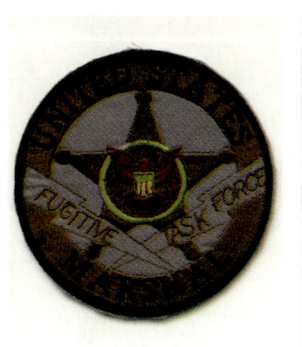

2467

2468
4½"

2469
3½"

2470
5"

2471
3"

2472
Fantasy

2473
USMS-FBI members
5"

2474
USMS-FBI members
3"

2475
Fugitive Teams
Arizona

2476
Calif. Districts

2477

2478
Pennsylvania

2479
Ohio

United States Marshal Service

2480 Ohio

2481 Approved version - 1993

2482 Prototype

2483 40 made - 1995 El Paso, Texas

2484 1991

2485 4" & 3" versions

2486 Posse New

2487 3" Arizona

2488 3" Arizona

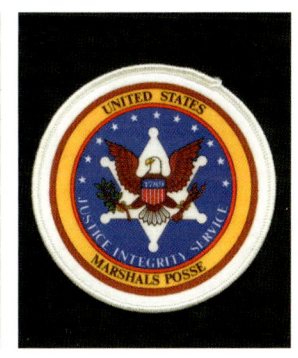

2489 3½" Arizona

2490 4"

2491 3½"

2492 Silver mylar 6" & 3½" versions

2493 3" Oklahoma

2494 Texas

2495

2496

2497

2498 Gold Alaska

2499 Silver Alaska

138   The Encyclopedia of Federal Law Enforcement Patches

2500 Arizona

2501

2502

2503 1996 - 200 made

2504 1997 - 200 made
Has been reproduced

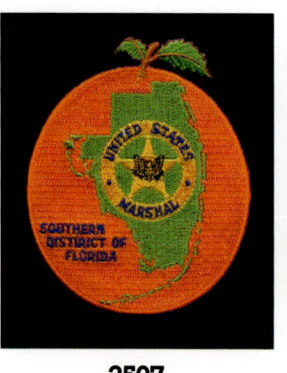

2505

2506 Extremely rare

2507

2508

2509 Beautiful set

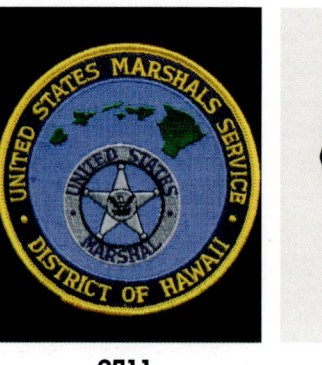

2510

2511

2512

2513

2514

2515 Variation

2516 Controversial set

2517 Controversial set

2518 WO/MI

2519 Red & blue versions

United States Marshal Service

139

2520
Final version - 1998

2521
Bicentennial Nebraska

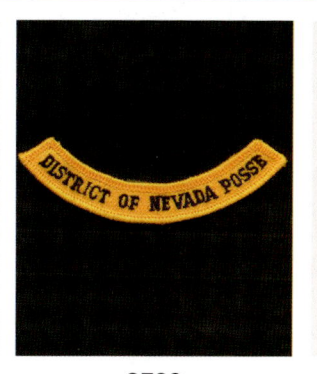

2522
Posse tab
Bottom of seal

2523
Silk-screened

2524
4"
1st edition - 1994

2525
3 1/2"

2526

2527
4"
1996 prototype

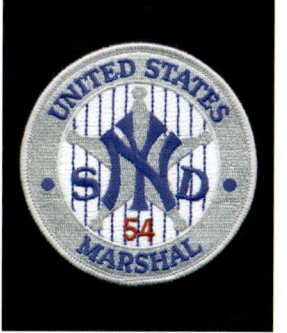

2528
3 1/2"
1996 prototype

2529
1996 official patch

2530

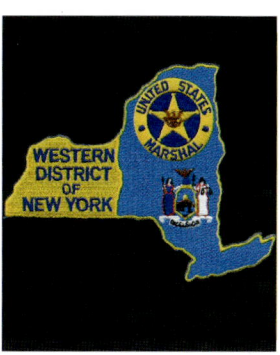

2531

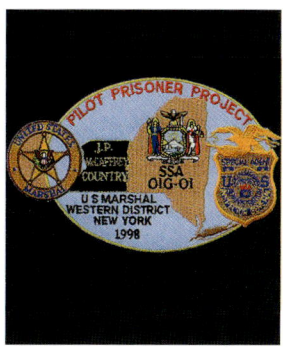

2532

2533

2534
4" & 3" versions

2535
Two color versions
1997 - gold & silver versions

2536
Gold & silver versions

2537

2538
Gold & silver versions

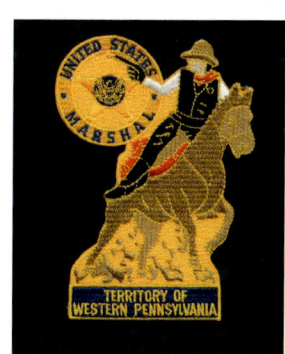

2539

The Encyclopedia of Federal Law Enforcement Patches

2540

2541

2542

2543

2544
1988 Bullion

2545
1988 - 20 made

2546
1988 - 20 made

2547

2548
V1/V2-500

2550

2551

2552

2553

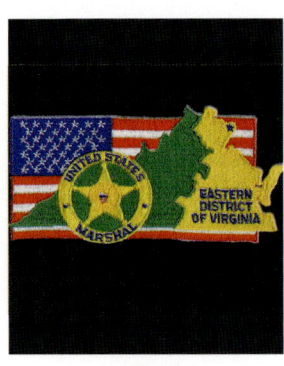

2554

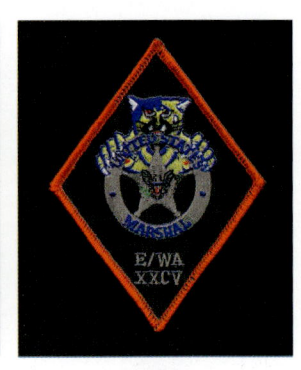

2555
Subdued

2556
Light

2557

2558

2559

2560

United States Marshal Service

2562 2¾" & 3" Glynco Trng. 
2563 SOG 
2564 Variation 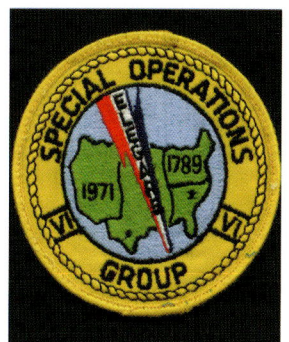
2565 SOG older version 
2566 Variation

2567 Bullion 
2568 3" bullion 
2569 Rare 
2570 4" bullion 1996 
2571 2571 & 2572 are a set

2572 
2573 5" 
2574 Rare - 3" x 5" Early 1980s SOG 
2575 
2576 SOG - Top/Explosives Below/Team leader

2577 SOG - Rt Years of service stripes
2578 More SOG strips 
2579 More SOG strips 
2580 More SOG strips 
2581 More SOG strips

142   The Encyclopedia of Federal Law Enforcement Patches

2582
V1/V2-499
Rare OD set

2583
V1/V2-502
Rare

2583a
USM

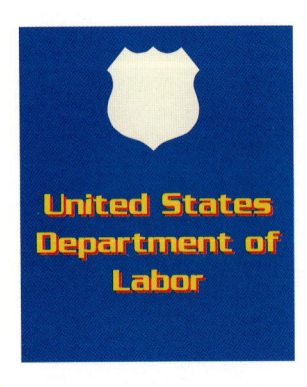

United States Department of Labor

2584
3"

2585
Bullion

2586
4"

2587
4"

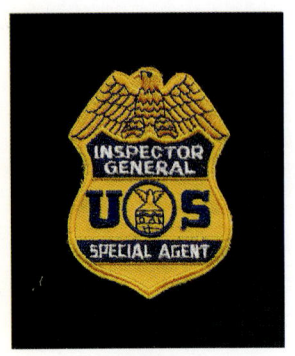

2588

2589
V1/V2-505

2590

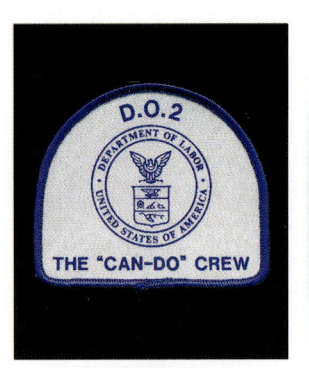

2591
Silk-screened

2592
V1/V2-506

2593
Silk-screened

2594

2595
California

2596
V1/V2-507

2597
V1/V2-508

United States Department of Labor

2598

2599

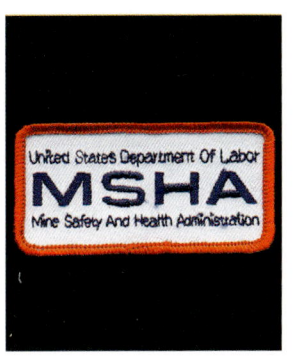

2600
2" x 4¼"

2601
1½" x 3" version

2602
V1/V2-509
2¼" x 4½" version

2602a
Labor Dept.

2602b
Labor Dept.
Investigator

2602c
Labor Dept.
Job Corps

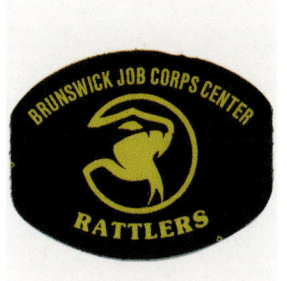

2602d
Labor Dept.
Job Corps

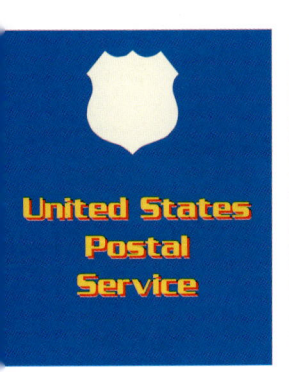

United States Postal Service

2603
O/S

2604
3¾" bullion
O/S

2605
3" bullion

2606
4"
Used on raid jackets

2607
3½" gold mylar

2608
3"

2609
3½" O/S

2610
V1/V2-741
3" silk-screemed

2611
5" O/S
Cincinnati raid jackets

144 The Encyclopedia of Federal Law Enforcement Patches

2612 — 3½" gold mylar

2613 — 4" Current

2614 — 3" Current

2615 — 5" prototype Cincinnati

2616 — 3½" & 2½" versions Current

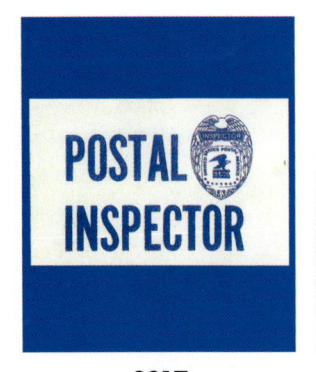

2617 — Rare armband

2618 — Never issued

2619 — Leather

2620 — Leather

2621 — 4"

2622 — 3"

2623 — SFO 4 variations exist

2624 — 2nd variation

2625 — Md. Drug TF

2626 — 1996 Olympics

2627 — 1996 Olympics

2628 — 1996 Olympics Variation

2629 — 1984 Los Angeles Games

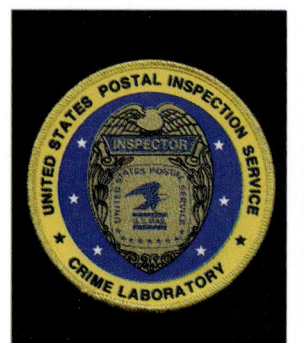

2630 — Current

2631 — Current

United States Postal Service

2632 Academy instructor

2633 Misprint - should be "Officer"

2634 Correct version

2635 "Headhunters"

2636 1st issue

2637 2nd issue

2638 Current

2639 Current

2640 New York Early 1970s

2641 New York Early 1970s

2642 5¼" - 1920s Extremely rare

2643 O/S Arizona

2644 O/S California

2645

2646

2647

2648

2649 O/S 2nd issue

2650 O/S 3rd issue

2651 Revenue Asset Protection Team

The Encyclopedia of Federal Law Enforcement Patches

2652 Current

2653 1st issue

2654

2655 1st issue RAPP Team

2656 2nd issue RAPP Team

2657 1st issue Info Tech div. - HQ

2658 Current

2659 1st issue

2660

2661 O/S

2662 Current

2663 O/S

2664 O/S

2665

2666 O/S 2nd issue

2667

2668 O/S - 1st issue

2669 O/S

2670 O/S Missouri

2671 O/S

United States Postal Service

2672 O/S 2nd issue

2673 O/S 1st issue

2674 4" & 3" versions O/S - 1st issue

2675 O/S 2nd issue

2676 Comm.

2677 Comm.

2678 Comm.

2679 Original 1st nat'l. approved Div. patch

2680

2681 O/S

2682 O/S 1st issue

2683 O/S 2nd issue

2684 O/S

2685 O/S 1st issue

2686 O/S 2nd issue

2687 O/S

2688 Two versions: Color & subdued

2689 O/S

2690 O/S

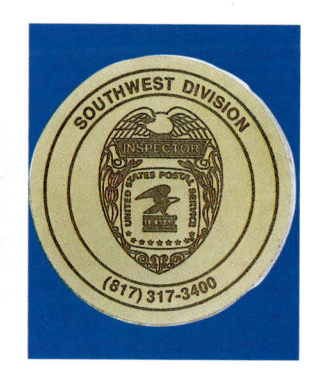

2691

The Encyclopedia of Federal Law Enforcement Patches

2692
O/S

2693
Original design
On felt

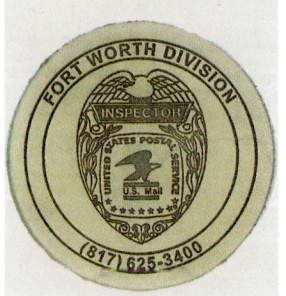

2694

2695
O/S
2nd issue

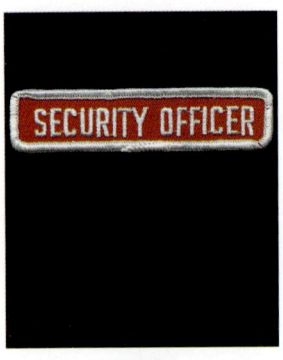

2696
O/S
1st issue

2697
O/S
1" x 4½"

2698
Contract Security

2699
V1/V2-249
1st issue

2700
V1/V2-742
2nd issue

2701
Current

2701a
Real?

2702

2703
O/S
P.O.D. now U.S.P.S.

2704
Current PPO Sgt.
stripes

2705
O/S

2706
Current

2707
V1/V2-743
Old

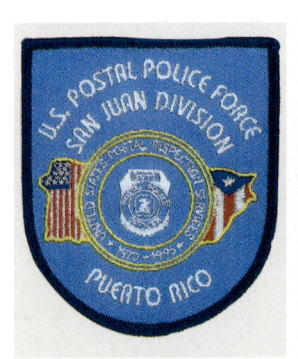

2708
O/S

2709
3" Bullion

2710
Postal Inspector

United States Postal Service

149

2711 V1/V2-807 1980 PPO Pistol Match	**2712** 1982 PPO Pistol Match	**United States Department of State**	**2713** Bullion	**2714** V1/V2-161 Bullion
2715 3"	**2716** 3"	**2717** V1/V2-510 3"	**2718** 3¼"	**2718a** V1/V2-514 3"
2719 Bullion	**2720** 4½"	**2721** 3"	**2722** 3" OD	**2723** 3" variation
2724 V1/V2-516 3"	**2725** V1/V2-517 4"	**2726** 3"	**2726a** Rarely seen	**2727**

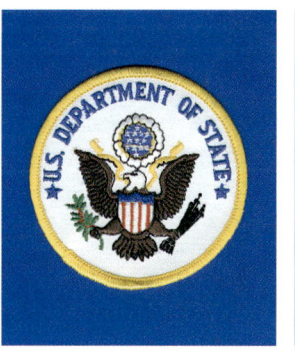

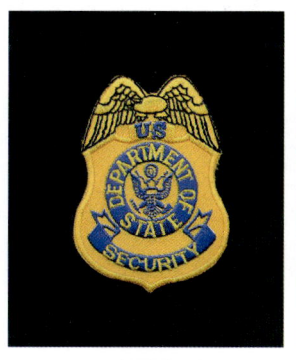

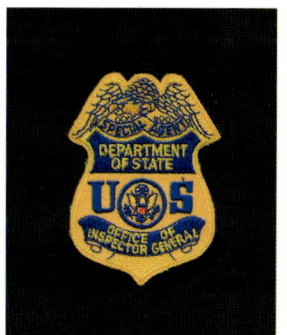

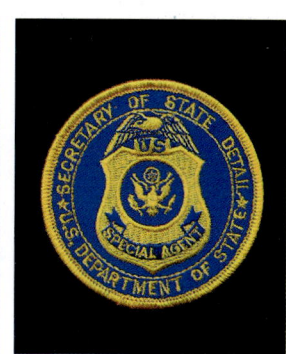

The Encyclopedia of Federal Law Enforcement Patches

2728

2729
Bullion

2730
3¼" silk-screened

2731
V1/V2-515v
Bullion

2732
4"

2733
4"

2734
3"

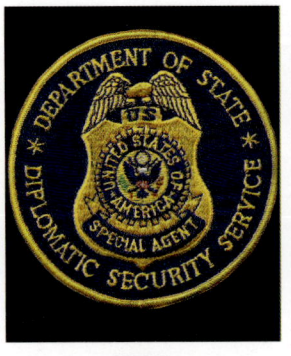

2735
5"

2736
3"

2737

2738

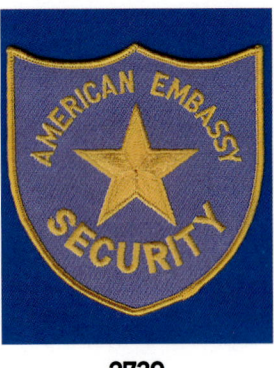

2739

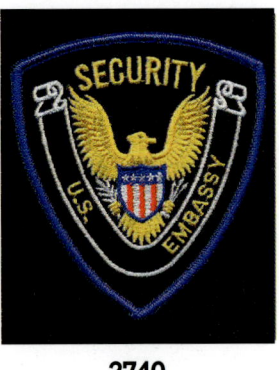

2740
Generic

2741

2742
2"

2743
V1/V2-513
3"

2744
4"

2745
Silk-screened

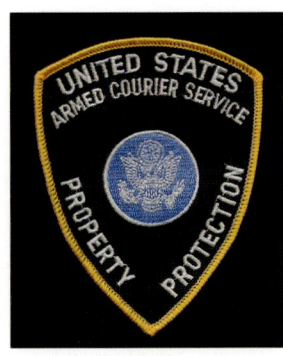

2746
Need additional info.

2747
3" OD

United States Department of State

2748
4"

2748a

2749
Riyadh, Saudi Arabia

2750
Trains embassy personnel

2751
V1/V2-512
Def. attaché - Laos

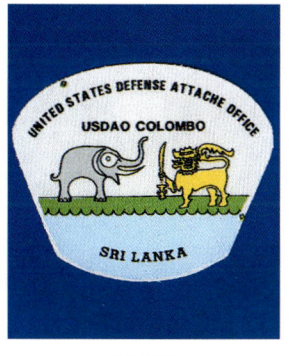

2752
Def. attaché - Sri Lanka

2753
Def. attaché - Laos

2754
V1/V2-518

2755
V1/V2-162

2756

2757
Variation

2758

2759

2760
Variation

2761
V1/V2-519

2762

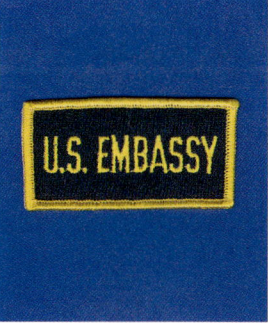

2763

2764
V1/V2-164

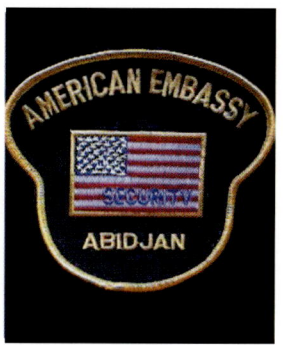

2765
Ivory Coast, Africa

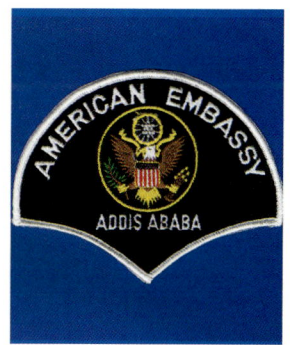

2766
Ethiopia

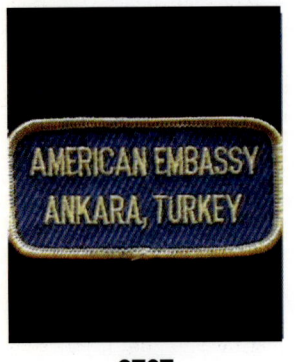

The Encyclopedia of Federal Law Enforcement Patches

2767

2768

2769
Gabon

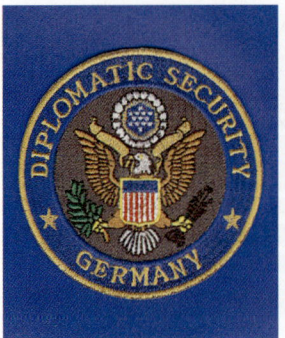

2771

2772

2773

2774

2775
Ireland

2776
Ireland

2777

2778
Lebanon

2779

2780

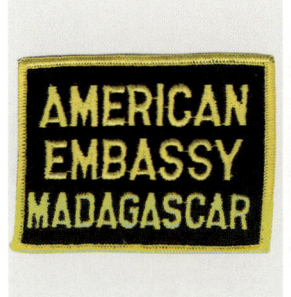

2781

2783
Russia

2784
Canada

2785
Canada
Customs attaché

2786

2787
Outer Mongolia
"Plum assignment!"

2788
Poland

United States Department of State

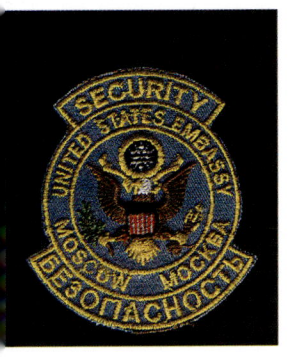

2789 Moscow

2789a State Dept. Embassy

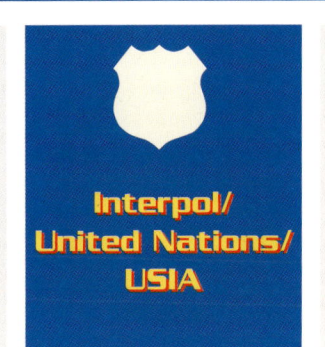

Interpol/ United Nations/ USIA

2790

2791 Bullion

2792 F/E

2793

2794

2795

2796

2797 V1/V2-165

2798

2799 V1/V2-520

2800

2801

2802

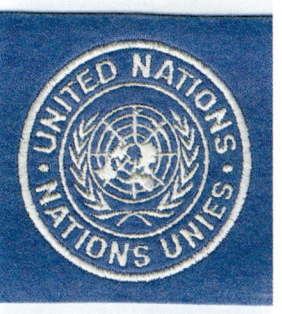

2803 V1/V2-521 Armband

2804

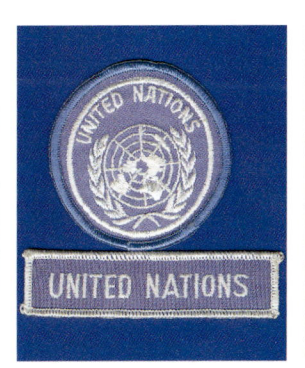

2805 V1/V2-522

2806 Bullion

153

The Encyclopedia of Federal Law Enforcement Patches

2807
V1/V2-259

2808
Possible misprint

2809
V1/V2-258

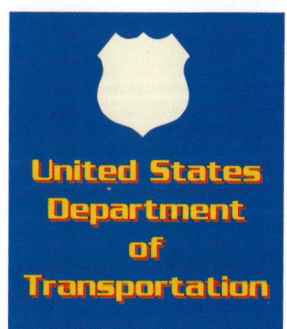

United States Department of Transportation

2810
4" seal F/E

2811
3¼" silk-screened

2812
3½"

2813
3"

2814
3½"

2815
Bullion

2816
2¾"

2817
Transportation Safety Inst.

2818
Back patch

2818a

2819
F/E

2820
Silk-screened

2821
1989 version lighter
1994 version darker

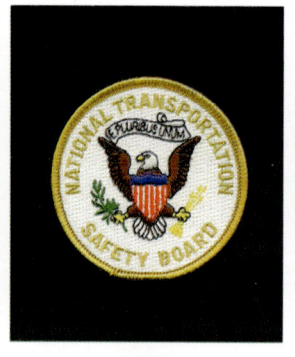

2822
F/E
Independent agency

2823
V1/V2-248
Twill

2824
3"

United States Department of Transportation

2825
V1/V2-530
3½" & 7½" versions

2826

2827
V1/V2-731
Abolished 1995,
7½" version also

2828
Many examples

2829

2830

2831
V1/V2-538

2832

2833
Merchant Marine
Academy - 1981

2834

2835

2836
Railroad Ret. Board

2837
V1/V2-170

2838
V1/V2-532
Old

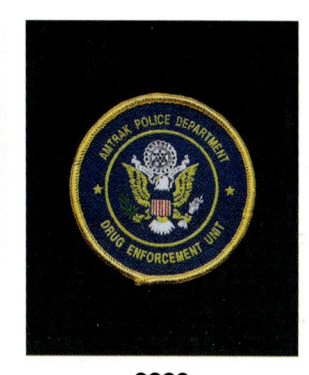

2839
Silk-screened

2840
1995 Task force

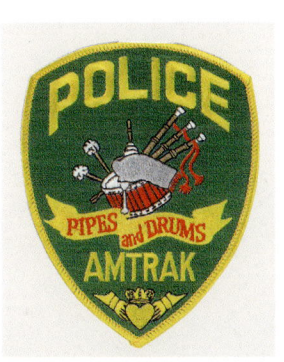

2841

2842
V1/V2-531
Bullion

2843
Bullion

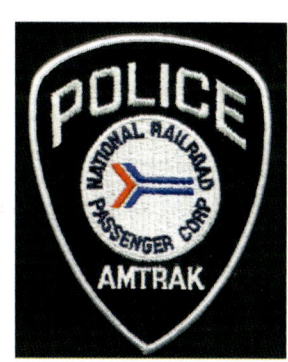

2844
V1/V2-171
5"

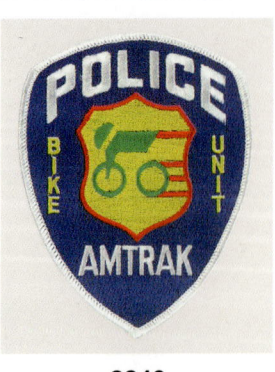

The Encyclopedia of Federal Law Enforcement Patches

2845
4"

2846
5"
Rider - left

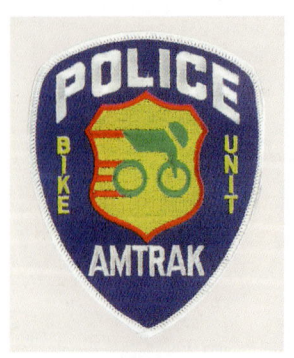

2847
5"
Rider - right

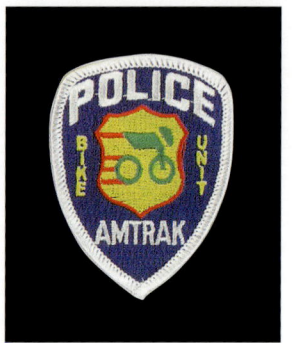

2848
2 3/4" cap

2849
Gold and silver thread versions

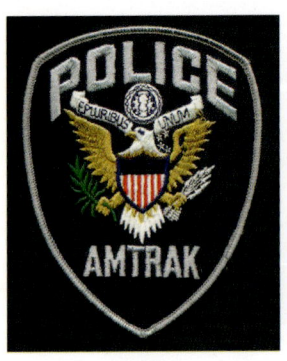

2850
V1/V2-534
5"

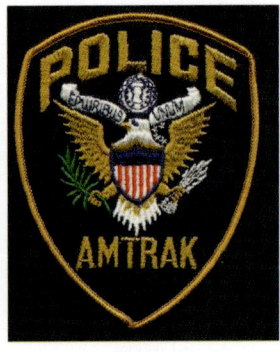

2851
V1/V2-533
5"

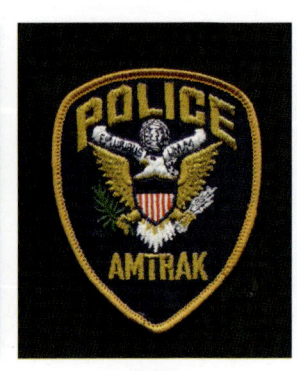

2852
3 1/2"

2853
5"
Northeast Corridor

2854
4"
Northeast Corridor

2855
Strip

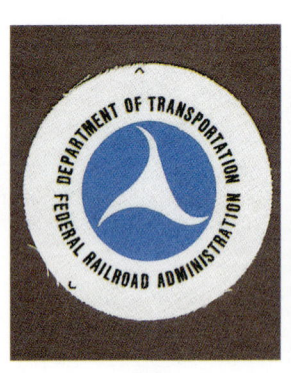

2856

2857
Silk-screened
Rare

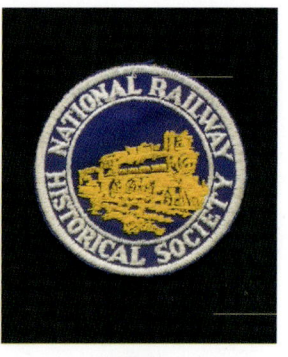

2858

2859

2860
4 3/4"

2861
3 1/4"

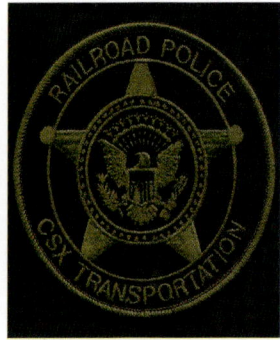

2862
Color version, too

2863

2864

United States Department of Transportation

157

2865

2866

2867
V1/V2-536
Penn-Central R.R.

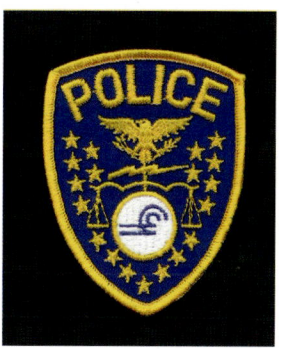

2868
V1/V2-535
4" & 3" versions

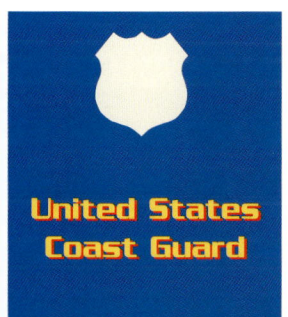

United States Coast Guard

2869
5"

2870
V1/V2-550
5" variation

2871
4½"

2872
3"

2873
V1/V2-551
4½"

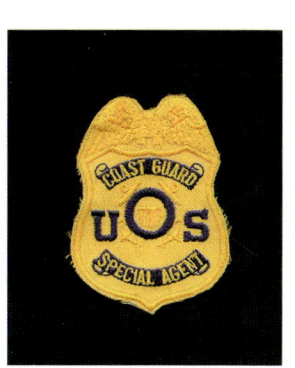

2874
3"

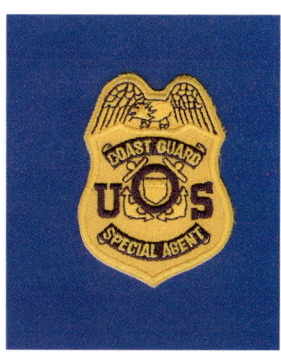

2875
2¾"

2876
Bullion

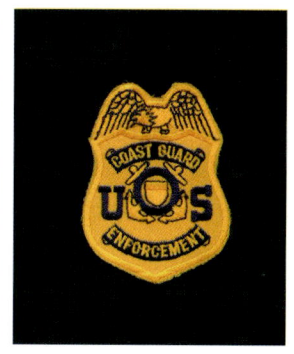

2877
2¾"

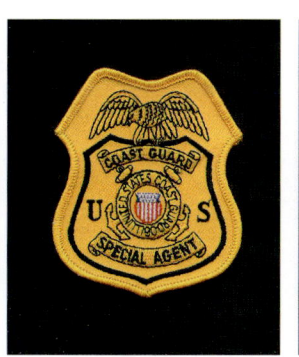

2878
3½" twill

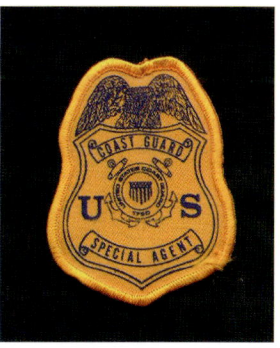

2879
3½" silk-screened

2880
V1/V2-543
3"

2881
V1/V2-544
3"

2882

The Encyclopedia of Federal Law Enforcement Patches

2883

2884
Law Enforcement
Detachment

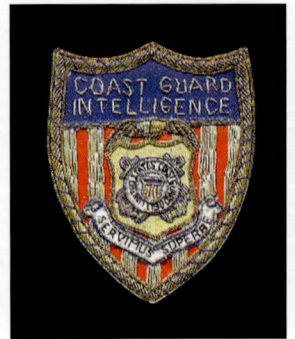

2885
3" & 4½" versions

2886
Bullion

2887
Life Saving Service
(Pre-USCG)

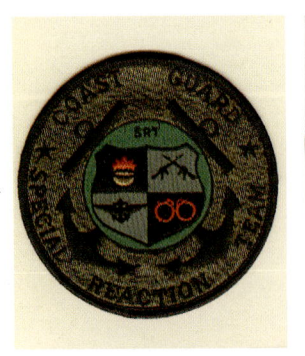

2888

2889
Old
Felt

2890
Felt armband
Old

2891

2892

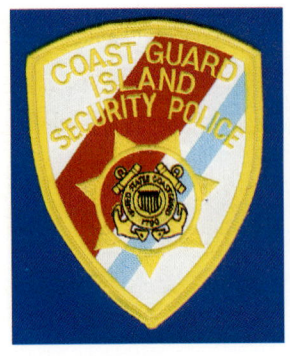

2893

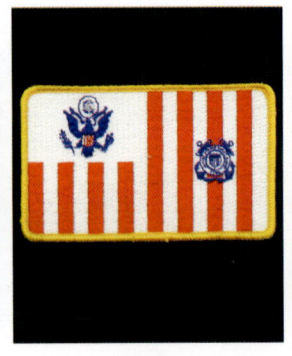

2894

2895

2896

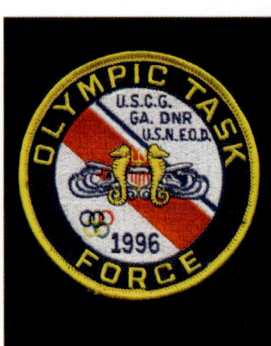

2897
1996 Olympics

2898

2899
Governor's Island, NY

2900
Governor's Island, NY
5" & 3" versions

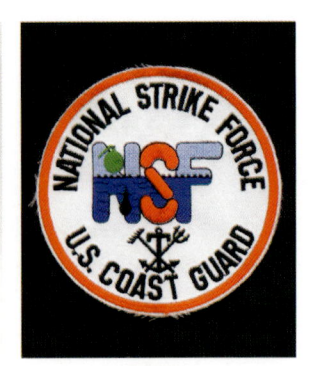

2901
V1/V2-540
Has rocker "Atlantic
Strike Team"

2902
Novelty

United States Coast Guard

2903

2904

2905

2906
Famous spelling error

2907

2908

2909

2910

2911
V1/V2-552

2912

2913

2914

2915

2916

2917

2918

2919
V1/V2-546

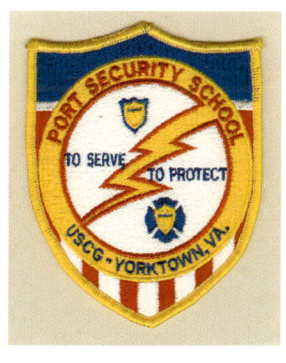

2921

2922

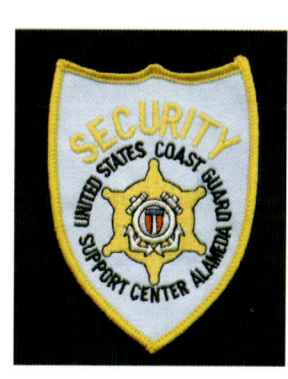

2923

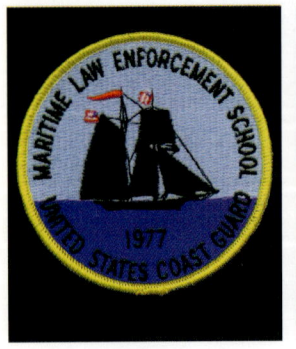

160   The Encyclopedia of Federal Law Enforcement Patches

2924

2925
Variation reads "Security"

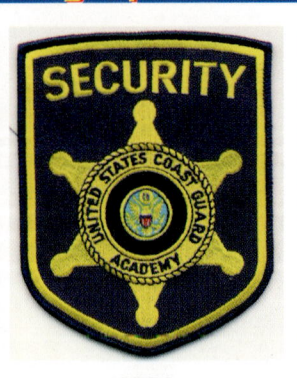

2926
5" & 3¼" versions

2927
5"

2928
5½", 4½", & 3" versions

2929
Old

2930
1943 - ?
Port Security
Chief 1st class

2931
Master-at-Arms
(Ship's cops)

2932
Rare

2933

2934

2935

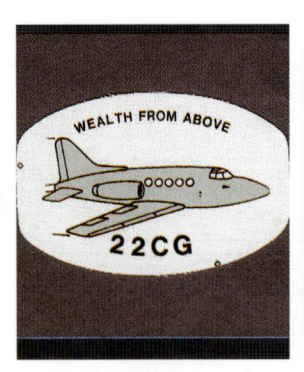

2936

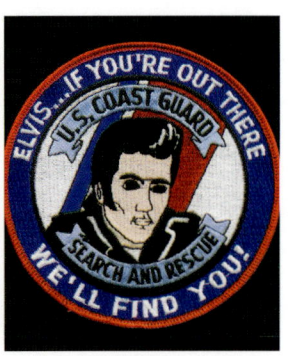

2937
"Just for grins"

Federal Aviation Administration

2938
4"

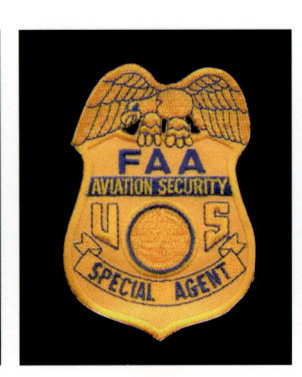

2940
4"

2941
3½"

2942
3"

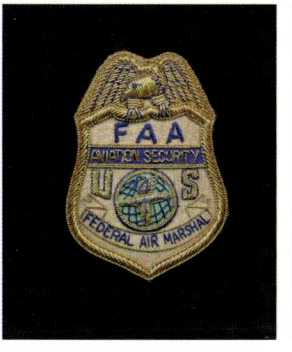

Federal Aviation Administration

2943
Bullion

2944
4"

2945
V1/V2-167
5½"

2946
V1/V2-168
3½"

2947
5½"

2948
V1/V2-169
4"

2949
V1/V2-526
2¾"

2950
V1/V2-527

2951
O/S

2952

2953
4" & 3" versions

2954

2955

2956

2957

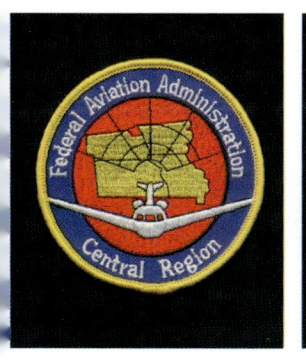

2958

2959

2960

2961
V1/V2-525
3½"

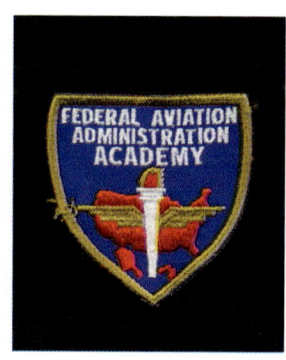

2962
3"

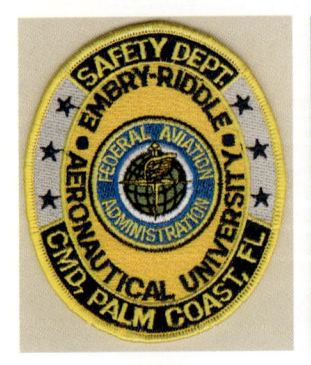

The Encyclopedia of Federal Law Enforcement Patches

2963

2964
V1/V2-528
3½" - National Av. Fac.
Ed. Ctr. - NJ

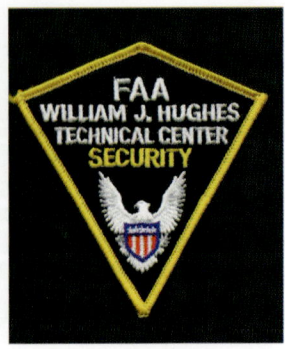

2965
4"

2966
3½"
Replaced #2964

2967
3"

2968

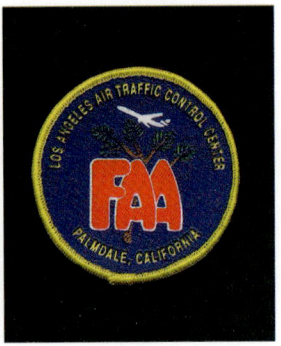

2969
3" silk-screened

2970

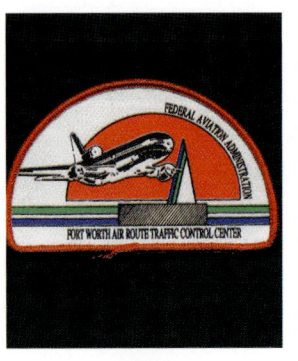

2971
Texas

2972

2973

2974
Texas

2975
V1/V2-523
3" & 7" versions

2976

2977
Bullion

2978
Gold mylar
3¼" & 3" versions

2979
V1/V2-166
3" twill

2980
3½" F/E

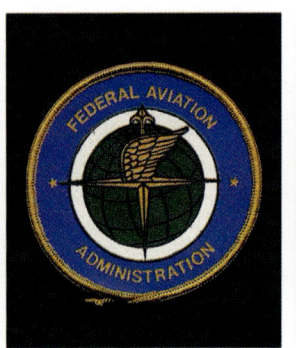

2981
3¼" & 2¾" silk-
screened versions

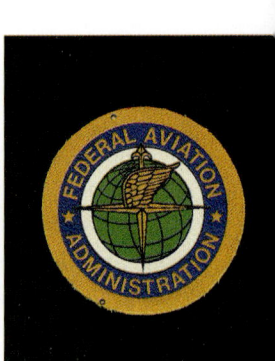

2982
3"
Old

Federal Aviation Administration

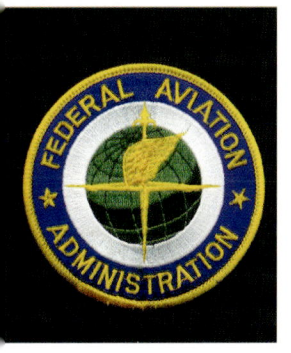

163

2983
3½" & 3" F/E versions
New

2984
5" & 6" versions

2985
V1/V2-524
3"

2986
1½" x 3¼"

2987

2988

2988a

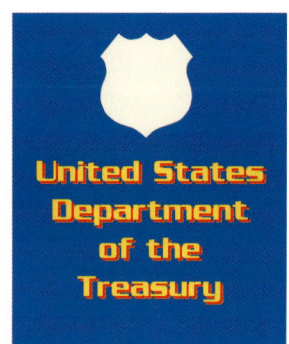

United States Department of the Treasury

2989
3½" & 3" versions
Seal

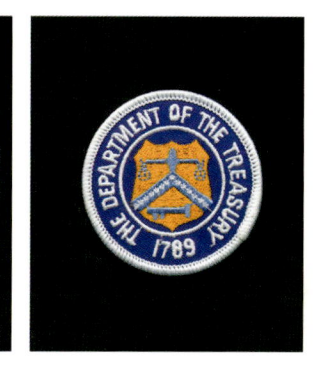

2990
2½"

2991
3" bullion

2992
V1/V2-177
3" variation

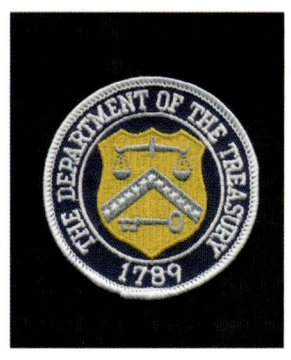

2993
Color variation

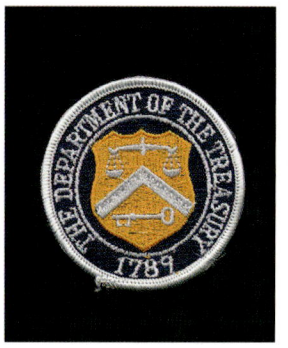

2994
Color variation

2995
V1/V2-176
3" variation

2996
Bullion I G

2997
Current I G
3½"

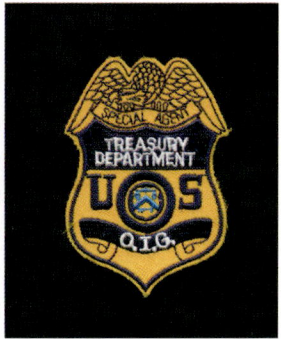

2998
3" O/S
Color varies

2999
Financial Crimes
Enforcement Network

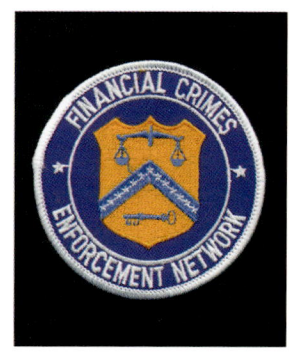

3000
3¼" & 2½" versions

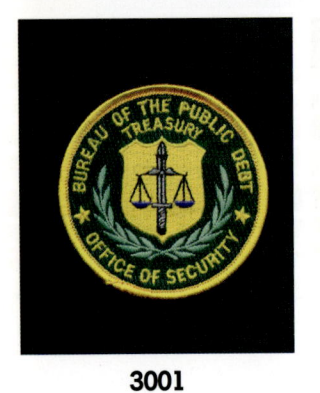

The Encyclopedia of Federal Law Enforcement Patches

3001 Little-known agency

3002

3003 Variation has silver badge

3004

3005 V1/V2-607

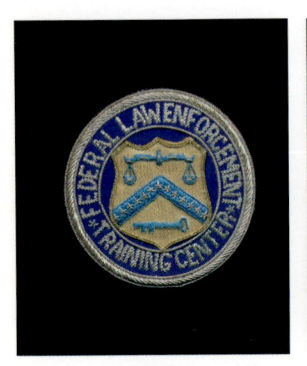

3006 3" bullion

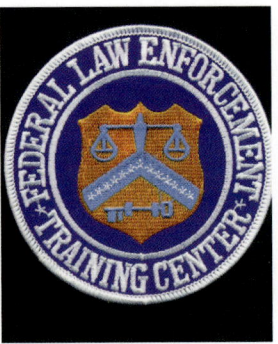

3007 4" & 2¾" versions

3008 V1/V2-189 3"

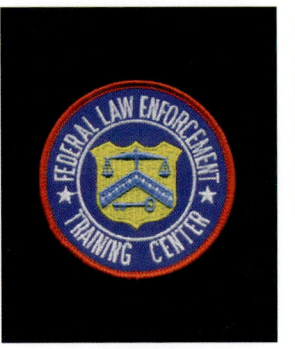

3009 2¾" twill

3010 3" twill

3011 V1/V2-576

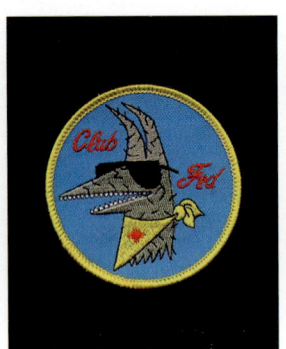

3012

3013 V1/V2-190

3014

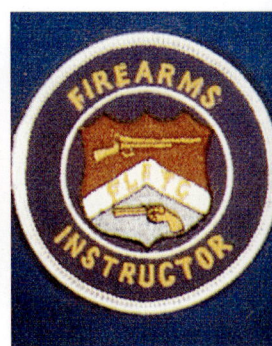

3014a V1/V2-191

3014b V1/V2-192

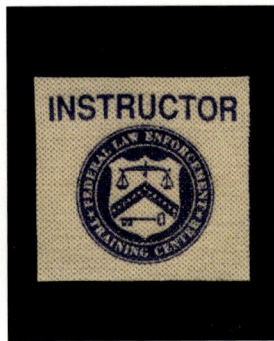

3015

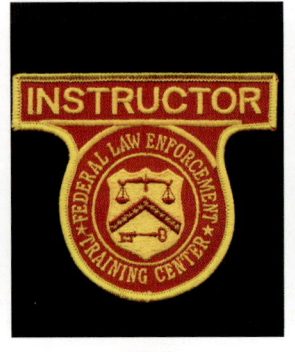

3016 4"

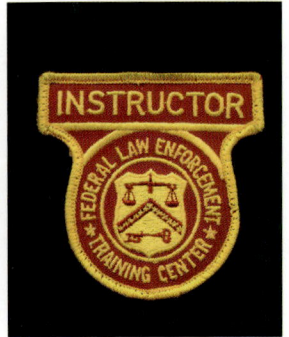

3017 3"

3018

United States Department of the Treasury

3019

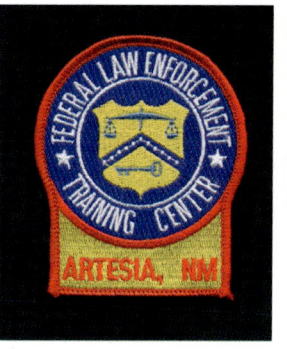

3020
3½" & 3" versions

3021

3022
V1/V2-194
4" twill

3023
4" twill

3024
V1/V2-571
3" bullion

3025
Bullion

3026
6" x 10" back patch

3027

3028
V1/V2-184

3029
Novelty

3030
V1/V2-567

3031

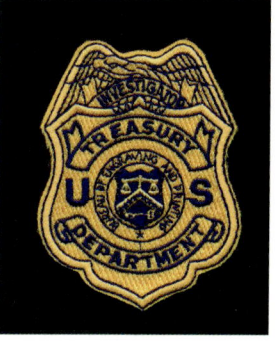

3032

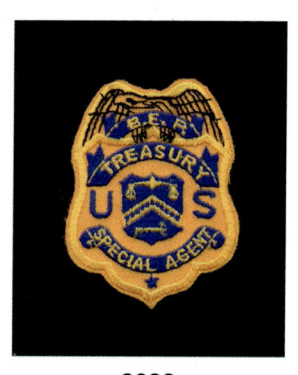

3033
V1/V2-570

3034

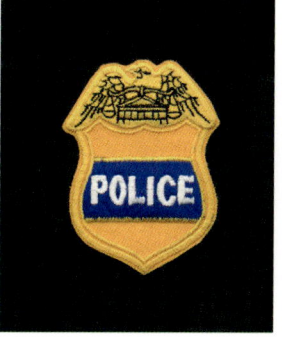

3035
V1/V2-569

3036
V1/V2-568

3037
V1/V2-186

3038
V1/V2-185

165

The Encyclopedia of Federal Law Enforcement Patches

3039

3040
5"

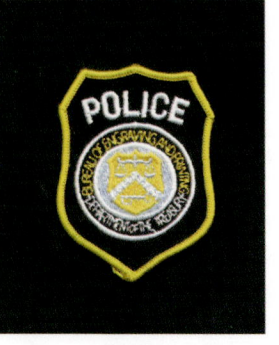

3041
3"

3042
Original

3043
Texas Reproduction

3044
Bullion

3045
Bullion

3046

3047
Bullion

3048
V1/V2-573

3049
V1/V2-187

3050

3051
V1/V2-574

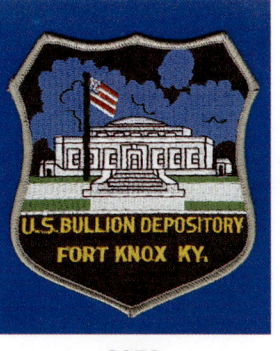

3052
V1/V2-575

3053

3054

3055
V1/V2-572

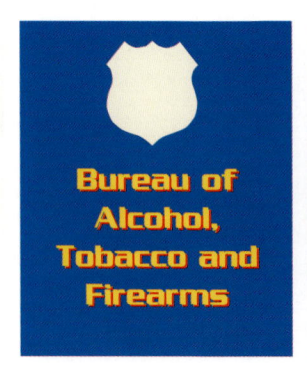

Bureau of Alcohol, Tobacco and Firearms

3056
V1/V2-181
Very old - front of #3089

3057
Front of early NRT jumpsuit

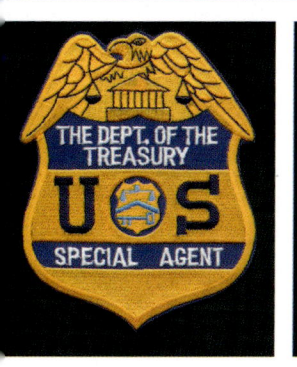

Bureau of Alcohol, Tobacco and Firearms

3058
V1/V2-178
Old raid jacket badge

3059
Variation of #3058

3060
V1/V2-556
Hat patch for #3058/59

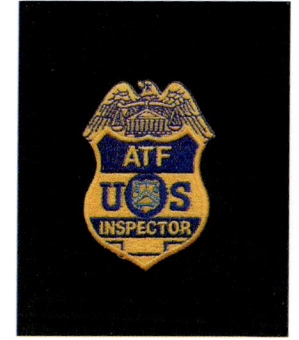

3061

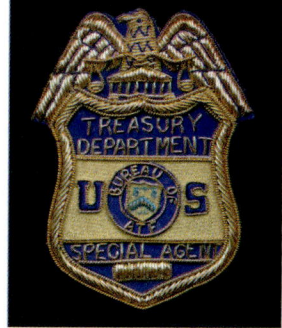

3062
3½" bullion

3063
V1/V2-557

3064
3¼"

3065
3" gold mylar

3065a
ATF

3066
4" OD

3067
3" NRT

3068
4½" variation

3069
3"

3070
3⅛"

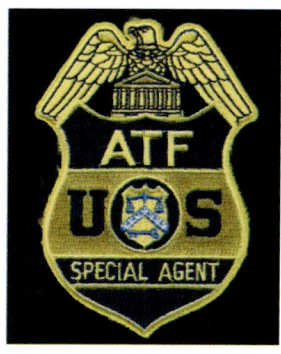

3071
4¼"

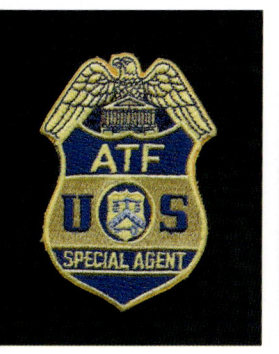

3072
3"

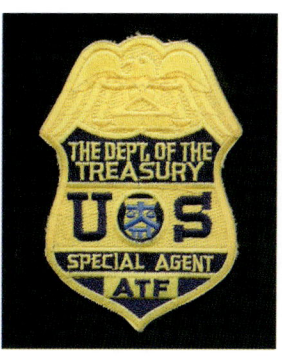

3073
V1/V2-180
4½"

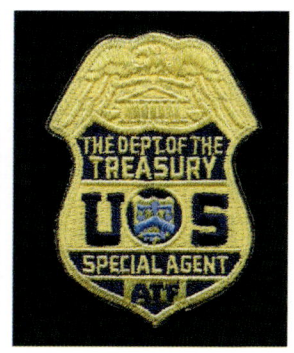

3074
4½" variation

3075
3"

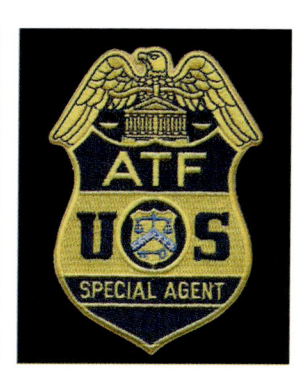

3076
4½"

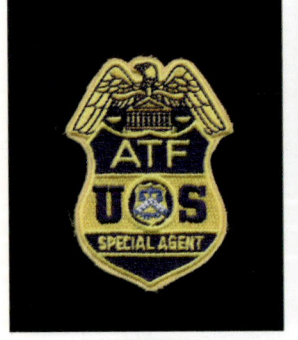

The Encyclopedia of Federal Law Enforcement Patches

3077
3"

3078
3"

3079
3 1/4"

3080
3 1/8"

3081
Two versions -
1991 & 1993

3082
Old
Silk-screened

3083
Bullion
1990s

3084
3" bullion

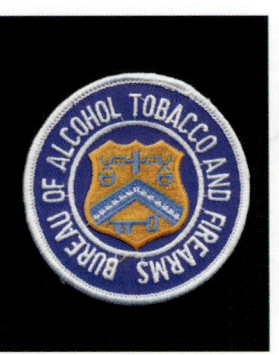

3085
V1/V2-179
3"

3086
3"

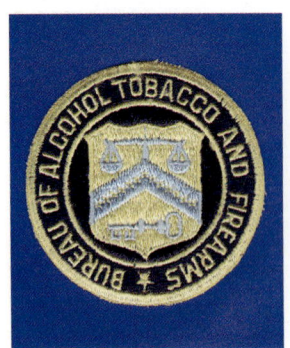

3087
V1/V2-555
3 1/4" - old

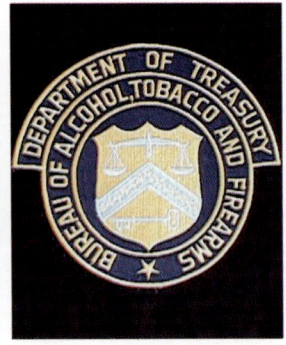

3088
8" x 9" back patch

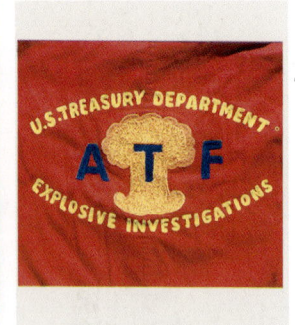

3089
Early NRT jumpsuit back

3089a
ATF

3090
V1/V2-560

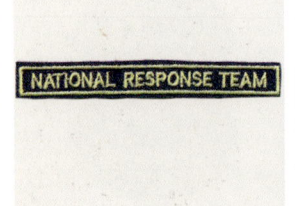

3091
Goes with #3067

3092

3093
V1/V2-182

3094

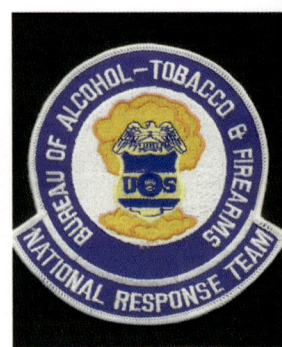

3094a
5" Rare

Bureau of Alcohol, Tobacco and Firearms

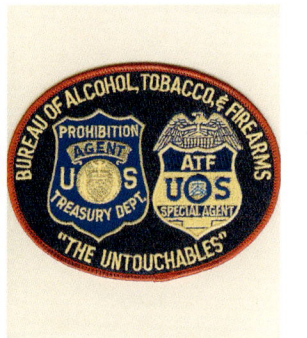

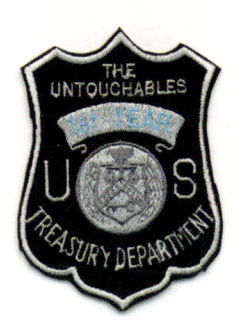

3095 Comm.

3096 TV show prop Rare

3097 Early 1970s Rare

3098 ATF trains here

3099

3100

3101

3102 Four good men died

3103

3104

3105 Issued only to agents on the raid

3106

3107 Bullion

3108 Two color schemes

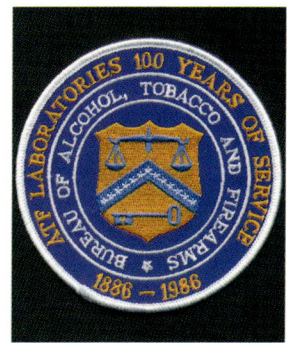

3109 Anniversary

3110 1996 bullion

3111

3112 Winnebago Co. Sher. Police

3113 Maryland

3114 Red and green versions

The Encyclopedia of Federal Law Enforcement Patches

3115 Special Response Team California

3116

3117

3118 1990 Issue Arizona

3119 Oregon

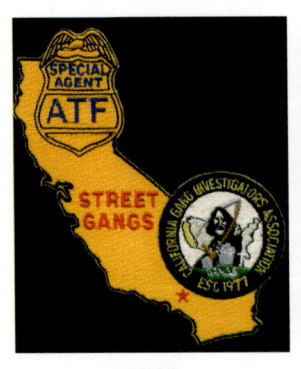

3120 California

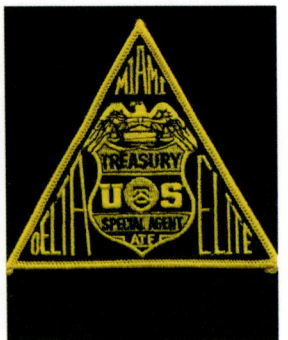

3121 Florida

3122 Illinois

3123

3124 Missouri

3125 Missouri From 1993 IACP

3126 Massachusetts

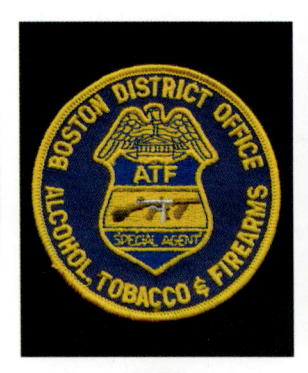

3127 Massachusetts

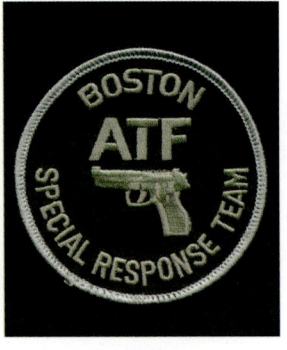

3128 Massachusetts

3129

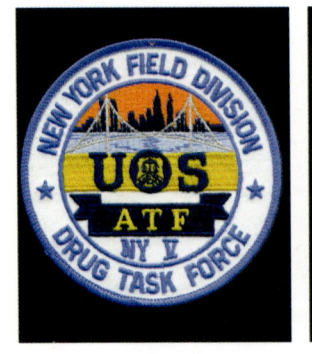

3130

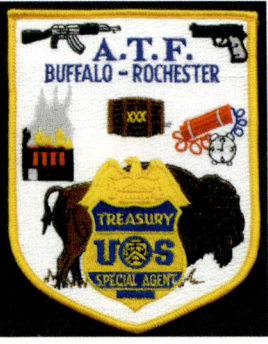

3131

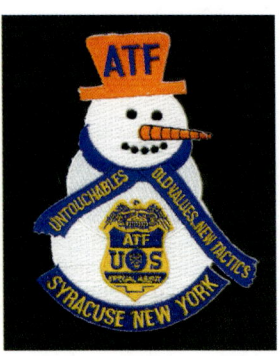

3132

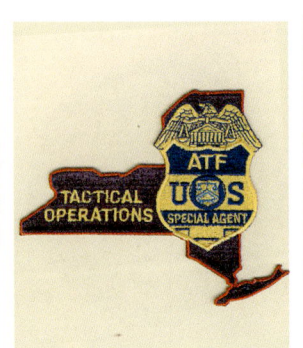

3133 New York

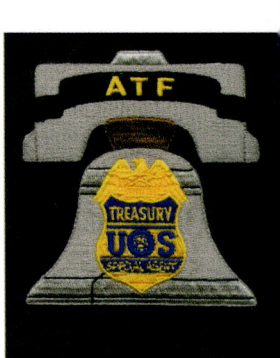

3134 Pennsylvania

Bureau of Alcohol, Tobacco and Firearms 171

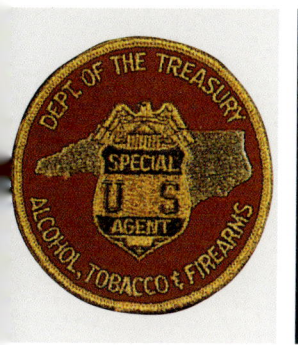

3135

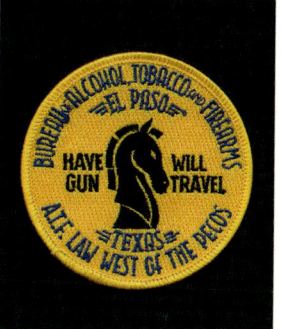

3136

3137

3138

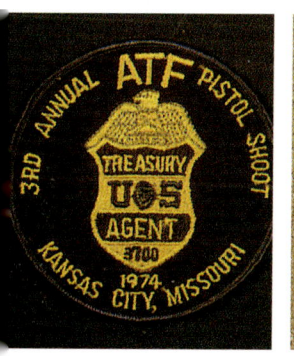

3139
4" x 10½"

3140
V1/V2-563

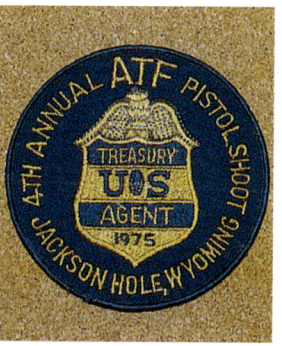

3141
V1/V2-564

3142
3" x 4½"

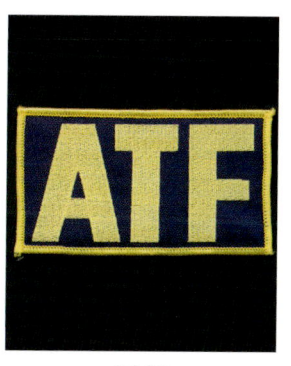

3143
2½" x 4½"
Two color variations

3144
4" x 7" armband

3145
4½" x 11" & 5" x 11"
back patches

3146
9½" x 9½" back patch
Two colors

3146a

3147

3148

3149

3150
3"

3151
4"

3152
4"

The Encyclopedia of Federal Law Enforcement Patches

3153
4"

3154
V1/V2-208
4" - Old

3155

3156
4"

3157
3"

3158
V1/V2-621
3½"

3159
3"

3160
3"

3161
5" new

3162
5"

3163
3"

3164
V1/V2-630
5" - Rare

3165
V1/V2-207
4" reproduction

3166
V1/V2-627
4½" gold mylar

3167
4"

3168
3"

3169
5"

3170
3"

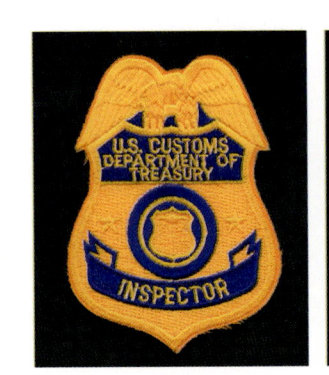

3171
4"

3172
3"

United States Customs Service

173

3173
3"

3174
V1/V2-623
3½"

3175
3"

3176
3"

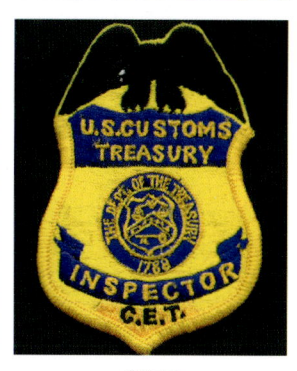

3177
3¾"
Contraband
Enforcement Team

3178
Silk-screened
Old

3179
V1/V2-209
5"

3180
5"

3181
5" new

3182
3"

3183
4" reproduction

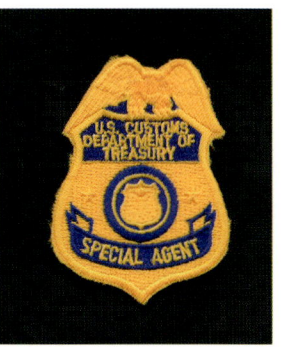

3184
3"

3185
V1/V2-210
3"

3186
V1/V2-633
3"

3187
4"

3188
3"

3189
V1/V2-634
3"

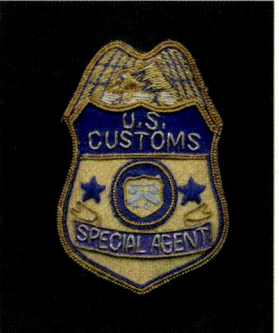

3190
3" bullion

3191
3" bullion

3192
3" gold mylar

The Encyclopedia of Federal Law Enforcement Patches

3193
V1/V2-202
3" & 2½" versions

3194

3195

3196

3197
Sr. Customs Rep.

3198

3199

3200

3201

3202
V1/V2-615

3203

3204

3205

3206
3¼"

3207
2½"
Also black version

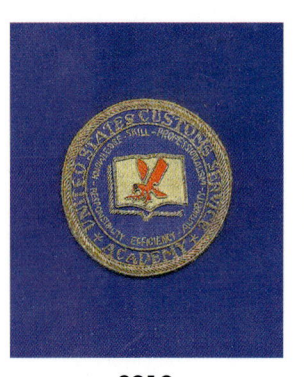

3208
Prototype

3209
Prototype

3210
Academy - bullion

3210a
Real?

3211
V1/V2-206
Sky Marshal Program

United States Customs Service

175

3212

3213
V1/V2-617

3214

3215
4½" prototype
100 made

3216
4"

3217
4¼"

3218
2" x 8¼"

3219
4" x 9½"
Reflectorized

3220
6" x 10¾" back patch

3221
1" x 4"

3221a

3222
V1/V2-618
Customs Court

3223
V1/V2-632
1986, 1987, 1988, 1989

3224
½" x 1½"

3225
1¼" x 3¼" bullion

3226

3227

3228

3229

3230
Velcro back

The Encyclopedia of Federal Law Enforcement Patches

3231 Velcro back

3232 5 patches, 1, 2, 3, 4, 5

3233 Air Smuggling Invest. Assn.

3234 V1/V2-635

3235 FLETC Training

3237 Staff patch

3238

3239

3240

3241

3242

3243

3244

3245

3246

3247

3248 V1/V2-649 4" & 3½" versions

3249 Old

3250

United States Customs Service

3251 V1/V2-638

3252

3253

3254

3255 V1/V2-636

3256

3257 Customs Surv. Group 1995

3258

3259

3260 Puerto Rico Air Branch

3261 Luke AFB

3262

3263

3264

3265

3266

3267

3268

3269

3270 Various color schemes

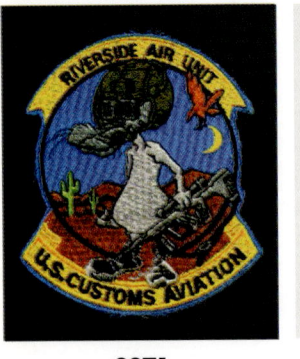

The Encyclopedia of Federal Law Enforcement Patches

3271	3272	3273	3274	3275 Silk-screened Old

3276 Color & subdued versions	3277	3278	3279	3280 4½" & 4" versions

3281	3282 Louisiana	3283 Louisiana	3284	3285

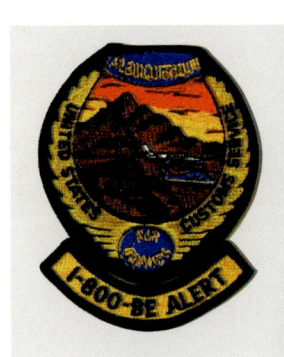

3286	3287	3288	3289 1997	3290

United States Customs Service

3291 El Paso Air Wing Pilot

3292

3293

3294 Anniversary

3295

3296

3297

3298

3299 "Entry" misspelled

3300 Finally got it right

3301

3302

3303

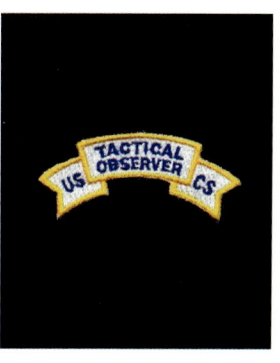

3304 Goes with #3305

3305

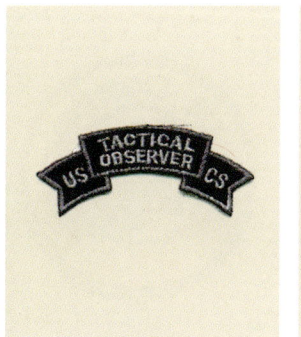

3306 Goes with #3307

3307

3308 "Costoms"?

3309

3310

180   The Encyclopedia of Federal Law Enforcement Patches

| 3311 | 3312 | 3313 | 3314 | 3315 |

| 3316 | 3317 | 3318 | 3319 | 3320 |

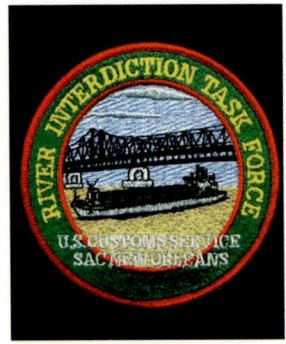

3321  | 3322 Freighter Invest. Surv. Team | 3323  | 3324 V1/V2-643 Florida | 3325

3326  | 3327   | 3328  | 3329  | 3330 V1/V2-639 Customs speedboats

United States Customs Service

3331

3332

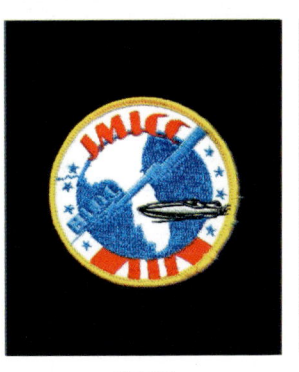

3333
V1/V2-640

3334
V1/V2-641

3335
V1/V2-625

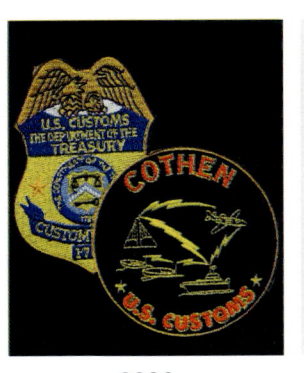

3336

3337

3338

3339
Old
Silk-screened

3340
Old
Silk-screened

3341
Old
Silk-screened

3342
Commo.

3343
"Descendants of Irish Kings"

3344
"Descendants of Irish Kings"

3345

3346
V1/V2-628

3347
Gold/Silver mylar version also exists

3348

3349

3350

The Encyclopedia of Federal Law Enforcement Patches

| 3351 | 3352 | 3353 | 3354 | 3355 |

| 3356 | 3357 | 3358 | 3359 | 3360 |
| Money-laundering Surveillance Team | Can you dig it! | | | V1/V2-619 |

| 3361 | 3362 | 3363 | 3364 | 3365 |

| 3366 | 3367 | 3368 | 3369 | 3370 |
| Badge & patch Very old | Very old | | | |

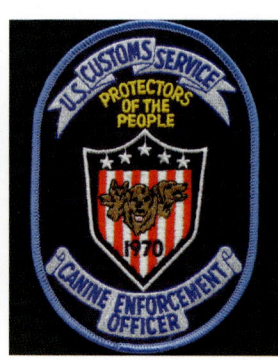

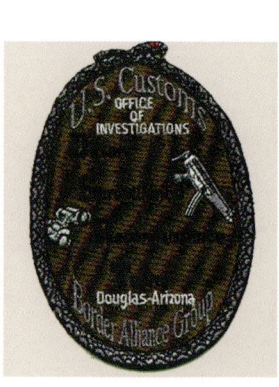

United States Customs Service

3371 Old Silk-screened

3372 D.C.

3373

3374

3375

3376

3377

3378

3379

3380 5" & 4" versions

3381

3382

3383

3384 V1/V2-637 5" & 4" versions

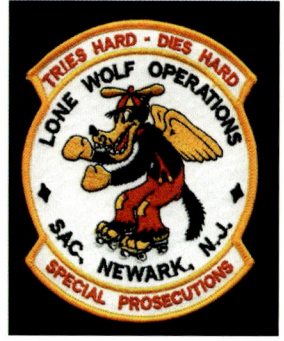

3385

3386

3387

3388

3389

3390

The Encyclopedia of Federal Law Enforcement Patches

3391

3392

3393

3394

3395

3396

3397
Yellow, blue & purple versions

3398

3399

3400

3401

3402

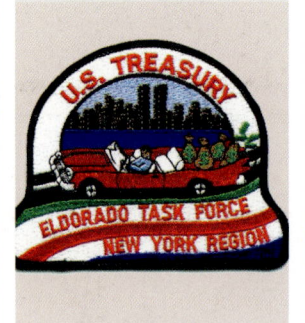

3403

3404

3405
V1/V2-626
All Treasury Agencies use in NYC

3406
White flag - 4th issue

3407
Blue flag - 3rd issue

3408

3409
Two versions - Untitled and Patrol Officer

3410
Surveillance Support Center

United States Customs Service

3411	3412 Old	3413	3414	3415 Two versions - 1st sword/2nd dagger
3416 V1/V2-642	**Internal Revenue Service**	3417 3" bullion	3418 V1/V2-578 3"	3419 V1/V2-577 2½"
3420	3421 Variation	3422 3⅛" bullion	3423 5 stars = 5 regions	3424 7 stars = 7 regions
3425 V1/V2-584 3"	3426 V1/V2-583 4½"	3427 3"	3428 4"	3429 3"

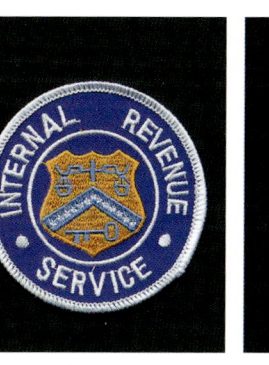

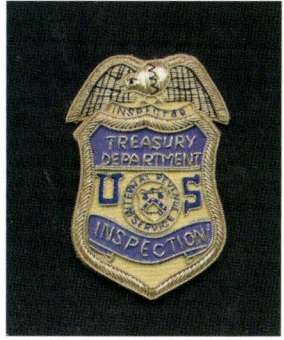

185

The Encyclopedia of Federal Law Enforcement Patches

3430
4"

3431

3432

3433

3434

3435
Comm.

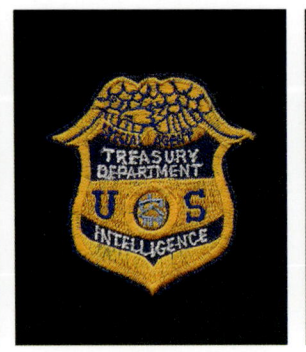

3436

3437

3438
V1/V2-200
Bullion

3439
Comm.

3440
Comm.

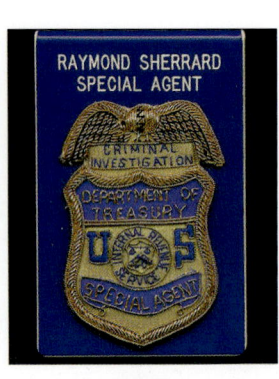

3441
V1/V2-199

3442
4" current

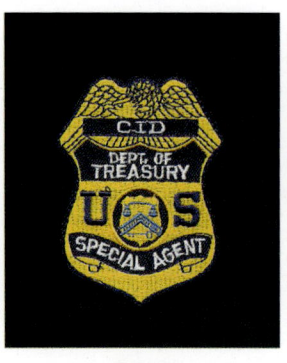

3443
3" current

3444
4 1/8" & 4 1/2" versions

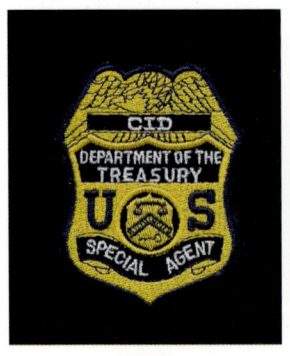

3445
3 1/2"

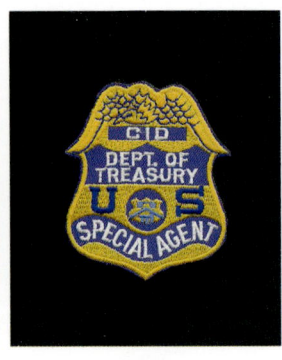

3446
V1/V2-196
3"

3447
V1/V2-197
4"

3448
V1/V2-201
4 1/8"

3449
3 1/8"

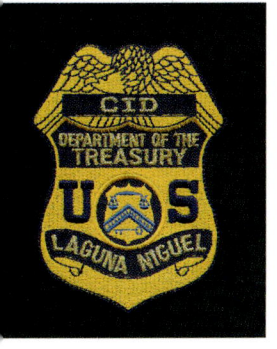

Internal Revenue Service

3450
1994

3451
Anniversary - Western Region Oval

3452
Anniversary - Western Region Star

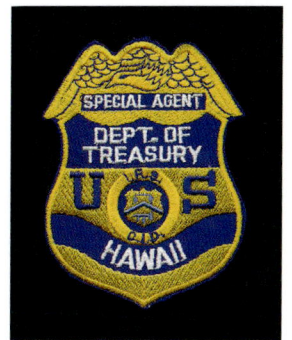

3453

3454

3455
V1/V2-579 National Ofc. "Giveaway" Patch

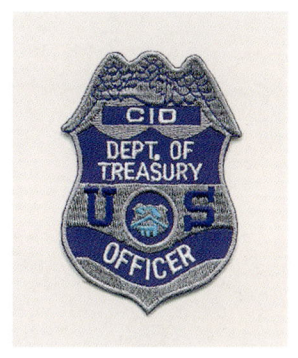

3456
Reproduction - Fantasy

3457
Reproduction - Fantasy

3458
Reproduction

3459
Reproduction

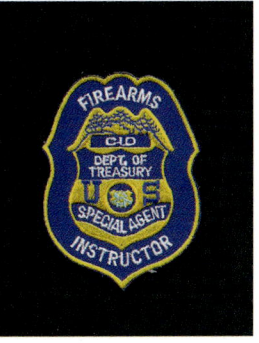

3460

3461
1" x 3" Raid jacket front

3462
IRS Uniformed Police West Virginia

3463

3464
IRS National Lab

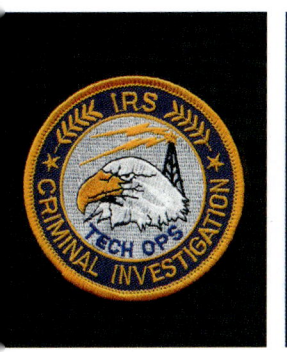

3465

3466

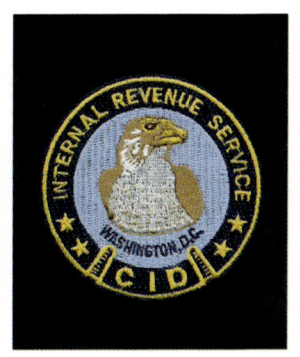

3467

3468

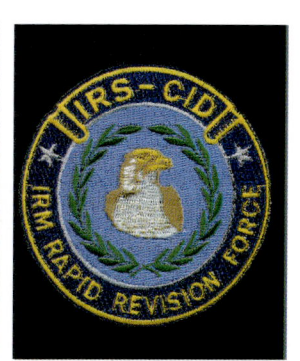

3469
Inside joke

188 The Encyclopedia of Federal Law Enforcement Patches

3471 Technical Operations Chicago

3472

3473 Michigan

3474 Brand new

3475

3476

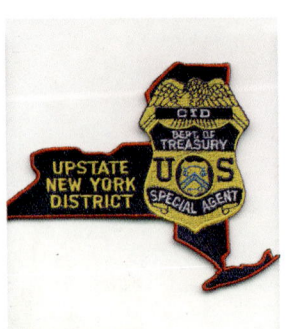

3477

3478

3479

3480 Raid jacket back patch

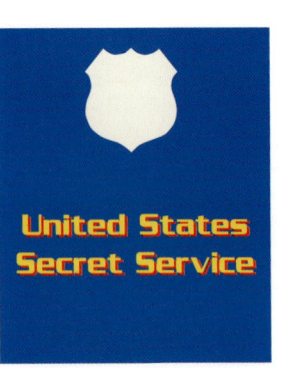

3481 Raid jacket back patch

3482 10" bullion

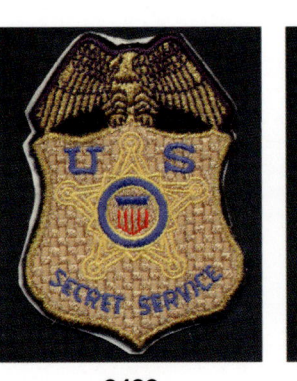

3483 Prototype

3484 Prototype

3485

3486 V1/V2-591 3"

3487

3488 V1/V2-211 3"

3489 3½"

United States Secret Service

3490

3491
Administration -
Non-uniform shirt patch

3492
Prototype of ERT C/B

3493

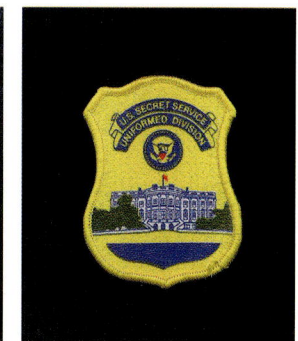

3494

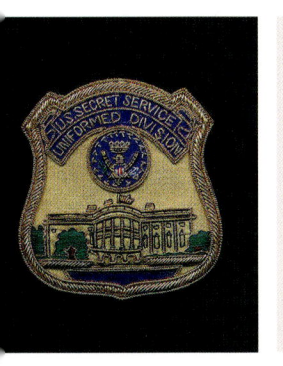

3496
3" bullion

3497
Hatpiece

3498
Motorcycle helmet insignia

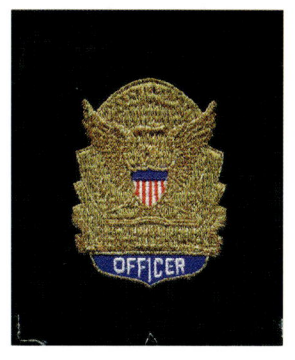

3499
V1/V2-590
Gold mylar

3500
6½" & 3½" bullion versions

3501
Ex-agents' association
Bullion

3502
4" & 3" versions

3503
V1/V2-594
3" peel-off backing

3504

3505
4" raid jacket

3506
3"
Oklahoma City hats

3507
3"

3508
2¾"

3509
V1/V2-592
FSD crime scene
jackets - 4"

3510
V1/V2-587
3¾"

The Encyclopedia of Federal Law Enforcement Patches

3511
3" WFO patch

3512
V1/V2-586
3¾" general use

3513
3" bullion

3514
4" reproduction

3515
O/S

3516
V1/V2-217
Western White House
Rare

3517
Original rare O/S
Counter-sniper
28 made

3518
Counter-sniper

3519
O/S Counter-Assault
Team

3520
Counter-Assault Team
Velcro

3521
Late 1970s
New York CAT team

3522

3523
ERT vest

3524
Old
EOD

3525
V1/V2-595
Embroidered hat patch

3526
Counter-Assault Team
(CAT) - 1995

3527
Counter-Assault Team
(CAT) - 1995

3528
Counter-Assault Team
(CAT) - 1995

3529
Gold mylar letters

3530
Original raid jacket
back patch 8" x 12½"

United States Secret Service

3531
2nd issue back patch
5" x 10½"

3532
Raid jacket front strip
2½" x 5"

3533
Raid jacket shoulder patch

3534

3535
V1/V2-606

3536
4½" & 3½" versions

3537
Worn on dress blues

3538

3539

3540

3541

3542

3543

3544

3545

3546

3547
V1/V2-604

3548
V1/V2-605

3549
V1/V2-213

3550

The Encyclopedia of Federal Law Enforcement Patches

3551
V1/V2-602
1976

3552
V1/V2-598

3553
Top - Presidential Yacht *Sequoia*

3554
V1/V2-612

3555
5¼" bullion

3556

3557
V1/V2-589
Original 2-pc twill + 1-pc F/E - current

3558
No info.

3559
V1/V2-609
3½"

3560
3½" OD

3561
4"

3562
Newer version

3562a
Newest version

3563
V1/V2-212

3564
V1/V2-603

3565
V1/V2-214

3566
V1/V2-596
Blue & black versions

3567
V1/V2-597
Also gold mylar version

3568

3569
Color & subdued versions - 4"

United States Secret Service

193

3570
Color & subdued versions - 4"

3571
4"

3572
3 1/4"

3573

3574
Bullion

3575
V1/V2-588
At least 3 variations

3576
V1/V2-601
O/S

3577
Protection Training
Local police

3578

3579

3580

3581

3582
For. Intell./Counter-Terr.

3583

3584

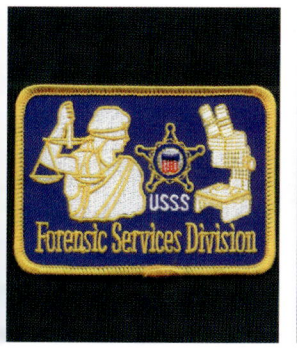

3585

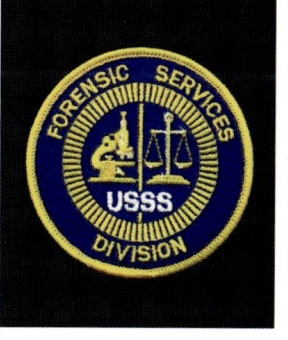

3586

3587

3588
1st version

3589
2nd version

The Encyclopedia of Federal Law Enforcement Patches

3590 Not USSS - but unique!

3591 1st version

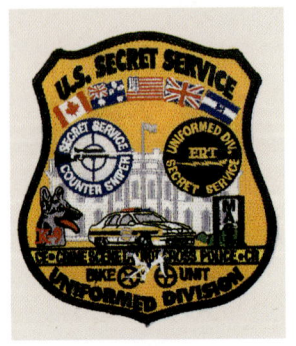

3592 Final version

3593 3½"

3594 4" HBR

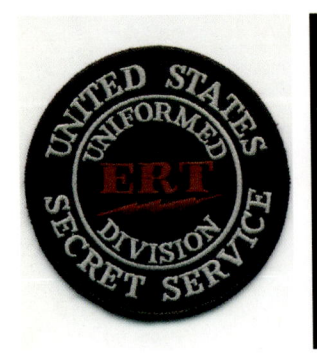

3595 4"

3596

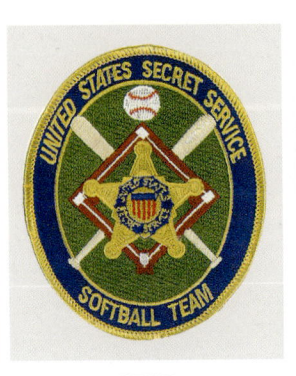

3597 Bats up

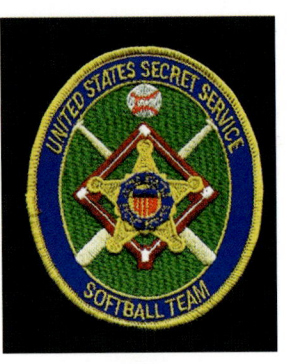

3598 Bats down

3599 EMT staff shirt patch

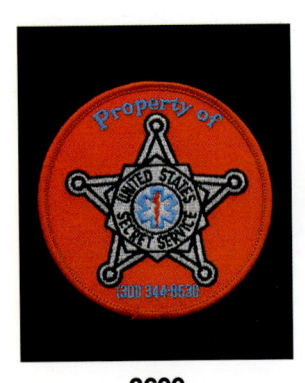

3600 EMT trauma kit patch

3601

3602

3603

3604 Final version

3605 1st version

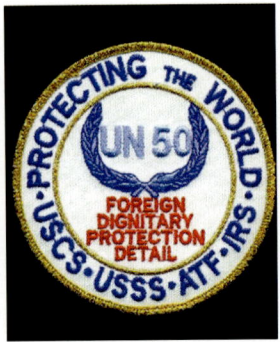

3606

3607

3608

3609

United States Secret Service

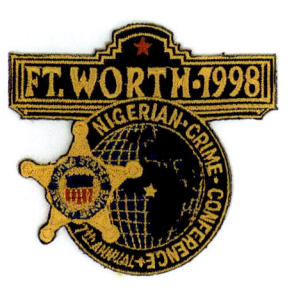

3610

3611

3612
Blue and black letter versions

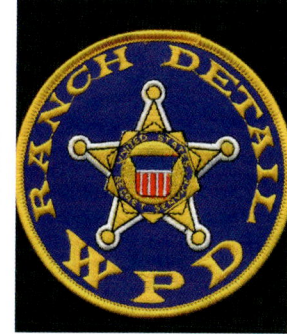

3613
Hard to get

3614
V1/V2-600
Extremely rare
Reagan Ranch

3615

3616

3617

3618

3619
May be reproduction

3620

3621
Worn by Cleveland PD

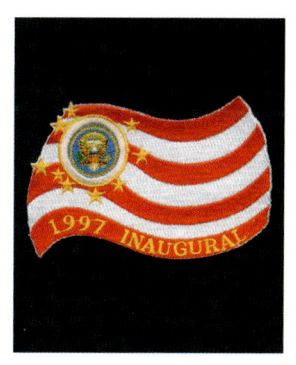

3622

3623

3624

3625

3626

3627

3628

3629

196 — The Encyclopedia of Federal Law Enforcement Patches

| 3630 | 3631 | 3632 | 3633 | 3634 |

| 3635 | 3636 | 3637 | 3638 | 3639 Washington, D.C. Field Office |

| 3640 | 3641 | 3642 | 3643 HBR | 3644 |

| 3645 Rare | 3646 | 3647 | 3648 | 3649 |

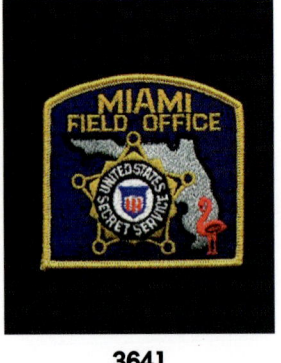

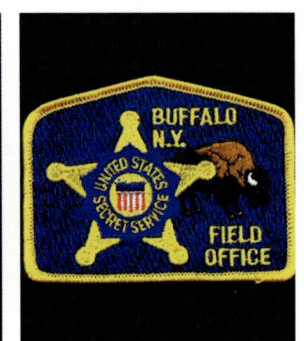

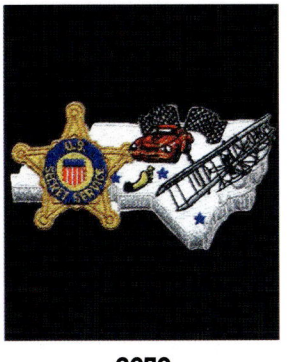

United States Secret Service

3650 North Carolina

3651

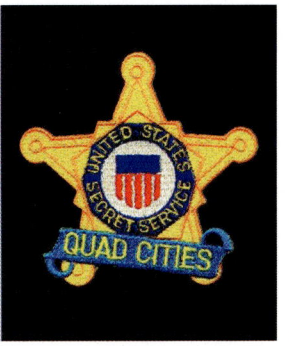

3652

3653

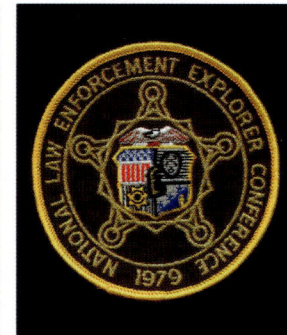

3654

3655 Silver mylar

3656

3657

3658

3659

3660 V1/V2-216

3661 V1/V2-215 4¾" - several variations

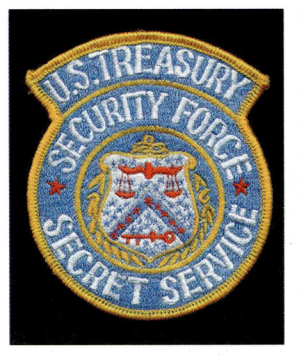

3662 4"

3663 Unofficial 4½" & 3" versions - 89th Airwing

3664 AF Test Team jackets

3665 AF Test Team jackets

3666 Boeing project personnel

3667 89th Air Force Wing jackets

3668 New - no info.

3669 New - no info.

The Encyclopedia of Federal Law Enforcement Patches

3669a
Air Force One

3670
V1/V2-608
9", 3½", 3", & 2¾"
versions

3671
9¼", 3½", & 3⅜"
versions

3671a
Old

3672
Bullion

3673

3674
3¼" movie prop

3675
2½" movie prop

3676
3" bullion

3677
Very rare

3678
V1/V2-611a
3½" twill

3679
Old

3680
No info. - silk-screened

3681
3½" & 3" versions

3682
Very rare

3683

3684
Bush Presidency

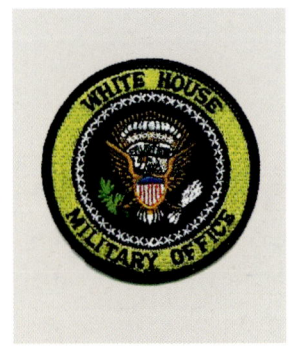

3685

3686
Military Office

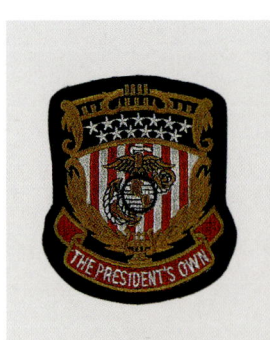

3687
USMC

United States Secret Service

3688

3689
Numbered 1-5

3690
Gold mylar

3691
Silk-screened

3692

3693
3" bullion
Presidential Seal

3694
4" bullion
Presidential Seal

3695
Large bullion

3696
Small bullion

3697
V1/V2-614
Vice-President Staff

3698
V1/V2-613
Vice-President

3699
Unif. Div. S/P

3700
Unif. Div. S/P

3701
Unif. Div. S/P

3702
Prototype

3703
3¾" twill
Old

3704
4" F/E gold mylar

3705
4" F/E gold mylar
Black & blue versions

3706
4" F/E gold mylar

3707
3¾" twill

199

200 The Encyclopedia of Federal Law Enforcement Patches

3708
4" UD F/E

3709
6¾" felt/gold mylar
4 versions

3710
4" variation

3711
3¾" felt

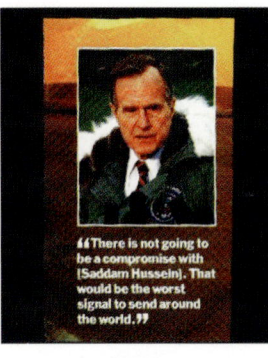

3712
3½" F/E

3713
"Prez" with his patch

3714
UD - dozens of variations 4" F/E

3715
V1/V2-219
3¾" Twill & F/E
Military Office

3716
3½" variation F/E

3717
3½" twill (felt, too)

3718
4" F/E

3719
4" twill

3720
4" twill
Blue background =
USAF Pres. Srvc. (Aide)
Black background =
Pres. Commd &
Travel Serv.
UD Patch - gold stars

3721
Of dubious origin

3722
May be fantasy

3723
Novelty

3724
Novelty

3725
Not a federal patch

3726
Old
Silk-screened

United States Secret Service

201

3727 Air Force One

Federal Courts

3728 Current C/B Gold mylar

3729 O/S S/P

3730 V1/V2-652 Current S/P

3731

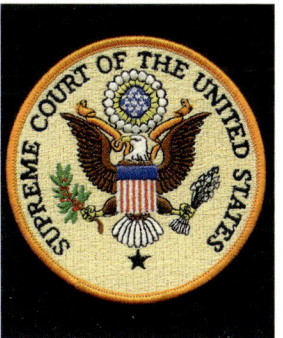

3732

3733 Bullion

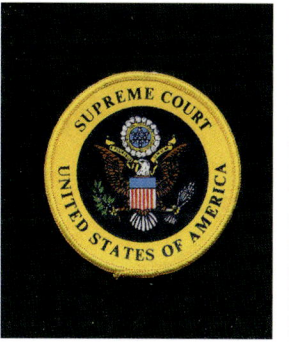

3734 Old Silk-screened

3735 1¼" x 3¼"

3736

3737 Bullion

3738 Bullion

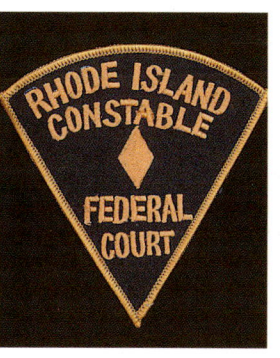

3739

3740 V1/V2-654

3741 3"

3742 5"

3743 5" variation

3744

3745

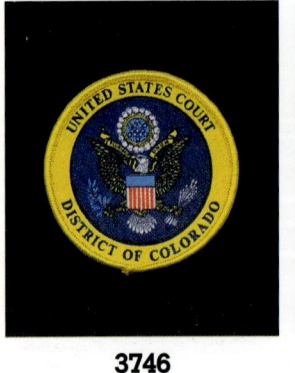

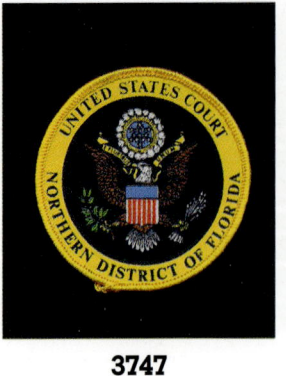

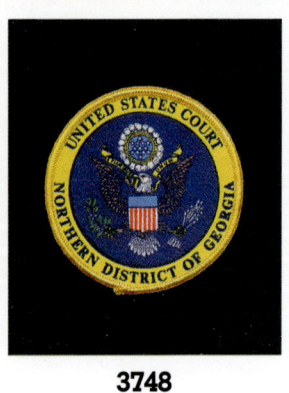

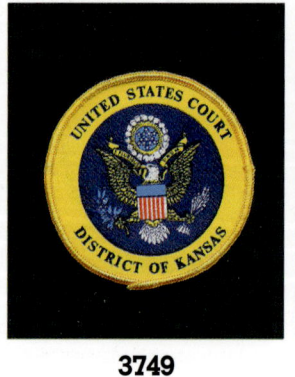

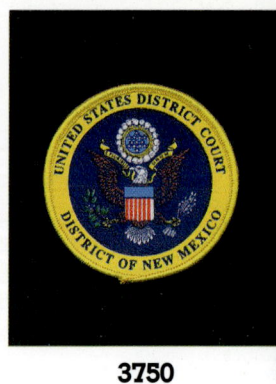

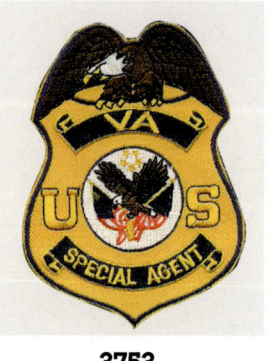

The Encyclopedia of Federal Law Enforcement Patches

3746

3747

3748

3749

3750

Veterans Administration/Department of Veterans Affairs

3751
3" bullion

3752
V1/V2-755

3753

3753a
VA - IG

3754
V1/V2-756

3755

3756
3½" & 3"

3757
2½" gold & silver versions

3758
V1/V2-262

3759
3¾"

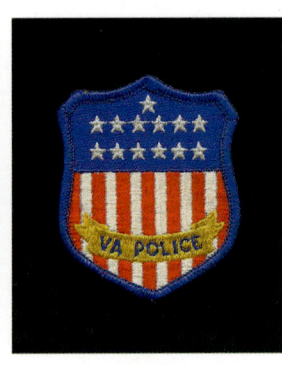

3760
V1/V2-263
3¾" & 3" versions

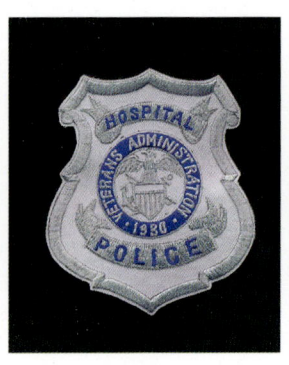

3761
V1/V2-266
Gold & silver versions

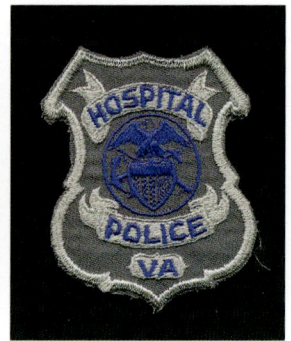

3762
V1/V2-757

3763
V1/V2-265
Wood, Wisconsin

Veterans Administration / Department of Veterans Affairs 203

3764

3765
Silk-screened

3766
Silk-screened

3767
V1/V2-759

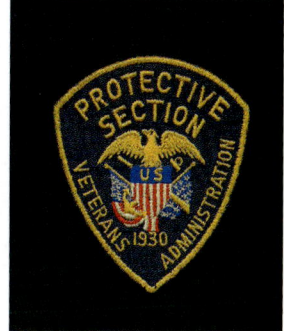

3768
V1/V2-264

3769

3770
V1/V2-260
U.S. Soldiers' Home

3771
V1/V2-754
U.S. Soldiers' and Airmen's Home

3772
V1/V2-267

3773

3774
3" F/E & bullion versions

3775

3776

3777

3778
Gold & silver versions

3779
Bullion

3780
Gold & silver 3" versions

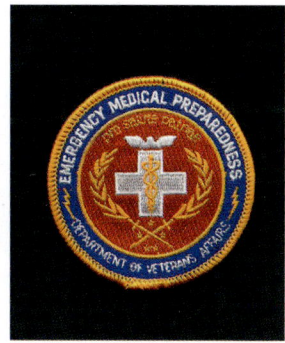

3781

3783
Used in Missouri, Connecticut, Florida, etc.

3784

The Encyclopedia of Federal Law Enforcement Patches

3785
V1/V2-261

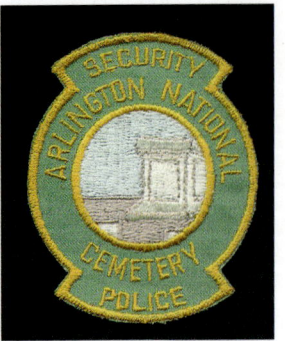

3786

3787
V1/V2-760/761
Style used at Rock Island, too

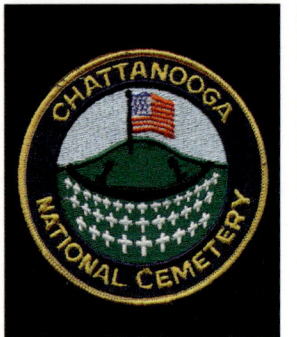

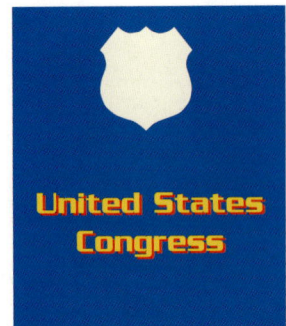

3788

3789

3790

3791

3792

3793

United States Congress

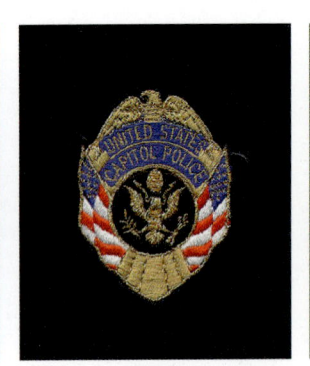

3794

3795

3796

3797
2½"

3798
V1/V2-226
4" Issue patch F/E

3799
OD

3800
Silver/black

3801
Black/silver

3802
Red border

United States Congress

| 3803 Olive border | 3804 V1/V2-225 | 3805 | 3806 4" F/E | 3807 V1/V2-228 3¼" |

| 3808 V1/V2-227 | 3809 V1/V2-658 | 3810 | 3811 | 3812 |

| 3813 | 3814 | 3815 V1/V2-657 | 3816 | 3817 |

| 3818 | 3819 | 3820 Old Silk-screened | 3821 Bullion | 3822 |

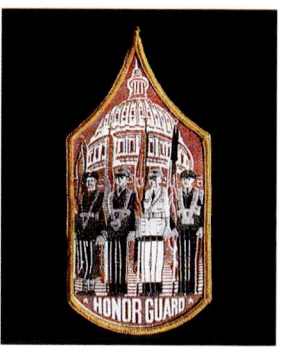

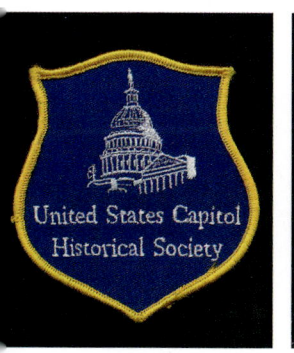

The Encyclopedia of Federal Law Enforcement Patches

3823

3824
Congressional Seal

3825
Government Accounting Office

3826
Bullion

3827
Bullion

3828
3¾"

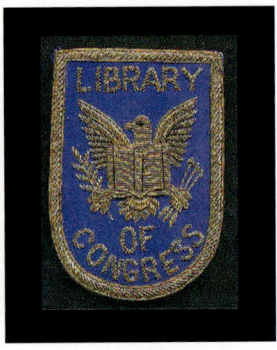

3829
V1/V2-246
3¼"

3830

3831
V1/V2-810

3832
V1/V2-659
Green & gold border version

3833
V1/V2-660

3834

3835
V1/V2-245

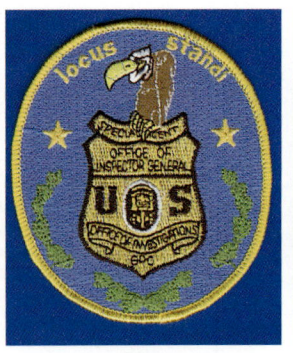

3836
4" & 3" versions

3837
4" & 3" versions

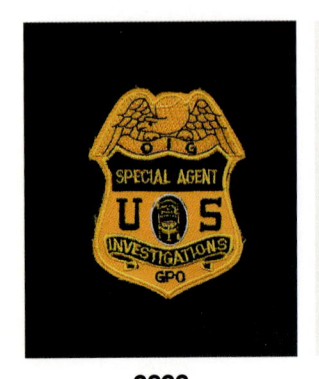

3838
4" & 3" versions

3839

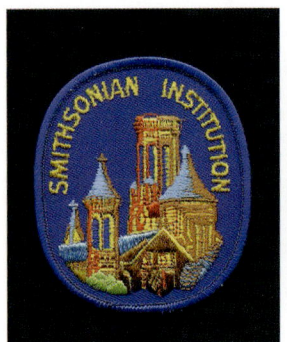

3840

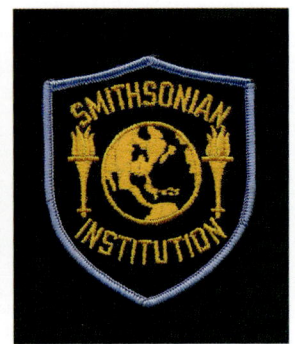

3841
V1/V2-255

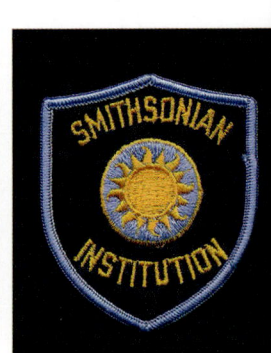

3842
V1/V2-256

United States Congress

3843
V1/V2-747

3844
V1/V2-254

3845
V1/V2-811
1973 issue

3847

3848
V1/V2-749
Old felt

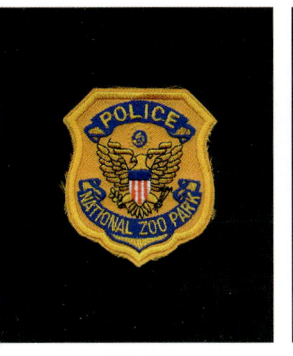

3849
V1/V2-748

3850

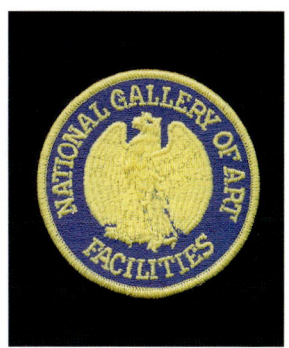

3851

3852

3853
See #0108 -
Agriculture

3854
Rare

3855

3856

3857

3858
V1/V2-664
3¼" & 3" versions

3859
V1/V2-662
3" & 2" T & F/E versions

3860

The Encyclopedia of Federal Law Enforcement Patches

Other Agencies

3861 Dubious origin

3862 Federal Deposit Insurance Co.

3863 5 variations known

3864 Bullion

3865 V1/V2-732

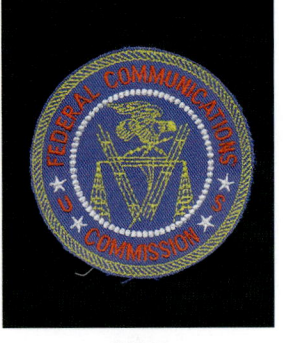

3866 Two variations

3867 Bullion

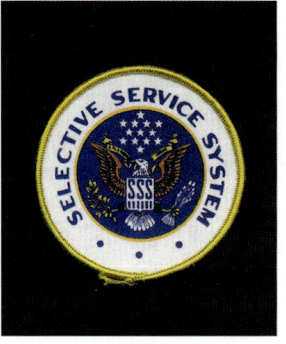

3868

3869 Bullion

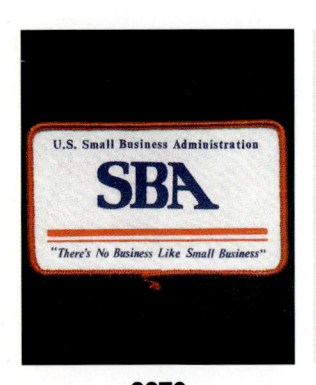

3870 Numerous variations

3870a Disaster team

3871 V1/V2-684/684a Regular & subdued versions

3872 3¾" bullion

3873 4" bullion variation

3874 V1/V2-687 5" & 3¼"

3875 V1/V2-231 5", 3¼", & 3" variations

3876

3877

3878 4"

Other Agencies

3879

3880
V1/V2-232
2nd issue Motorman

3881
Felt - old

3882
Variation reads
"S.O.D."

3883

3884
V1/V2-679/680
Gold & silver versions

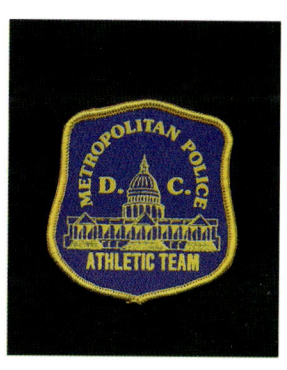

3885
V1/V2-682

3886

3887

3888

3889

3890

3891

3892

3893

3894

3895
6" x 10½"

3896
Silk-screened

3897

3898
3" silk-screened
Old

The Encyclopedia of Federal Law Enforcement Patches

3899
V1/V2-681
3"

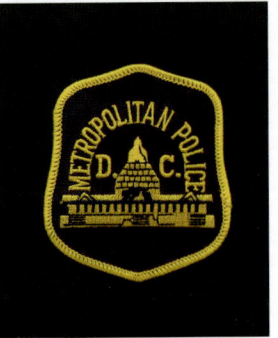

3900
3 1/4"

3901
V1/V2-678
3"

3902
12+ titles in this style

3903

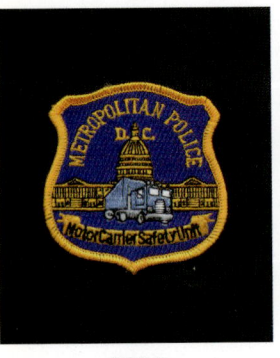

3904

3905

3906

3907

3908

3909

3910
Two versions

3911
Alternate version
"Boys Club"

3912

3913
60 years old
Felt

3914

3915
Dispatchers

3916
"Up the Irish"

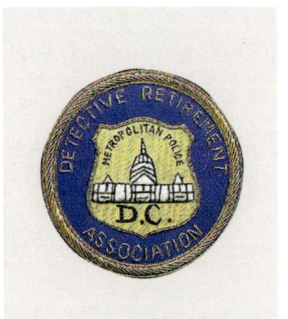

3917
Bullion

3918
Novelty

Other Agencies

3919 1st issue Novelty

3920 2nd issue 1991 Novelty

3921 V1/V2-672

3922 V1/V2-235

3923 V1/V2-672a 4 versions

3924 V1/V2-675

3925

3926

3927

3928 Unofficial

3929 Current

3930

3931 V1/V2-234

3932

3933

3934

3935 V1/V2-667 3 versions

3936 Old

3937 V1/V2-670

3938 Old

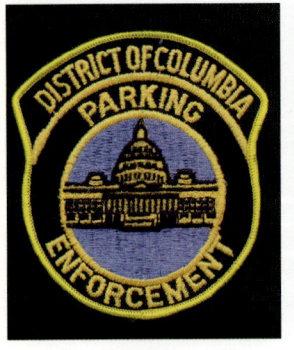

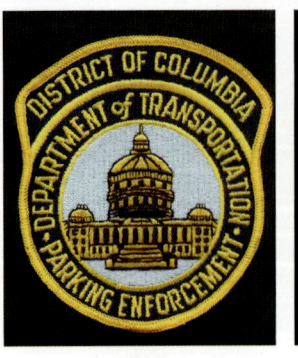

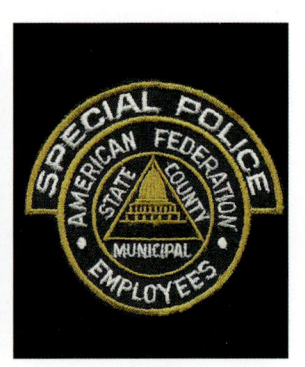

The Encyclopedia of Federal Law Enforcement Patches

3939

3940
V1/V2-673

3941

3942
V1/V2-674

3943

3944

3945

3946

3947

3948

3949

3950

3951

3952

3953

3954

3955

3956
Over 3 dozen titles

3957
Special police variation

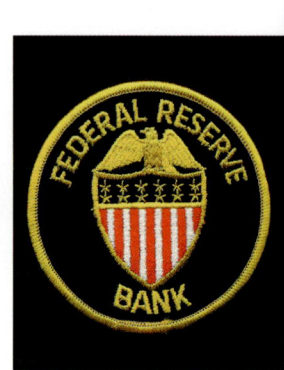

3958
V1/V2-702
3½" & 3" versions
(SLC)

Other Agencies 213

3959
V1/V2-709
Detroit

3960
V1/V2-705

3961
V1/V2-704

3962
V1/V2-703

3963
V1/V2-715
2 versions - tan & blue

3964

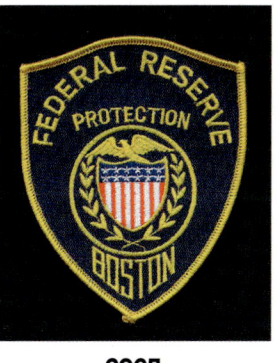

3965
4½" & 3" versions

3967

3968

3969
V1/V2-710
Variation reads "Dallas"

3970

3971

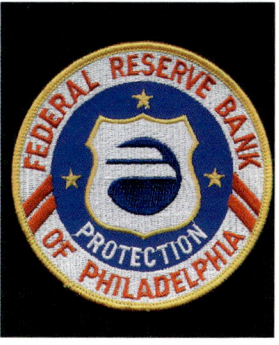

3972

3973
V1/V2-713

3974
V1/V2-714

3975

3976

3977

3978

3979
V1/V2-711

214 The Encyclopedia of Federal Law Enforcement Patches

| 3980 | 3981 | 3982 | 3983 V1/V2-707 | 3984 |

| 3985 | 3986 | 3987 | 3988 | 3989 V1/V2-712 Black & blue border versions |

| 3990 | 3991 | 3992 | 3993 V1/V2-706 | 3994 |

| 3995 | 3996 V1/V2-708 | 3997 | 3998 | 3999 |

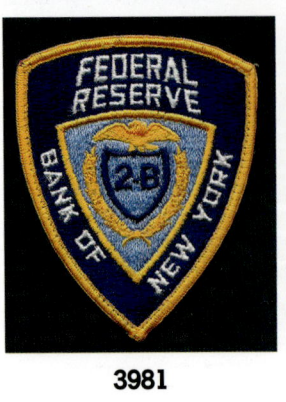

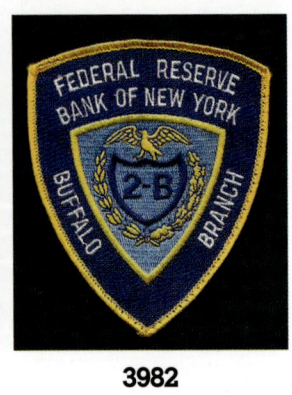

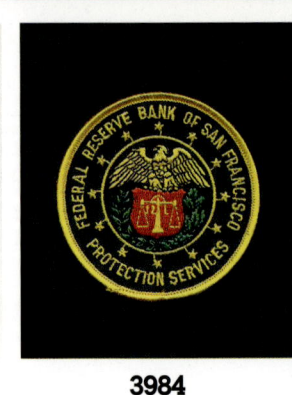

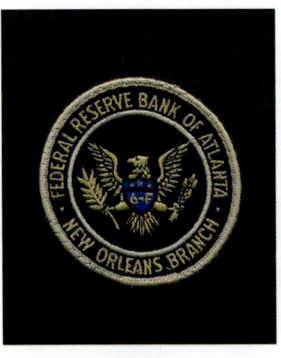

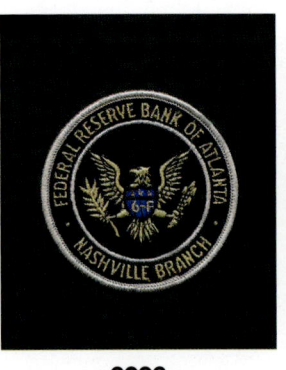

Other Agencies 215

| 4000 | 4001 3" bullion | 4002 | 4003 3" bullion | 4004 Boston Unauthorized |

| 4005 V1/V2-720 | 4006 4" jumpsuit Adhesive back | 4007 | 4008 | 4009 Variation of #4007 |

| 4011 | 4011 V1/V2-244 | 4012 | 4013 | 4014 |

| 4015 V1/V2-242 4" & 2½" versions | 4016 V1/V2-723 Gold & silver mylar | 4017 4" felt - jackets | 4018 V1/V2-241 3½" twill - shirts | 4019 4" twill |

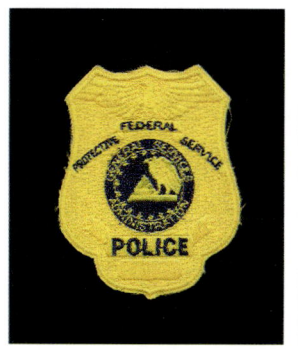

The Encyclopedia of Federal Law Enforcement Patches

4020
V1/V2-730
4½" & 5" versions
Old - felt

4021
V1/V2-240
4½", 4", & 3" versions

4022
V1/V2-718
Prototype

4023
V1/V2-721
Blazer patch - D.C.

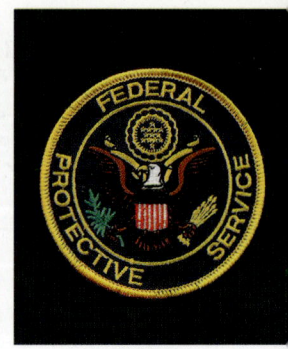

4024
"Saigon Sally" item

4025
V1/V2-722v

4026
V1/V2-724
Felt

4027
3" & 2" variations

4028
V1/V2-239
2" baseball cap patch

4029

4030
Regular & subdued versions

4031
Rare

4032
Rare

4033

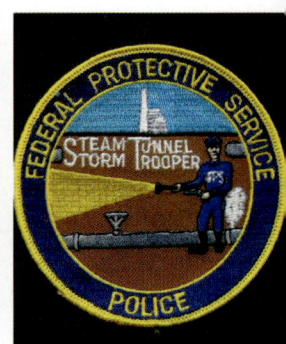

4034
4" & 3¼"
Novelty

4035
V1/V2-716
4½"

4036
V1/V2-717
4¾"

4037
4½" & 3" versions

4038
4½"

4039
4½" & 3" versions

Other Agencies 217

4040	4041	4042	4043	4044
3"	4½"	V1/V2-729	V1/V2-727 Color & subdued versions	V1/V2-728

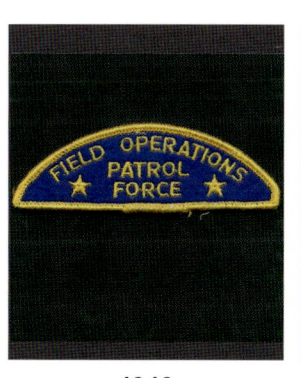

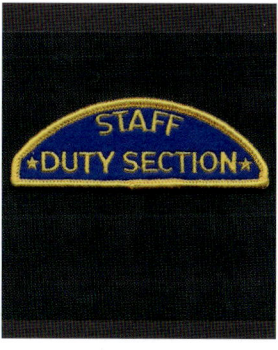

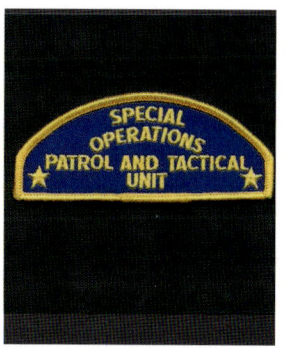

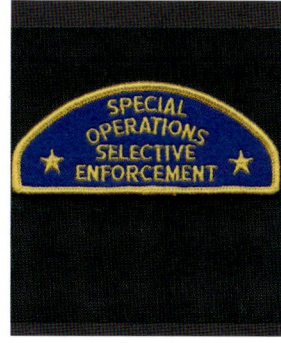

4045	4046	4047	4048	4049
	V1/V2-725	V1/V2-726		

4050	4051	4052	4053	4054
			Federal Supply Service	Abortion Clinic Novelty

4055	4056	4057	4058	4059
	Not Police O/S		No info. available	

The Encyclopedia of Federal Law Enforcement Patches

National Aeronautics and Space Administration

4060 Variation reads "Fleet Center"

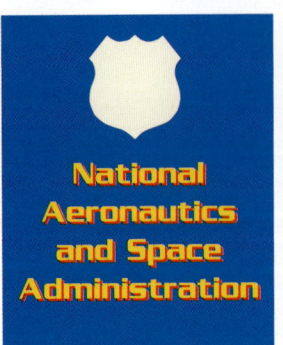

4061

4062

4063 Bullion

4064

4065

4066 V1/V2-734

4067 V1/V2-738

4068

4069

4070

4071

4072 Old - twill

4073

4074

4075 V1/V2-737

4076

4077 V1/V2-247

4078

National Aeronautics and Space Administration

219

4079

4080

4081

4082
Two versions -
Dot/no dot

4083

4084

4085

4086

4087
Variation reads
"Alert/Protection"

4088
3½" & 4" versions

4089
Two versions -
Silk-screened/twill

4090

4091

4092

4093
V1/2735

4094

4095

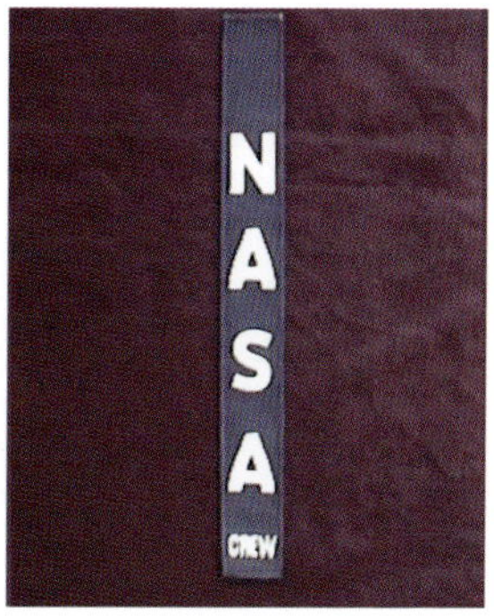

4096

4097

4098
Movie prop

The Encyclopedia of Federal Law Enforcement Patches

4099 Movie prop

4100 Movie prop

4101 V1/V2-733

4101a

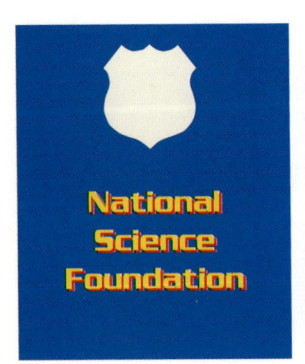

4102 V1/V2-736

National Science Foundation

4103

4104 V1/V2-740

4105

4106

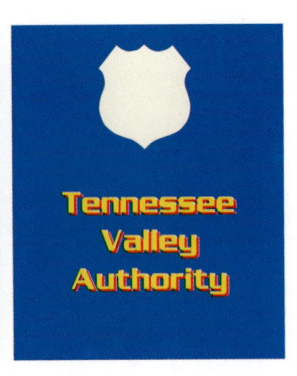

4107

Tennessee Valley Authority

4108 4" & 3" versions

4109

4110 V1/V2-751

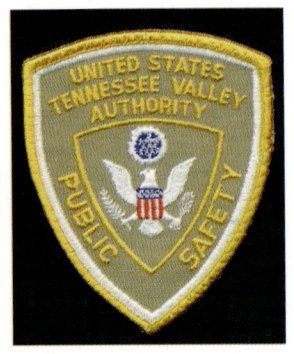

4111 V1/V2-752

4112

4113

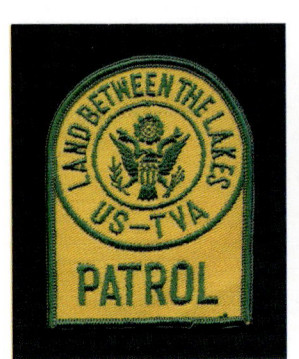

4114

4115 V1/V2-753

Trusts, Territories and Possessions

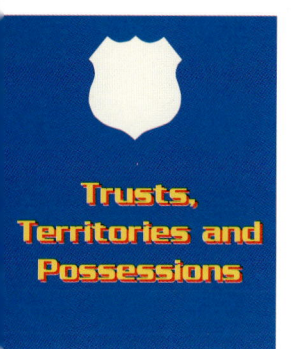

Trusts, Territories and Possessions

4116
V1/V2-284

4117
3½" & 2¾" versions

4118

4119
Rare - twill

4120

4121
V1/V2-285

4122

4123

4124

4125

4126
Gold & blue seal versions
Blue = fake?

4127
V1/V2-223
Variation reads "Customs"

4128
V1/V2-221

4129
V1/V2-224

4130
V1/V2-222

4131
V1/V2-764

4132
V1/V2-765

4133

4134

221

The Encyclopedia of Federal Law Enforcement Patches

4135

4136

4137
V1/V2-768v
Var. reads "Department of Corrections"

4138

4139

4140

4141

4142
V1/V2-268

4143
V1/V2-772v
Var. reads "Port Authority Security"

4144
V1/V2-270

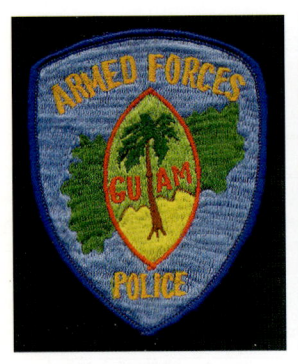

4145
V1/V2-766

4146
V1/V2-269

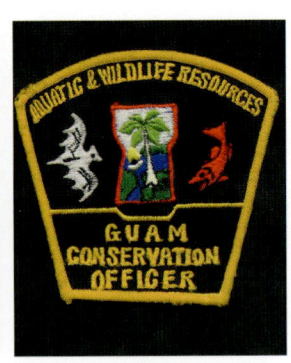

4147
V1/V2-767

4148
V1/V2-771

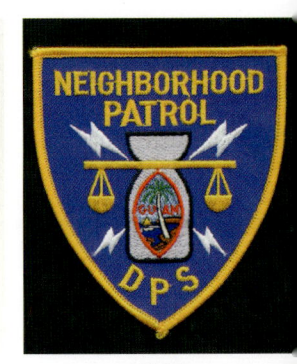

4149
V1/V2-271

4150

4151
V1/V2-769

4152

4153
V1/V2-274-276
Variations - Saipan/Tinian

4154
V1/V2-773

Trusts, Territories and Possessions

4155

4156
V1/V2-278

4157
3½" & 3" versions

4158

4159

4160

4161
Very rare

4162
V1/V2-273

4163

4164

4165
1947-1955

4166

4167

4168
V1/V2-272

4169
V1/V2-776

4170
V1/V2-279

4171
V1/V2-775

4172
5" & 4½" versions

4173
V1/V2-778

4174
V1/V2-777

The Encyclopedia of Federal Law Enforcement Patches

4175 V1/V2-277v Variation is #277

4176 Old Silk-screened

4177 V1/V2-782

4178 V1/V2-780

4179 V1/V2-779

4180 V1/V2-784

4181

4182 V1/V2-785

4183

4184 V1/V2-288

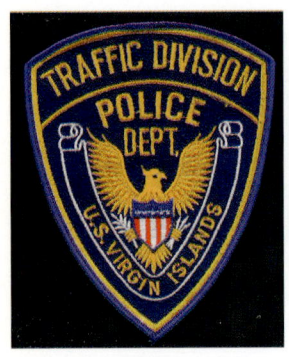

4185

4186 V1/V2-286 3 variations

4187

4188 V1/V2-800 5½" & 5" versions

4189 V1/V2-287/803 #803 reads "Bureau of Corr."

4190 V1/V2-804

4191 V1/V2-801

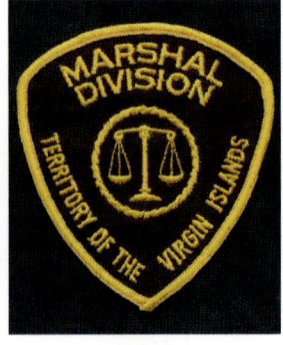

4192 V1/V2-805

4193 V1/V2-806

4194

Trusts, Territories and Possessions

225

4195

4196
V1/V2-281/282
5" & 4" versions

4197

4198
V1/V2-280

4199
V1/V2-797

4200
V1/V2-791

4201
SWAT Team

4202
V1/V2-798
SWAT Team

4203

4204
V1/V2-795

4205
V1/V2-796
Mounted police

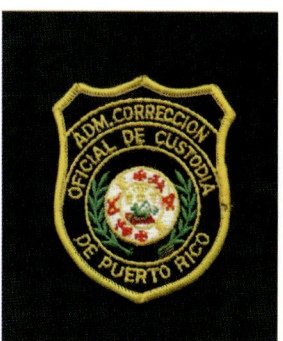

4206
V1/V2-790
Corrections

4207
V1/V2-792

4208
Fire Inspector

4209
V1/V2-789

4210
Traffic/Hwy.

4211

4212

BORDER PATROL
POLICE U.S. MARSHAL
DEA
IRS-CID POLICE
POLICE U.S. AGENT
DEA
U.S. MARSHAL
POLICE
IRS
FEDERAL AGENT
FBI
SAFETY FIRST
EYE WASH FOUNTAIN
FBI-NYPD JOINT TERRORIST TASK FORCE
U.S. CUSTOMS POLICE
U.S. AGENT
U.S. AGENT

Sources of Insignia

This section is shorter than the ones in previous RHS books, for these reasons: More than a few of the previously-listed sources have gone out of business, and with over 4,000 photo exhibits I was forced to greatly cut the text.

The very best source of insignia is, and remains, *Police Collector News* (*PCNews*—see ad inside front cover). Generally, insignia reference books currently being offered are shown there as well as hundreds of display and bulletin-board ads which offer a wide variety of items available. New sources appear each month. In addition, if you read the "Letters to the Editor" sections, you'll get a sense of who the schlockmeisters—as well as the good guys—are in the hobby.

Listed below are just a few of the many sources of supply for federal patch collectors; they are the companies and individuals with which I am familiar. Be aware that even the best-intentioned firms or individuals sometimes pass along bogus or repro patches, mostly through not knowing what is and what isn't real. I am sure that, with the advent of computerized patch manufacturing (see page 1) it is becoming harder and harder to tell "what's live, and what's Memorex"...to quote the old advertising line. I too have occasionally got stuck with bogus items when I've acquired collections or single pieces.

Insignia Suppliers

A.T. EMBLEM CO.
Post Office Box 382, Ramsay, NJ 07446 (201) 327-9060
Sells to collectors

BOOK 'EM
Route 5, 166 Seneca Avenue, Canastoga, NY 13032-9465
Send for catalog

BRIGADE QUARTERMASTERS
1025 Cobb International Blvd., Kennesaw, GA 30144-4349 (404) 428-1234
Sells insignia and insignia reference books

"BRONC" OF RIDLEY PARK
Box 255, Ridley Park, PA 19078 (610) 522-0840
Has large stock of state and federal patches for sale

JIM BURTON
1614 Ridgewood Rd., Neosho, MO 64850-6821 (417) 455-2347
Large supply of patches for sale

DOVER ARMY & NAVY STORE, INC.
222 W. Loockerman St., Dover, DE 19904 (302) 736-1959
Dealer in patches

FLETC EXPRESS STORE
Building 86, Federal Law Enforcement Training Center, Glynco, GA 31524 (912) 265-2048
Accepts mail orders

G-MAN EMBLEMS
1400 O'Hennesey Ln, Lenoir, NC 28645-9595 (828) 759-0751
Designs, produces, and trades patches

BILL HEDGES
P.O. Box 6983, Buena Park, CA 90622
Large supply of patches and badges for sale

J & G. ENTERPRISES
P.O. Box 3176, Fort Lee, NJ 07024 (201) 986-1017
Sells Feds

LOS ANGELES POLICE REVOLVER AND ATHLETIC CLUB (LAPRAC)
P.O. Box 1591, Main Post Office, Los Angeles, CA 90053
LAPD and other cloth insignia for sale

GENE MATZKE
2345 South 28th St., Milwaukee, WI 53215 (414) 383-8995
Large supply of patches for sale

MEAN STREETS OF BOSTON
P.O. Box 88 Astor Station, Boston, MA 02123 (617) 846-5558
Has military police and other items for sale to collectors

METRO USA
1950 North West 88 Court, Miami, FL 33172 (305) 477-6671
Police and military supplies

PROFESSIONAL POLICE PRODUCTS CATALOG
6300 Yarrow Dr., Carlsbad, CA 92009-1597 (800) 854-6449
Catalog of police supplies, books, and gear

QUARTERMASTER
750 Long Beach Bl., Long Beach, CA 90813 (800) 444-8643
Patches, uniforms, and equipment dealer

RHS ENTERPRISES
Post Office Box 5779, Garden Grove, CA 92846-0779
(714) 892-9012
Dealer of police insignia books; catalog of federal patches, pins

R&R UNIFORMS, INC.
517 E. Jefferson St., Louisville, KY (502) 584-8261
(Write for catalog)

SALLY'S COP SHOP
6203 Altama Avenue, Brunswick, GA 31525 (912) 265-8303
T-shirts, ball caps, etc.

H.J. SAUNDERS
U.S. Military Insignia, Inc., 5025 Tamiami Trail East, Naples, FL 34113 (941) 774-3323
Write for catalog

SHOMER-TEC
Post Office Box 28070, Bellingham, WA 98228
Major law enforcement supply dealer

SILVER STAR POLICE INSIGNIA
Post Office Box 51, Hastings, NE 68902-0051
Catalog of insignia

SOMES UNIFORMS
65 Route 17, Post Office Box 306, Paramus, NJ 07653-0306

STAR PACKER BADGES
Neil Swendsboe
P. O. Box 3422, Nashua, NH 03061-3422 (603) 888-4714
Sells marked replica Old West badges, $40 to $70 each; catalog $5

WILLIAM D. SIMMONDS
2407 East 15th Street, Brooklyn, NY 11235 (917) 457-2014
Specializes in U.S. Marshals Service patches

BOB TUCKER ENTERPRISES
3642 Diablo Street, Napa, CA 94558 (707) 255-2202
LAPD patches and memorabilia

US CAVALRY STORES, INC.
1375 N. Wilson Road, Radcliff, KY 40106 (502) 351-1164
Patches and insignia reference books (send for catalog)

WES WESSLING
9437 NE 146th Circle B-205, Bothell, WA 98011-4571 (425) 486-4534
Write for catalog of US Coast Guard books and patches

WEST END UNIFORM
4650 Arrow Hwy B-1, Montclair, CA 91763 (909) 621-7444
Owner Gene Gianuzzi also is a collector of Police and Fire items

VICKI and STEVEN WHITE
508 Pheasant Ridge Circle, Lancaster, PA 17603
(717) 299-6774
Designers, collectors; specialty USSS and FBI pins and patches

WORLDWIDE INSIGNIA, INC.
Post Office Box 259, Hope, NJ 07844 (908) 459-4403

Collectors

Listed below are a few individuals who are both knowledgeable and honest, and who have given permission for their addresses to be listed.

DARRELL L. HAYNES
Post Office Box 9072, Wichita, KS 67277-0072
Emblems@INAME.com
Police officer, designer, collector

PAUL W. LUTTON
804 Mockingbird Drive, Port Orange, FL 32127-4725

DAVID KOLBERSON
7157 Alameda #14, El Paso, TX 79915

GARY GRANT
223 East Lynn Creek Drive, Arlington, TX 76002-2777

STEVE PETRO
9 Twin Circle Drive, Rochester, NY 14624

RYDER LUSK
2410 Chas Drive, Rolling Meadows, IL 60008-2066

STEVE and VICKI WHITE
508 Pheasant Ridge, Lancaster, PA 17603
Design FBI and USSS pins, patches; collectors also

Insignia Collector Associations

ASMIC — American Society of Military Insignia Collectors
c/o George Duell, 526 Lafayette Ave., Palmerton, PA 18071-1621

IPA — International Police Association U.S. Section
Post Office Box 3212, Auburn, CA 95604-3212
(530) 885-9420

PICAA — Police Collectors Insignia Association of Australia
Post Office Box 56, Forestville NSW 2087, Australia

PICAGB — Police Insignia Collectors Association of Great Britain
17 Kingsway Drive, Kidlington, Oxford OX5 2LZ, England

Related Reading

In my previous books I included extensive bibliographical material. This time, however, the list is much shorter, for two reasons: Lack of space; going from 500 to over 4,000 photo exhibits lessened the amount of text that can be used; and many of the prior listings are now out-of-print, and it is difficult if not impossible to locate copies today.

Those readers who have copies of previous RHS titles (some of which are still available; see the last page in this volume) can access the larger bibliographic listings.

The books in this section were of help in the author's collecting and writing.

Airport Police
by Jim Karas and William Delgado
4503 Saratoga Woods Drive, Louisville, KY 40299-8331
(502) 452-5091

An American Elite
by Dan Meany
56 Park Avenue #1, Winthrop, MA 02152-2558
New book will feature major US and foreign S.W.A.T. emblems, etc. Write for publication date

Badges and Ornamentation of the National Park Service
by R. Bryce Workman
The best federal law enforcement insignia book to date. To be published in the near future; check ads in *PCNews*

Badge Hallmarks For Collectors
by Steve Knight
2588-D El Camino Real Suite 285, Carlsbad, CA 92008
(619) 434-8074
1996. Helpful listing of literally hundreds of badge hallmarks

Badges of the United States Marshals
by Raymond H. Sherrard and George Stumpf
See RHS Enterprises ad at end of this book (very limited supply of softcovers).

Stan Benjamin
8401 South Kolb Road #101, Tucson, AZ 85706 (520) 574-8397
Write for list of patch reference manuals

Book 'Em
Route 5, 166 Seneca Avenue, Canastoga, NY 13032-9465
(315) 697-5100
Sell promotional insignia, mugs, keychains, and related items

The Bureau Trader
182 Daniel Dr., Tooele, UT 84074-1597,
BureauTrader@yahoo.com
Features FBI patches and pins. $25.00/year

Caliber Press, Inc.
666 Dundee Rd. Suite 1607, Northbrook, IL 60062-2760
Write for book catalog

The California Patch Book
by Randall Grago
2901 Via Toscana Suite 103, Corona, CA 92879-6582
(909) 734-2712
2-volume CD set shows color pictures of all California patches in use since the 1920s. Over 10,000 exhibits. Includes a licensed copy of Thumbs Plus browser. $99.00 per volume

California Police and Sheriff Shoulder Patches
by Will Berry
Post Office Box 132, Burbank, CA 91503 (818) 348-2516 ext. *3 Patches shown in color. Approximately $20.00

Casey's Travel Guide to Police & Fire Museums
by Jim Casey
Casey Publishing Company, Post Office Box 937, Orangevale, CA 95662-0937 (916) 539-4613

The Centurions' Shield
by Raymond H. Sherrard, Keith D. Bushey, and Jacob A. Bushey
1996. History of the LAPD, its badges and insignia. $49.95 hardcover, $29.95 softcover. See RHS Enterprises ad at end of this book

Coast Guard Patch Books
Wes Wessling, 122 Timber Ridge, Durham, NC 27713 (919) 493-5989
Write for list of titles and availability

A Collectors Guide to Police Memorabilia
by Mike Bondarenko
Available from PCNEWS, 2392 US Highway 12, Baldwin, WI 54002 (715) 684-2216

Gerard R. Davis, Ltd.
P.O. Box 1424, Woonsocket, RI 02895 (401) 766-8760
Write for catalog of commemorative/anniversary items

The Encyclopedia of Collectibles
Time-Life Books, 541 North Fairbanks Ct., Chicago, IL 60611
One volume in this series contains an excellent "Police Memorabilia" section

Federal Law Enforcement Patches, Volume Two
by Raymond H. Sherrard, 1987
See RHS Enterprises ad at end of this book. All-color. $20.00

Fire Magazine
Rue Montoyer 1, B-1000, Brussels, Belgium
(02) 511-88-34
French language, but lots of federal patches shown in color. Editor Rene Smeets is a federal collector

Handbook of Federal Police and Investigative Agencies
by Donald A. Torres
Greenwood Press, Westport, CT, 1985
40 pictures of federal patches, and a brief description of every federal agency. $49.95

Bill Hedges
P.O. Box 6983, Buena Park, CA 90622 (714) 952-3304
Write for list of patch reference manuals

Indian Tribals
by Donald Brockman
6629 West Bennett Avenue, Milwaukee, WI 53219-4126
1990. Hundreds of tribal patches are shown

The Langenbecker Spotter's Guide
by Dave Arnold
1200 East Davis S. Suite 115-172, Mesquite, TX 75149 (972) 288-2887
Guide to reproduction badges. Very useful for collectors!

Law and Order Magazine
1000 Skokie Blvd., Wilmette, IL 60091 (312) 256-8555
Many emblems diplayed in articles. $15.00/year

Law Enforcement Memorabilia Price and Identification Guide
by Monty McCord
1201 N. Juniata Avenue, Post Office Box 302, Juniata, NE 68955, or from Krause Publications (715) 445-2214
550 photos, 208 pages, $19.95 plus $3.25 P&H

Law Enforcement Product News
100 Garfield Street Suite 300, Denver, CO 80206-5550
(800) 291-3911

Wes Maroney
Cal-Coast Insignia
1248 Woodmere Road, Santa Maria, CA 93455
(805) 937-7775
Write for list of patch reference manuals

Modern Police Cars
Dodge, Plymouth, and Chrysler Police Cars
by Robert Genat
Motorbooks International, Post Office Box 2, Osceola, WI 54020 (909) 889-8644
Both books feature many color photos of police vehicles

National Reporter
International Police Association
Post Office Box 3212, Auburn, CA 95604-3212
(530) 885-9420
Has "Hobby Page" for collectors. Must be a police officer to join the association. $25.00/year

NIC
500 Flournoy Lucas Road Building 3, Post Office Box 5950, Shreveport, LA 71135-5950
Write for their catalog

Police Collector News (PCNEWS)
2392 US Highway 12, Baldwin, WI 54002 (715) 684-2216
The MUST-READ monthly collector's magazine. $24.00/year

Police the Law Officers Magazine
Post Office Box 847, Carlsbad, CA 92018-0847
Monthly; good articles; lists collectors worldwide. $21.95/year

The Police Marksman
6000 East Shirley Lane, Montgomery, Al 36117
Bi-monthly; for police shooters; insignia displayed in articles

Police Product News
6200 Yarrow Drive, Carlsbad, CA 92008-0996
Articles and photos relating to police insignia

Police Relics
Police Collectibles Pictorial Guide
Badges of Law & Order
by George Virgines
Post Office Box 13761, Albuquerque, NM 87192
Police Relics has a section on patches, price guide. $6.95

Postal Insignia
by J.R. Mundy
320 West Main Street, Eaton, OH 45320
Privately printed, 1992

Railroad Police Patch Reference Book
by Jim Karas
4503 Saratoga Woods Drive, Louisville, KY 40299-8331

Rangers of California State Parks
by Michael G. Lynch
Post Office Box 3212, Auburn, CA 95604-3212
Many badges and patches are shown. Write for price

Seals and Other Devices in Use at the Government Printing Office
Superintendent of Documents, U.S. Government Printing Office, Washington, DC 20402
Has clear drawings of most U.S. Government seals

Sheriffs Insignia of the United States
by James V. Claflin
Post Office Box 4682, Hinsdale, IL 60522-4682
Over three thousand color photos depicting patches from every sheriff's department in the USA. $49.95 hardcover, $32.95 softcover

Shomer-Tec
Post Office Box 28070, Bellingham, WA 98228
(360) 733-6214
Write for their huge catalog of law enforcement supplies including patches, badges, and books. Owner Joel Jaffe is himself a collector of federal patches

Silver State Law Enforcement Cloth Insignia
by Dave Underwood
1216 Heather Ridge Road, North Las Vegas, NV 89031-1520
Massive three-ring binder containing hundreds of color photos of federal, state, and local Nevada patches. Updated periodically. Write for prices and availability

Southern Lawman Magazine
507 Walnut Street, Paris, TN 38242 (901) 642-5435
$15.00/year

S.W.A.T. Magazine
Post Office Box 16598, North Hollywood, CA 91615-9962
Has articles dealing with S.W.A.T. collectibles

The Tactical Edge
Post Office Box 529, Doylestown, PA 18901
Quarterly journal of the National Tactical Officers Association; has articles showing S.W.A.T. insignia. $12.00/year

United States Air Force Police Insignias
by MSGT Paul Block and Col. Charles Piver
5718 Cambridge Lane #1, Racine, WI 53406
(414) 886-9409
$21.45

The United States Government Manual 1998/99
U.S. Government Printing Office, Superintendent of Documents, Mail Stop: SSOP, Washington, DC 20402-9328
Indispensable working tool for researching federal agencies. $41.00

Appendix

Excerpts from United States Code, Title 18, Section 700 Relating to Emblems, Insignia and Names

Title 18 Section 701. Official badges, identification cards, other insignia

Whoever manufactures, sells, or possesses any badge, identification card, or other insignia, of the design prescribed by the head of any department or agency of the United States for use by any officer or employee thereof, or any colorable imitation thereof, or photographs, prints, or in any other manner makes or executes any engraving, photograph, print, or impression in the likeness of any such badge, identification card, or other insignia, or any colorable imitation thereof, except as authorized under regulations made pursuant to law, shall be fined not more than $250 or imprisoned not more than six months, or both.

Section 709. Whoever, except with the written permission of the Director of the Federal Bureau of Investigation, knowingly uses the words "Federal Bureau of Investigation" or the initials "F.B.I.", or any colorable imitation of such words or initials, in connection with any advertisement, circular, book, pamphlet or other publication, play, motion picture, broadcast, telecast, or other production, in a manner reasonably calculated to convey the impression that such advertisement, circular, book, pamphlet, or other publication, play, motion picture, broadcast, telecast, or other production, is approved, endorsed, or authorized by the Federal Bureau of Investigation;

Shall be punished as follows: a corporation, partnership, business trust, association, or other business entity, by a fine of not more than $1,000; an officer of member thereof participating or knowingly acquiescing in such violation or any individual violating this section, by a fine not more than $1,000 or imprisonment for not more than one year, or both.

Section 713. Use of likenesses of the great seal of the United States and the seals of the President and Vice President

(a) Whoever knowingly displays any printed or other likeness of the great seal of the United States, or of the seals of the President or the Vice President of the United States, or any facsimile thereof, in, or in connection with, any advertisement, poster, circular, book, pamphlet, or other publications, public meeting, play, motion picture, telecast, or other production, or on any building, monument, or stationery, for the purpose of conveying, or in a manner reasonably calculated to convey, a false impression of sponsorship or approval by the Government of the United States or by any department, agency, or instrumentality thereof, shall be fined not more than $250 or imprisoned not more than six months, or both.

(b) Whoever, except as authorized under regulations promulgated by the President and published in the Federal Register, knowingly manufactures, reproduces, sells, or purchased for resale, either separately or appended to any article manufactured or sold, any likeness of the seals of the President or Vice President, or any substantial part thereof, except for manufacture of sale of the article for the official use of the Government of the United States, shall be fined not more than $250 or imprisoned not more than six months, or both.

(c) A violation of subsection (a) or (b) of this section may be enjoined at the suit of the Attorney General upon complaint by any authorized representative of any department or agency of the United States.

Law Enforcement Collector Books

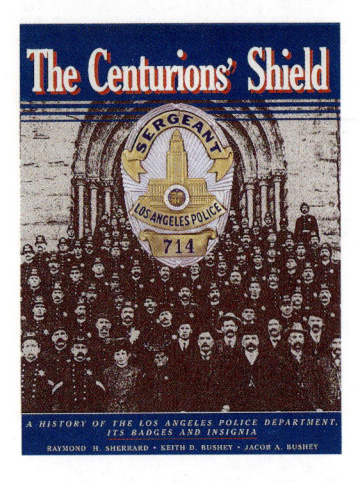

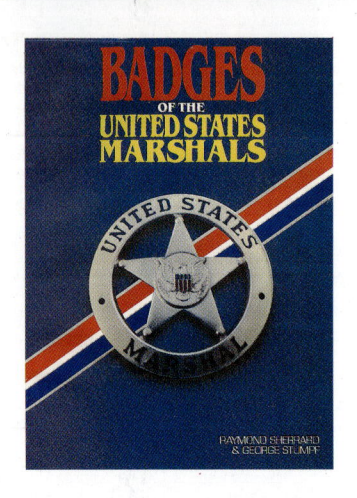

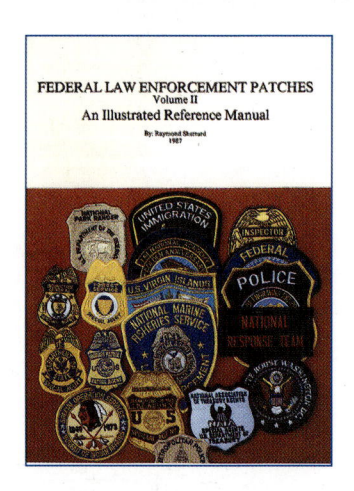

The Centurions' Shield — Comprehensive pictorial history of the Los Angeles Police Department, its badges and insignia. Hundreds of variations shown, plus guide to badge hallmarks, LAPD career info, collecting hints, "Reel Cops," and much more. 320 pages, 8 in full color, profusely illustrated, color cover and dustjacket, 8½ x 11. Hardcover, softcover, and collector's editions.

Badges of the United States Marshals — Contains over 500 color and black & white photos of U.S. Marshals' badges, credentials, pins, patches, etc., going back to the Civil War. Also, history of U.S. Marshals, Career as a U.S. Marshal, spotting fakes and reproductions, How to Collect, Movie Marshals, SOG and other elite groups 144 pages, 8½ x 11. **LIMITED QUANTITY!**

Federal Law Enforcement Patches Volume II — Over 500 U.S. government law enforcement agency patches are shown in full color, and identified. Takes up where Volume I left off. 72 pages, all in color, profusely illustrated, 8½ x 11, softcover only. **LIMITED QUANTITY!**

Patches, Pins, Badges — I also publish from time to time lists of patches, pins and badges that I have for trade or for sale. Write for information. Note: to obtain a badge list, please furnish proof of your active or retired law enforcement employment. Thank you.

Book Order Form

Name _____ Telephone _____

Address _____

City _____ State _____ Zip _____

____ copy(s) **The Centurions' Shield** Hardcover Edition at $49.95 each .... $ _____

____ copy(s) **The Centurions' Shield** Softcover Edition at $29.95 each .... $ _____

S&H $3.00 domestic; $5.00 surface/$30.00 air foreign (hardcover)/$10.00 air foreign (softcover) ...... $ _____

____ copy(s) **The Centurions' Shield** Collector's Edition with leather cover & slipcase at $129.95 each .... $ _____

S&H $4.50 domestic; $10.00 surface/$30.00 air foreign .... $ _____

____ copy(s) **Badges of the United States Marshals** Softcover Edition at $25.00 each .... $ _____

____ copy(s) **Federal Law Enforcement Patches Volume II** at $20.00 each .... $ _____

____ copy(s) **Encyclopedia of Federal Law Enforcement Patches** at $39.95 each .... $ _____

S&H $2.50 domestic; $5.00 surface/$10.00 air foreign .... $ _____

Total Enclosed (Payment other than by credit card must be made in U.S. funds drawn on a U.S. bank, preferably international or postal money order. Send cash by Registered Mail.) .... $ _____

If ordering by Visa or MasterCard: Credit Card # _____ Exp. Date _____

Name on card _____ Signature _____